KNOWING
GOD
Intimately

KNOWING
GOD
Intimately

Being as Close to Him as You Want to Be

JOYCE MEYER

New York Boston Nashville

FaithWords
Hachette Book Group
237 Park Avenue
New York, NY 10017
www.HachetteBookGroup.com

FaithWords is a division of Hachette Book Group, Inc.
The FaithWords name and logo are trademarks of Hachette Book Group, Inc.

The Hachette Speakers Bureau provides a wide range of authors for speaking events. To find out more, go to www.hachettespeakersbureau.com or call (866) 376-6591.

The publisher is not responsible for websites (or their content) that are not owned by the publisher.

Printed in the United States of America

Originally published in hardcover by Hachette Book Group
First international mass market edition: November 2013

10 9 8 7 6 5 4 3 2 1
OPM

This book is dedicated to the Holy Spirit who leads and guides me and who is ever teaching me how to grow spiritually and dwell in the presence of God.

CONTENTS

~

INTRODUCTION: IS THERE MORE?

Many Christians go to church, do what they think they should be doing to follow all the rules, and live what they think is the Christian life; but inside they are wondering, *Is this it? Is this all there is?*

I spent many years as a Christian just going through the motions of serving God. In my heart I felt that something was missing from my relationship with the Lord, although I didn't know what it was. God had done many wonderful things for me, but my life was frustrating and not really much different from the lives of those I knew were not Christians. I had many problems in my personality and life. I wanted to see a change, but somehow I was powerless to do anything to bring about that change. I could not believe that my life was meant to be a meaningless existence.

I finally asked God to give me whatever it was I was missing; I wanted more of Him in my life. In response to my desire and request, even though I didn't know what it was I was seeking, God gave me the answer! I learned that growing in the knowledge of who God is and seeking intimate fellowship with Him is a vital necessity of enjoying His purpose for our lives.

Had I not learned the importance of seeking fellowship

with God *daily* many years ago, I wouldn't be here writing this book today. Neither would I be the founder and director of a world outreach center which now employs nearly five hundred people dedicated to spreading the gospel of Jesus Christ. Each year thousands of people receive Christ as their personal Savior and experience the baptism of the Holy Spirit during our national and international conferences.

In addition to the millions of books distributed by my publisher, our ministry, *Life in the Word,* has printed more than 1.7 million books in forty-three foreign languages. One year we distributed more than five million cassette tapes and books. Each day, a potential audience of 2.1 billion people receives life-changing biblical teaching from our *Life in the Word* broadcast aired on more than 250 radio stations and 350 television stations, spanning nearly two-thirds of the globe.

New churches and Bible schools are built each year through the support of *Life in the Word* partners. New ministries to prisons, nursing homes, orphanages, feeding projects, and to troubled teens continue to spring forth as a result of the provision God has made for our ministry. Thousands of testimonies confirm that the Word of God we are sharing is changing people's lives.

Nobody builds a ministry like ours on a "charismatic personality." God is the One behind this world outreach, and God is the One who has to keep it up and running. God is the One who has to pay the bills and touch people's hearts; it's not about a personality at all. If God stopped supporting us, we would all be out on the street within a month. We understand that God is a *vital necessity* in our lives.

We all start out at the same place with God. The longer we are with Him, the deeper we want to go with Him. My husband, Dave, and I are as ordinary as anyone can be. If God can use us, He can use anyone to accomplish His mission. I know that if God's anointing of power to teach His Truth doesn't come upon me, I may as well sit down and be quiet. People don't come by the thousands to my conferences to see a television personality—they come only because through me God's anointing—His manifest presence—is revealed to meet their needs.

If God did not anoint what I say, everyone would go to sleep. So I realize it's not my clever delivery that draws people to our meetings; it's simply God's anointing on the message He imparts through a willing vessel.

Intimate fellowship with God releases His anointing of power to help us accomplish what He has called us to do. He anoints each of us for specific tasks that He has entrusted to us, whether we are to run households, businesses, or worldwide ministries.

Pressure is intensifying in the world to such an unbelievable degree that I believe we need the presence of God even to get in and out of the grocery store and to remain calm in these troubled days! We never know when someone who is having a "bad day" will feel like taking it out on us. People who don't have fellowship and intimacy with God through the Holy Spirit are unhappy—and unhappy people make life miserable for those around them.

I believe the lives of people in the body of Christ are going to get better and better, but the lives of those who are still in bondage to the world will get worse and worse as they sink deeper and deeper into despair and depression. In Isaiah 60:2 God says, "Darkness will become gross darkness, but My glory shall shine upon My people" (paraphrase). That brightness will intensify in us as we allow Him to work *in* us to make us the kind of vessels through which His glory can shine.

God wants us to know Him more intimately. His Word teaches that we can purposefully enter into His anointed presence. When Moses said, "God, You've sent me to deliver Your people from bondage, but You've not told me who will go with me" (paraphrase), God said to him, "My *Presence* shall go with you, and I will give you *rest*" (Exodus 33:14). When God is with us, He makes things easy. I often refer to God's anointing as "Holy Ease."

In this book, we will look at Old and New Testament parallels of four levels of intimacy available to all believers as illustrated through Moses and the children of Israel, and through those who followed Jesus.

Jesus said that no one can see the kingdom of God unless he is born again (see John 3:3). So, obviously, the first experience of knowing God intimately is found through the indwelling presence of His Holy Spirit, who comes to us through salvation. *God anointed us, set His seal of ownership on us, and put His Spirit in our hearts as a deposit, guaranteeing what is to come* (see 2 Corinthians 1:21-22). God wants us to ask Him for our daily bread and for wisdom (see James 1:5), and then listen for His voice to guide us. He has promised to answer us if we call on Him, assuring us, "Whether you turn to the right or to the left, your ears will hear a voice behind you, saying, 'This is the way; walk in it' " (Isaiah 30:21 NIV).

In the second part of this book, we will study the gift of God's transforming power that Jesus spoke of in Acts 1:4-5 NIV when He said to His born-again disciples,

"Wait for the gift my Father promised, which you have heard me speak about. For John baptized with water, but in a few days you will be baptized with the Holy Spirit." Knowing that the Holy Spirit is *in* us gives us confidence for our salvation, but many of us will struggle in our desire to do good works if we do not receive the gift of the Holy Spirit's power spoken of by Jesus in Acts 1:8: "But you shall receive power (ability, efficiency, and might) when the Holy Spirit has come upon you." When the Holy Spirit comes *upon* us, He gives us ability, efficiency, and might to do His work with Holy Ease.

Finally, we will examine the evidence of God's presence that is reflected through our lives as we learn to simply do whatever He tells us to do. Obedience takes us deeper into an understanding of who God is. First John 2:3 says, "And this is how we may discern [daily, by experience] that we are coming to know Him [to perceive, recognize, understand, and become better acquainted with Him]: if we keep (bear in mind, observe, practice) His teachings (precepts, commandments)." When we obey God, the glory of His goodness which He pours out upon us is a visible demonstration to others of the great things He wants to do for them. As we let His gifts work in and through us, we will be a blessing to others.

But there is still more, for in Matthew 5:8 KJV Jesus says, "Blessed are the pure in heart: for they shall *see* God" (emphasis mine). God is willing to purge us and to cleanse us of the things in our life that are not like Christ, if we will welcome His fire into our life. Like a gardener who prunes off dead limbs, God will work in us to bear fruit, if we will humble ourselves before Him and admit our dependence on Him to do the work for us and in us.

The Bible says, "Now the man Moses was very meek (gentle, kind, and humble) or above all the men on the face of the earth"(Numbers 12:3). Moses talked to God face to face, which indicates intimacy (see Exodus 33:11). The Bible says that at the Last Supper, John rested his head upon the breast of Jesus (see John 13:23), which is another way of describing intimacy. Moses and John shared a passion to know God more intimately than the others around them. Seeing the face of God is the reward of those who crave God's presence more than anything else on earth. God's Word says, "Serve Him with a blameless heart and a willing mind. For the Lord searches all hearts and minds and understands all the wanderings of the thoughts. If you seek Him [inquiring for and of Him and requiring Him as your first and vital necessity] you will find Him"(1 Chronicles 28:9).

Throughout this book, we will review God's original plan to walk beside us and talk with us like a friend as He did with Adam in Genesis 2. We will examine how the presence of sin in our life makes us want to hide from God, and we will observe God's passionate pursuit to remain close to us.

Under the old covenant, He dwelled in nearby mountaintops, in tents, and in a sanctuary where He could hide His face behind a sacred veil to separate His powerful presence from the ones He loved. Without Christ's blood to atone for our sins, we cannot stand in the full presence of God.

But when Christ made final atonement for our sins, God immediately invited us into the Holy of Holies because our sin and shame are now cleansed by Christ's blood sacrifice. God wants us to come close to Him and see that His attitude is filled with love toward us. We no longer have to hide behind the veil that once separated God from His people. We can now enjoy intimate fellowship with God!

We need God's presence in our lives; we need intimate fellowship with Him. The world in which we live can be a frightening place. Often we find ourselves in situations that we don't know how to handle, but God is ready to lead and guide us by His Spirit if we have made ourselves an available sanctuary in which He can dwell.

He not only desires to help us, but through us He desires to help others as well. I believe God has strategically placed His people all over the world, in every company, every marketplace, every hospital, school, etc. As the darkness in the world becomes darker in these last days, His glory will shine brighter on those who truly belong to Him. They will be able to help the lost find their way.

This is the day for laypeople to shine and be used by God as never before. The world will not be won through a handful of preachers. We desperately need an army of people available for one-on-one ministry in their neighborhoods, at their work, and in the marketplace. This is why I implore you to seek God to the highest level of intimacy that He is willing to reveal to you so that you are full and overflowing with His presence. Not only do you need God, but He needs you!

Don't discount yourself by believing that God could not possibly use you. " 'In the last days,' God says, 'I will pour out my Spirit on all people. Your sons and daughters will prophesy, your young men will see visions, your old men will dream dreams. Even on my servants, both men

Introduction

and women, I will pour out my Spirit in those days, and they will prophesy'" (Acts 2:17-18 NIV). This prophetic word from the Lord must include you and me.

In chapter 47 of the biblical book by his name, the prophet Ezekiel talks about a vision in which he saw waters issuing from the threshold of God's temple. I believe these waters represent an outpouring of God's Spirit. First the water was only ankle deep to Ezekiel; then it reached his knees; and then it reached all the way to his loins. Soon the waters could not be passed through, for they had risen deep enough to swim in.

Even here we see a picture that could represent four levels of commitment to God. Some people only want to get close enough to God that they are ankle-deep in water. They like to feel their feet on solid ground so they can be sure they are still in control. They are not willing to abandon themselves totally to the point that the river (representing God's Spirit) is in control.

The Lord pleads with us, "Here I am! I stand at the door and knock. If anyone hears my voice and opens the door, I will come in and eat with him, and he with me" (Revelation 3:20 NIV). He wants us to enjoy the fullness of His plan for us. But we must have His presence—His anointing, His grace, His power—every day in order to enjoy fully His work in us that is vitally necessary to our life.

How far up the "the mountain" of God's presence are you willing to climb? How close to the heart of Jesus are you willing to lay your head? How far into the River of Life are you willing to let the Holy Spirit lead you?

Those who seek, crave, and long to see God will find Him and will enjoy His everlasting fruit of peace that passes all understanding (see Philippians 4:7 KJV). If you are looking for God, or if you know Him but are not experiencing the fullness in your relationship with Him that you know He has available for you, you *can* experience that fullness. I have written this book to help show you, as God showed me, the way to experience that deep, intimate relationship with Him.

As you read to the end of this book, I am praying God's Word over you from Ephesians 1:17 NIV:

> I keep asking that the God of our Lord Jesus Christ, the glorious Father, may give you the Spirit of wisdom and revelation, so that you may know him better.

INTIMACY LEVEL
1

~

God's Manifest Presence

May He grant you out of the rich treasury of His
glory to be strengthened and reinforced with mighty
power in the inner man by the [Holy] Spirit [Himself
indwelling your innermost being and personality].
May Christ through your faith [actually] dwell (settle
down, abide, make His permanent home) in your
hearts! May you be rooted deep in love and founded
securely on love, that you may have the power and be
strong to apprehend and grasp with all the saints [God's
devoted people, the experience of that love] what is the
breadth and length and height and depth [of it]; [that
you may really come] to know [practically, through
experience for yourselves] the love of Christ, which
far surpasses mere knowledge [without experience];
that you may be filled [through all your being] unto all
the fullness of God [may have the richest measure of
the divine Presence, and become a body wholly filled
and flooded with God Himself]! Now to Him Who,
by (in consequence of) the [action of His] power that
is at work within us, is able to [carry out His purpose

and] do superabundantly, far over and above all that we [dare] ask or think [infinitely beyond our highest prayers, desires, thoughts, hopes or dreams]—to Him be glory in the church and in Christ Jesus throughout all generations forever and ever.

—EPHESIANS 3:16-21

1

Something Seems to Be Missing

~

I remember the emptiness I felt in 1976 when, as a young Christian, I realized that *doing* the right things brought temporary happiness but not deep, satisfying joy. In those early days of my friendship with God, I could only see Him from a distance, much like the children of Israel who remained at the foot of Mount Sinai might have seen Him when He talked face to face with Moses on the top of the mountain. They could hear His voice, but to them He looked like a consuming fire.

Without a doubt, I saw God as big and powerful, and I wanted to remain safely within the borders of His provision, so I lived by the law of the church. I showed up for every meeting and signed up for multiple opportunities to serve Him, but my life was still full of irritations and aggravations that robbed me of true contentment.

Many people frustrate their search for fulfillment, as I did, because they don't know where to look for that *one thing* that will satisfy their desire for something more. Like most people, the children of Israel thought of satisfaction as the sense of enjoyment, security, and well-being that comes from having their physical needs met; but it is more than that. I was a Christian for several years before I understood that true inner satisfaction is the most important thing in life and that it is the result of enjoying life through the abiding presence of God.

One day I read these words of the psalmist David, who summarized life's one requirement, the one he felt was more important than anything else: "One thing have I asked of the Lord, that will I seek, inquire for, and [insistently] require: that I may dwell in the house of the Lord [in His presence] all the days of my life, to behold and gaze upon the beauty [the sweet attractiveness and the delightful loveliness] of the Lord and to meditate, consider, and inquire in His temple" (Psalm 27:4).

David had enjoyed many opportunities to find self-worth and inner satisfaction. Empowered by the presence of God, he had killed a lion and a bear with his bare hands, and then an imposing giant although armed only with a slingshot and five small stones. God chose this anointed songwriter to become king of Israel even though he was the youngest brother of a family of men who were all more prominent than he was. His eventual fame and wealth offered all that most people might think would bring inner satisfaction.

David's pursuit of more of God, even after experiencing God's presence through many extraordinary events in his life, gave me confidence that there was much more to know about God than what I already knew. After all, even David felt the need to know God more intimately. I believe we need to *continually* desire intimate fellowship with God if we want to experience lasting inner joy.

I emphasize the word *seek* when meditating on Psalm 27:4 ("One thing have I asked of the Lord, that will I *seek,* inquire for, and [insistently] require: that I may dwell in the house of the Lord [in His presence] all the days of my life") because that word appears many times in the Bible, but some people may not fully understand what it means. To *seek* is to desire and require, which is to crave, pursue, and go after something with all of your might.

Many people want guidance from God, but they don't crave and pursue Him or lay aside other things in order to go after a word from Him. But David narrowed down all the things that he wanted in his life to this one thing—more of God *all* the days of his life. David's words in Psalm 27:4 have become my favorite life Scripture. I often sign it after my name when autographing books because I believe that the only thing that truly satisfies the longing within us is to know God more intimately today than we did yesterday.

More than likely, you can reflect on a moment with God that was more satisfying than any other event in your life. But if that moment was years ago, or even yesterday, then you are missing out on the rich pleasure that comes from fellowshipping daily with the Father, through His Holy Spirit. The Lord says, "I love those who love me, and those who seek me early and diligently shall find me" (Proverbs 8:17), and, "You will seek Me, inquire for, and require Me [as a vital necessity] and find Me when you search for Me with all your heart" (Jeremiah 29:13).

No matter what we own, where we go, or what we do, nothing can give us true gratification but the presence of God. Money, trips, vacations, houses and furniture, clothes, open doors of opportunity, marriage, children, and many other blessings are all things that can certainly excite us and give us a degree of happiness for a period of time. But happiness is based on what is happening at the moment, while joy is based on an internal assurance independent of outward circumstances.

The Greek word translated *joy* in the New Testament means "calm delight."[1] It's not necessarily hilarity, although it can include that, but to be calm and delighted is wonderful. I don't think there's anything better than just to be satisfied. To wake up in the morning and think, *Life is good, praise God, I'm satisfied,* and then to go to bed at night still satisfied, that is truly living an abundant Spirit-filled life.

We will never be permanently, consistently satisfied if we seek things to do or own in order to quench that void inside of us instead of seeking the inner satisfaction that comes only from time spent with God. I am pressing this point because I believe there are too many unhappy born-again and so-called Spirit-filled believers who are without knowledge of what to do about their dry, unfulfilled lives. I say "so-called" because to be filled is to *remain full* of the Spirit of God by acknowledging Him and pursuing His ways on a daily basis.

God's Word says, "But ever be filled and stimulated with the [Holy] Spirit"(Ephesians 5:18). *Ever* means always, anytime, daily. Our stomachs never stay filled if we don't keep eating and drinking. One good book, one classroom study, or one good conversation with someone can never satisfy our thought life, and one-time encounters with God are never going to keep us contented spiritually.

We spend time and money, we make careful plans and elaborate provisions to feed ourselves each day. Sometimes we even know today where and what we're going to be eating tomorrow! Just as our physical body must be fed, our spirit man must also be fed. But somehow we seem to think we can have a great relationship with God without feeding ourselves with His Word and filling ourselves with His presence.

Jesus said, "Man does not live and be upheld and sustained by bread alone, but by every word that comes from the mouth of God" (Matthew 4:4, paraphrase). Then in John 6:33 He said, "For the Bread of God is He Who comes down out of heaven and gives life to the world." Yet we starve ourselves of life's most important requirement—this Daily Bread from God.

We were created to enjoy a living, vital relationship with God. There's something supernaturally wonderful about reading the Word of God and hearing Him speak His promises to us. His Word to us has inherent power in it; His words are spirit, and they are life (see John 6:63). If we don't seek God and spend time feeding our spirit with His truth, we will never be content. I don't think there's anything worse than being in a low-level state of spiritual dissatisfaction all the time.

YOU ARE AS CLOSE TO GOD AS YOU WANT TO BE

It's obvious that some people are closer to God than others. Some people have a reverent familiarity with God that seems foreign to other Christians. These "close friends" of God share stories of talking to Him as if they know Him personally. Their faces shine with enthusiasm as they testify, "And God told me…" while skeptical onlookers grumble to themselves, "Well, God never talks to me like that!"

Why is that? Does God have favorites? Is God a respecter of persons? No, Scripture teaches that we, not God, determine our own level of intimacy with Him. We have all been extended the open invitation to "fearlessly and confidently and boldly draw near to the throne of grace (the throne of God's unmerited favor to us sinners), that we may receive mercy [for our failures] and find grace to help in good time for every need [appropriate help and well-timed help, coming just when we need it]" (Hebrews 4:16). At this moment, each one of us is as close to God's throne of grace as we choose to be.

Looking first at God's dealings with the Israelites beginning in Exodus chapter 19, we see four levels of intimacy that we can choose to have with God. Moses went alone to the top of the mountain to speak with God, but God established borders at three more levels on the mountain to which others could also ascend in order to draw near to Him. The borders coincided with their corresponding level of maturity and commitment to pursue Him.

The first border was at the foot of the mountain:

And the LORD said to Moses, "Behold, I come to you in the thick cloud, that the people may hear when I speak with you, and believe you forever." So Moses told the words of the people to the LORD. Then the LORD said to Moses, "Go to the people and consecrate them today and tomorrow, and let them wash their clothes. And let them be ready for the third day. For on the third day the LORD will come down upon Mount Sinai in the sight of all the people. You shall set bounds for the people all around, saying, 'Take heed to yourselves that you do not go up to the mountain or touch its base. Whoever touches the mountain shall surely be put to death.' " (Exodus 19:9-12 NKJV)

Then the Lord invited Aaron, Nadab, Abihu, and seventy of the elders of Israel to come closer to His mountain habitat and worship at a distance, thus demonstrating a second level of relationship with God. Joshua was allowed to climb up to the third level before Moses left him to approach the Lord alone. Exodus 24:9-17 NIV explains:

Moses and Aaron, Nadab and Abihu, and the seventy elders of Israel went up and saw the God of Israel. Under his feet was something like a pavement made of sapphire, clear as the sky itself. But God did not raise his hand against these leaders of the Israelites; they saw God, and they ate and drank. The LORD said to Moses, "Come up to me on the mountain and stay here, and I will give you the tablets of stone, with the law and commands I have written for their instruction." Then Moses set out with Joshua his aide, and Moses went up on the mountain of God. He said to the elders, "Wait here for us until we come back to you. Aaron and Hur are with you, and anyone involved in a dispute can go to them." When Moses went up on the mountain, the cloud covered it, and the glory of the LORD settled on Mount Sinai. For six days the cloud covered the mountain, and on the seventh day the LORD called to Moses from within the cloud. To the Israelites the glory of the LORD looked like a consuming fire on top of the mountain.

Why would God let some people only into a certain level of His presence, but allow others to come closer, and some, like Moses, to see Him face to face? In Exodus 32 we see that the level of commitment each group demonstrated to God parallels the level of intimacy each group experienced on God's mountain. We decide what depth of His presence we will enter by our level of obedience to His instruction in our lives.

To everyone at the first border, God was saying, "I'm coming to visit you, but you can only come this far into My presence." And they were comfortable remaining at the foot of the mountain where they could hear God's voice as He talked to Moses. They didn't move beyond that boundary because to them God looked like a consuming fire. Remember, this was the same group of people who later pooled their gold jewelry to make a golden calf to worship because they grew tired of waiting for Moses to come back from his visit with God. Think of it—they worshiped the earrings God had given them when they left Egypt (see Exodus 32:1-6)!

Aaron was among the priests and elders who ascended to the second level and were privileged to see the beauty of God's feet (see Exodus 24:9, 10), yet he later helped the children of Israel prepare an altar for their unholy sacrifices. And his sons, Nadab and Abihu, who shared this encounter with God, eventually lost their lives for making an unauthorized sacrifice to Him (see Numbers 3:1).

Joshua, an aide to Moses, was allowed to ascend into

the third level of intimacy with God where he watched Moses enter the cloud of God's presence. We see Joshua's humility and dedication to serve the Lord as we watch him faithfully assist Moses whenever he was needed. When Joshua wasn't running an errand for Moses, he could be found praying (see Exodus 33:10-11). He was one of the twelve spies sent into the promised land, and one of two who came back with a good report of faith in God's ability to give them the land (see Numbers 13). God chose Joshua to replace Moses when it came time to take the people into the land God had promised them.

RELATIONSHIP REQUIRES COMMITMENT

But only Moses went to the top of the mountain and into the intimate presence of God. It is clear from Scripture that Moses had taken great personal sacrifices and risks to obey God. He had turned down opportunities for personal promotion in order to see God's people blessed. When he found out that he was not an Egyptian but an Israelite, he refused to be known as the son of Pharaoh's daughter (see Hebrews 11:24-29). What a momentous decision that was for him! Since he had grown up in the house of Pharaoh, he was rich with every earthly treasure that anybody could possibly have. The Israelites, on the other hand, were poor slaves who enjoyed none of the luxuries that he was used to.

Hebrews 11:25 says of Moses: "He preferred to share the oppression [suffer the hardships] and bear the shame of the people of God rather than to have the fleeting enjoyment of a sinful life." Now that's a powerful Scripture! Moses could have kept on having fun in the flesh, but he chose to seek something more. Not everyone would have paid that price.

Moses passed the test of ambition and selfishness. He wanted intimacy with God more than anything else. Moses spent time with God for forty days and forty nights and received the Ten Commandments. God spoke with Moses face to face, as a man speaks with his friend (see Exodus 33:11). The manifest glory of God shone on Moses' face in such intensity that he had to wear a veil because the brightness of his countenance blinded the people (see Exodus 34:30-35).

These same four levels of intimacy are demonstrated in those who knew Jesus. We know that Jesus appointed at least seventy people to travel ahead of Him to every city and place where He Himself was going (see Luke 10:1). From the seventy, Jesus chose twelve disciples to share a deeper level of intimacy with Him, and out of the twelve there were three—Peter, James, and John—who were taken by Jesus into situations that none of the others could share. But of these three who were closest to Jesus, only John felt comfortable enough to rest his head on Jesus' chest as he listened to the Lord teach and talk of the kingdom of God.

Jesus had seventy acquaintances, twelve disciples, three close friends, and one who loved Him like a brother. Jesus loved them all, and they all loved Jesus, but not everyone was willing to make the same level of commitment as those who entered into a more intimate relationship with Him.

Not everybody is willing to pay the price it takes to be

close to God. Not everybody is willing simply to take the time to be close to the Lord. God doesn't ask for *all* of our time. He wants us to do other things besides engaging in spiritual activities. He designed us with a body, a soul, and a spirit, and He expects us to take care of each area of our being.

Exercising our bodies takes time and effort. Our soul needs to be taken care of. Our emotions need to be ministered to, we need to be entertained and have fun, and we need to enjoy fellowship with other people. Likewise, we have a spiritual nature that needs attention. If any area of our being gets out of balance, the spiritual begins to suffer; then our lives quickly become lopsided, and things just don't work as they should.

I believe the whole issue of intimacy with God is a matter of time. We say we don't have time to seek God, but we take time to do the things that are the most important to us. "I'm busy" can be an excuse. We all have to fight distractions every day to protect our time to seek God. He is the most important requirement in our lives, so why doesn't He have that place of importance in our time? Perhaps it's because when we start making a spiritual investment, we want instant gratification. But to seek God means to continue looking for Him.

We won't experience instant gratification. We must sow before we reap; we must invest before we get a return. In other words, we must lose before we gain; we must give up time before we can experience intimacy with God.

TIME WITH GOD IS A VITAL NECESSITY

We may have to deal sternly with our flesh to resist the spirit of passivity that tries to keep us from growing in the knowledge of God. A commitment to spend time with God is as serious as any commitment that we could ever make.

God's Word says, "Seek My face [inquire for and require My presence as your vital need]. My heart says to You, Your face (Your presence), Lord, will I seek, inquire for, and require [of necessity and on the authority of Your Word]" (Psalm 27:8). God promises, "Then you will seek Me, inquire for, and require Me [as a vital necessity] and find Me when you search for Me with all your heart" (Jeremiah 29:13). I love that Scripture—it tells us we are to require God as a vital necessity in life.

My uncle, who is now home with the Lord, had a pacemaker in his heart that had to be charged every so many days. One Saturday Dave and I invited my aunt and uncle out for a nice steak dinner, but they couldn't go because my uncle had to charge his pacemaker that day.

At first I didn't understand why my aunt said they couldn't go. I said, "Well, he can charge his pacemaker tomorrow!"

She said, "Joyce, he won't be here tomorrow if he doesn't charge his pacemaker today."

If my uncle didn't take time to recharge his pacemaker, his heart would stop beating. It was a *vital necessity* for him to keep his appointment with his lifeline to that machine. If we looked at our time with God as the opportunity to recharge the pacemaker of our heart, it would be important enough for us to make sure that we took time to do it. If we would even keep our appointment with God as we keep other appointments, we would be in good shape. But things come up, and all of a sudden we're off doing something else.

If I needed dialysis due to kidney disease and had to be at the hospital twice a week for treatment at 8:00 A.M., I certainly would not accept an invitation to do anything else, no matter how appealing it might seem. I would know that my life depended upon keeping my appointment. That is the way we should view our time with God. The quality of our life is greatly affected by the time we spend with God, and it should have a place of priority in our schedule.

Perhaps because God is ever available we think we can spend time with Him later, so we choose to respond to what seems urgent, instead of giving God a place of priority in our lives. But if we spent more priority time with God, we wouldn't have so many emergencies that rob us of our time. We are to redeem time through prayer.

When you sit in the presence of God, even if you don't feel like you are learning anything new, you are still sowing good seed into your life that will produce a good harvest. With persistence, you will get to the point where you understand more of the Word, where you are having great fellowship with God, where you are talking to Him, and He is talking to you. You will sense His presence and begin to see changes in your life that will amaze you. Don't spend your time chasing blessings. Chase God, and the blessings will chase you.

The blessings of God are released to us according to our level of maturity in Him. Third John 1:2 KJV says, "Beloved, I wish above all things that thou mayest prosper and be in health, even as thy soul prospereth."

Maturity is demonstrated through our daily lifestyle, through the way we treat our family and friends. True spirituality is not only evident on Sunday mornings at church, but throughout the week as we do what God tells us to do whether we feel like it or not. Our maturity will be tested by people capable of bringing out the worst that is still in us.

When you spend time with God, everybody else knows it. You become calmer, you're easier to get along with, and you don't lose control of your emotions as quickly. Your patience increases, and your heart soon understands what God likes and what offends Him. As with any friend, the more time you spend with God, the more like Him you become.

Spending time with God causes you to be sensitive to the love He wants to demonstrate to you and to others through you. Your conscience alerts you to His presence when you're talking to someone in a wrong way. Your heart grieves when He grieves, and you quickly pray, "Oh God, I'm sorry. Please forgive me." Desire fills your heart to apologize to the person you have offended. You soon discover that saying, "I'm sorry; I didn't mean to hurt your feelings," isn't so difficult after all.

The desires of your heart and the way you treat others reveal more about you and your relationship with God than any other outward sign. Moses enjoyed a deep level of intimacy with God, and he desired for God to bless His people. When God told Moses that he had favor in God's eyes (see Exodus 33:12), Moses understood that meant he could ask for whatever his heart desired. (What would you have asked for if you had been in Moses' place?)

Moses said to God, "If I have found favor in Your sight,

show me now Your way, that I may know You [progressively become more deeply and intimately acquainted with You, perceiving and recognizing and understanding more strongly and clearly] and that I may find favor in Your sight. And [Lord, do] consider that this nation is Your people" (Exodus 33:13). Moses had already seen God perform history's most magnificent miracles, yet he wanted to learn more of God's ways so that he could continue to find favor with the Lord. And he remembered to ask God to bless the people He had put in his care.

Staying at the same level of intimacy with God can't satisfy us. Three obvious distractions that keep us from spending time with God are our desire for entertainment, our work, and the demands of other people. All of these are unavoidable—and even necessary—so we have to make a quality decision to want more of God than anything else and to learn balance in taking time to seek Him.

It is awful to want to be somewhere, but not be able to find a way to get there. I want to help you get to where you want to be. People read books and go to seminars to learn how to live successful lives, get promotions, and enjoy better relationships. God has answers to every need; all we have to do is cooperate with Him. God is not going to tell you to do something that is beyond your ability—all He wants is your willingness, and then He will do the work.

TRUST COMPLETELY IN GOD

I remember when the Lord told me to quit my full-time job where I was making as much money as my husband. In addition, I was "the boss," so I enjoyed many benefits because of my high position. But the Lord began to deal with me, saying, "You're going to have to lay that down and stay home and prepare for ministry."

Outside of my job, I was a housewife in Fenton, Missouri, with three little kids. How did I even know for sure that I was hearing from God? God dealt with me, and dealt with me, but I was afraid to quit work. Finally I tried to make a deal with God, saying, "I'll tell You what; I won't work full-time anymore, but I'll work part-time."

So I went to work part-time for a company because I was afraid to trust God all the way. Dave and I didn't have as much income as we had before, but I found we could survive on the smaller amount of money that we were making. We had to cut down on expenses, but we could pay our bills—and that was okay with me. It seemed like a good plan to me, but it was not God's plan.

I learned that God doesn't want to make "deals," and I ended up getting fired! I wasn't the kind of person who got fired from a job. I had never been fired before. I had always been in charge. I used to fire other people, and now I had been fired. After I lost my job, I was where God wanted me to be all along—totally dependent on Him.

When I no longer had a job, I had to learn to trust God for little things like socks, underwear, a skillet, washcloths, and my kids' tennis shoes. This situation continued for six years, and during those years I learned a lot about the faithfulness of God. Now Dave and I must trust God on a much higher level for what we need to run our ministry. If I had not gone through those years of testing and stretching my faith, I would not be where I am today.

Many people give up during the testing years. They never pass their tests, so they spend their entire life going around and around the same mountains (see Deuteronomy 2:3). You may not understand what you are going through right now, but later on you will see the purpose, if you refuse to give up.

I am not telling you to quit your job to get ready for ministry. I only tell this story to explain that my husband and I didn't just roll out of bed one morning and begin working for God with thousands of people in a worldwide ministry. The Bible says that Jesus gained experience through what He suffered and was equipped for His office as High Priest. Even Jesus went through things that helped Him in His ministry in later years (see Hebrews 5:5-10).

God told *me* to quit work so I could gain experience in trusting Him for everything I needed. But please don't quit your job and try to do something in the flesh. God doesn't tell many people to just quit what they are doing, but He had to teach me to live by faith because of the things He knew Dave and I would have to believe Him for now. Only experience can equip us for the faith we need on a daily basis to continue doing what God has called us to do.

In the early days of my walk with God, my desire to know Him grew into this life prayer, which I encourage you also to pray if you are hungering for more of God:

> *God, if I have found favor with you, show me your ways. I want to think and be like you. I want to know you and the power of your resurrection. Help me, God, to walk in the fruit of the Spirit. Help me not to mistreat people. Help me to be a blessing everywhere I go today.*

I decided that *if anybody can get more of God, I want more, too.*

2

Yes, There Is More!

~⌒~

On a Friday morning in February 1976, I was driving to work and feeling discouraged. My husband and I had had an argument before we left for work, something that happened quite often.

It seemed to me that I was doing everything the church said I should do. I was expecting my routine of good works to bring me the peace and joy promised in the Scriptures. Instead, I found myself quite disheartened that nothing seemed to be working.

Dave and I both were involved in church work. He was an elder, and I was on the church board—the first and only woman at that time to serve on that board. Helping make decisions in the church was extremely frustrating because of all the bureaucracy. It often took several meetings just to decide a small, almost insignificant matter.

Dave and I were both on the Evangelism Team; one night a week we went door-to-door telling others about Jesus. Our life revolved around the church. Our children went to school there. We joined all the right social clubs and sports teams and attended all the church dinners. We had friends I thought were good friends, but I was soon to discover otherwise.

Even though I was doing what I thought God required of me, I still felt that I needed change in my life, but I didn't know exactly what I needed. I was searching, but I didn't know what I was searching for.

That morning out of sheer frustration and desperation I cried out to God, stating that I felt I couldn't go on any longer with the way things were. I remember saying, "God, something is missing. I don't know what it is, but something is missing."

I was like a starving person. I was so spiritually hungry I was ready to receive anything as long as I knew it was from God. People can be hungry but still picky about what they eat; however, if they get hungry enough, they will eat whatever is put in front of them. Because of my great spiritual hunger, I was totally open to God at that point in my life.

To my surprise I heard the audible voice of God that morning in my car. He called my name and spoke to me about patience. From that moment, I knew with certainty that God was going to do something about my situation. I didn't know what He would do or when, but I knew that He was about to move in my life.

After work on Fridays, I had my hair done. Afterward, Dave and I always went bowling as part of a league. On that Friday afternoon, I drove home from the beauty shop, turning off Highway 270 onto the Gravois exit to go to Fenton, the St. Louis suburb where we lived. As I sat in the car at a red light, I felt my heart fill with faith about what God was going to do. Even though I had no idea what it would be, I began to thank Him for it.

At that very moment, Jesus filled me with the presence of the Holy Spirit in a way that I had never before experienced. I didn't know what was taking place, but I certainly knew that God had manifested Himself in a different and powerful way.

The best way I can describe my feeling at that moment is to say it was as if someone had poured me full of liquid love. For about three weeks I felt as if I was drunk on the love of God. It affected my behavior. I was peaceful, happy, excited, and easy to get along with. I felt as if I loved everything and everyone.

I remember driving past a field of weeds and thinking how beautiful they were, simply because I knew God had made them. Everything that God had anything to do with looked beautiful to me. People I hadn't wanted to be around before suddenly seemed pleasant and likeable to me. I was actually the one who was different, but when we change, everyone and everything else seems to us to have changed.

I got up that morning feeling as if everything had come to a discouraging end. I went to bed that night knowing I was at a place of new beginnings. That is how God is. He moves *suddenly* in our lives. I believe if you are reading this book you have a "suddenly" coming into your life.

Open your heart to God in a greater way than ever before. Ask Him to change you and your life however He sees fit and proper. None of us can afford to stand still without change. If we aren't moving forward with God, we are drifting backward.

After that experience with God, my behavior changed to the extent that people began asking me what had happened. I didn't know what to call it, but soon God put material into my hands that taught me what had taken place.

FAITH VERSUS EXPERIENCE

In sharing my experience with you I don't mean to imply that you should seek an experience with God. I share my story with you simply to illustrate that if you are not satisfied with your relationship with God, there is always more to know about Him. We are to seek the Lord, not an experience, and He alone decides how and when to manifest His presence in our life. He deals with each of us individually, but He does promise that if we seek Him, we will find Him. If we ask the Father to give us the Holy Spirit in a greater measure, He will do it.

Jesus said to His followers:

> So I say to you, Ask and keep on asking and it shall be given you; seek and keep on seeking and you shall find; knock and keep on knocking and the door shall be opened to you. For everyone who asks and keeps on asking receives; and he who seeks and keeps on seeking finds; and to him who knocks and keeps on knocking, the door shall be opened. What father among you, if his son asks for a loaf of bread, will give him a stone; or if he asks for a fish, will instead of a fish give him a serpent? Or if he asks for an egg, will give him a scorpion? If you then, evil as you are, know how to give good gifts [gifts that are to their advantage] to your children, how much more will your heavenly Father give the Holy Spirit to those who ask and continue to ask Him! (Luke 11:9-13)

God is faithful and ever true to His Word (see Hebrews 10:23). He is no respecter of persons (see Acts 10:34 KJV). What is available to one is available to all. God may not answer each of us exactly the same way, but He will answer our prayers and meet our needs.

Our seeking must be sincere and we should always be ready to make a deeper commitment. When that is the case, God will move and send His Holy Spirit to touch each of us in a special way. Ask and believe by faith that God will do something wonderful. While you wait for Him to do it, thank Him, and offer Him praise.

Do you look forward to church and find it interesting, or are you attending out of obligation, looking forward to it being over? Do you have a degree of success, or even a great deal of success, in your life but realize there is something missing? Perhaps you are a Christian just going through the motions as I was.

There are many people who have received Jesus as Savior and Lord who will live their Christian lives and go to heaven without ever drawing on the full capacity of the Holy Spirit available to them, never experiencing the true success God intends for them. People can be on their way to heaven and yet not be enjoying the trip.

We often look on those who have wealth, position, power, fame, and other attributes associated with material acquisition and consider them to be totally successful. But many people who are viewed as successful still lack good relationships, good health, peace, joy, contentment, and other true blessings that are available only in a personal relationship with God through Jesus Christ. Such people are still independent; they have never learned to be totally dependent upon the ability of the Holy Spirit.

Some people who are self-sufficient think it is a sign of weakness to depend on God. But by drawing on the ability of the Holy Spirit, they can accomplish more in their lives than they could by working in their own strength. And people who depend on their own strength sometimes find there are times when they seem powerless to help others, but the Holy Spirit can empower and work through them.

God created us in such a way that although we do have strengths, we also have weaknesses and need His help. We know He is willing to help us because He sent a Divine Helper to live inside us (see John 14:16; 1 Corinthians 6:19).

There are countless things we struggle with when we could be receiving help from the Holy Spirit. Many people never find the right answers to their problems because they seek out the wrong sources for advice and counsel instead of asking the Divine Counselor within them. It is amazing how many people can give us advice that has no effect upon us. But when God tells us something, it is full of power, and peace comes with it.

Jesus did not die to give us a religion. He died so that through faith in Him we could have an intimate relationship with God. Our worst day with God is still better than our best day without Him.

Many people live every day tormented by fear. Sadly, most of them don't realize help is available to them through the ability of the Holy Spirit. The Holy Spirit wants to help us by comforting us when we need it. He will comfort us when we have been disappointed, hurt, or mistreated, or when we have experienced loss. He will also comfort us during changes in our life, when we are simply tired, or when we have failed in some way. Some people never experience this comfort because they don't know it is available for the asking.

I had a lot of emotional pain in my life that resulted from rejection. Like everyone else, I hate the lonely feeling that comes with being rejected. As human beings, we all desire acceptance, not rejection.

For many years I suffered from rejection because I didn't know there was anything I could do about it, but thank God all that has changed. Not too long ago something happened that brought back those old pains of rejection. I reached out to someone who had hurt me a great deal in my childhood. Instead of an apology, I received blame for something that wasn't my fault, as well as a clear message that the person had no real interest in me. I instantly experienced that old feeling of wanting to retreat into a corner somewhere and nurse my wounds.

The pain in my emotions was intense. I wanted to hide and feel sorry for myself, but thank God I now know there is a solution for such situations. I immediately asked God for the comfort of the Holy Spirit. I asked Him to heal my wounded emotions and to enable me to handle the situation exactly the way Jesus would handle it. As I continued to lean on God, I felt warmth inside me. It was almost like soothing oil was being poured on my wounds.

I asked God to help me forgive the person who had hurt me, and He gave me the grace to remember what I tell others: "Hurting people hurt people." His intimate, personal response brought healing to my wounded spirit.

In 2 Corinthians 1:3-4 it says God is a Father of sympathy (of pity and mercy), and He is the Source of every comfort. It says He comforts, consoles, and encourages us in every trouble, calamity, and affliction. Ask yourself,

"Do I have a close, personal relationship with God? Do I know Him intimately?"

Jesus wants to come into our lives to establish us in a personal relationship with God. He will strengthen us and enable us to do with ease what we would struggle to do, and never could do, without Him. Through Jesus, God has provided the Holy Spirit to deepen our relationship with God into an intimate one by making real to us everything that God is. For example, God doesn't want just to *give* us strength; He wants to *be* our strength through the Divine Strengthener.

If God created you to need Him, and if you act as though you don't, how can you ever be fulfilled? Don't you want to experience the presence and the full ability of the Holy Spirit in your life? To know God intimately you must receive Jesus as your only Savior and Lord by being born of the Spirit.

BORN OF THE SPIRIT

In John chapter 3, Jesus told Nicodemus who came to Him asking questions:

> Unless a person is born again (anew, from above), he cannot ever see (know, be acquainted with, and experience) the kingdom of God. (Verse 3)

Nicodemus said to Him:

> How can a man be born when he is old? Can he enter his mother's womb again and be born? (Verse 4)

Jesus answered:

I assure you, most solemnly I tell you, unless a man
is born of water and [even] the Spirit, he cannot
[ever] enter the kingdom of God. (Verse 5)

When any person accepts Jesus Christ as Savior,
believing in His substitutionary work on the cross,[1] that
person is born of the Holy Spirit or *born again* (see
v. 3). This is not based on any good deeds the person
has done or ever could do, but solely on the grace (or
power), mercy, and election (or choice) of God. The Bible
tells us:

For by grace you have been saved through faith, and
that not of yourselves; it is the gift of God, not of
works, lest anyone should boast. (Ephesians 2:8-9
NKJV)

In Titus 3:5 NKJV, the Word of God teaches that we
are saved "not by works of righteousness which we have
done, but...through the washing of regeneration and
renewing of the Holy Spirit." The Holy Spirit is involved
in our salvation, and He will be with us until the end.
God has assigned the Holy Spirit to walk with each of us
believers through this world and deliver us safely to God
in heaven at the appointed time.

Have you been born of the Spirit? If not, pray the following prayer right now, knowing that as you sincerely
surrender your life to Jesus Christ, you will be born of the
Spirit or born again. Then you can begin to experience
true *intimacy with God* through His Holy Spirit.

PRAYER FOR A PERSONAL RELATIONSHIP WITH THE LORD

God wants you to receive His free gift of salvation. Jesus wants to save you and fill you with the Holy Spirit more than anything. If you have never invited Jesus, the Prince of Peace, to be your Lord and Savior, I invite you to do so now, and if you are really sincere about it, you will experience a new life in Christ. Simply pray this prayer out loud:

Father,

You loved the world so much, You gave Your only begotten Son to die for our sins so that whoever believes in Him will not perish, but have eternal life.

Your Word says we are saved by grace through faith as a gift from You. There is nothing we can do to earn salvation.

I believe and confess with my mouth that Jesus Christ is Your Son, the Savior of the world. I believe He died on the cross for me and bore all of my sins, paying the price for them. I believe in my heart that You raised Jesus from the dead.

I ask You to forgive my sins. I confess Jesus as my Lord. According to Your Word, I am saved and will spend eternity with You! Thank You, Father. I am so grateful! In Jesus' name, amen (see John 3:16; Ephesians 2:8-9; Romans 10:9-10; 1 Corinthians 15:3-4; 1 John 1:9; 4:14-16; 5:1,11,12,13).

IMMERSED IN THE HOLY SPIRIT

What had happened to me that Friday in February 1976 when I was driving home from the beauty shop was the experience written about in Acts chapters 1 and 2, as well as in many other places in the Holy Scriptures. I had been immersed in or filled with the Holy Spirit.

Before Jesus was taken up into heaven following the forty days He spent on earth alive after He was resurrected from the dead (Acts 1:3), He gathered the disciples and told them not to leave Jerusalem, but to wait for the promise of the Father: "Of which [He said] you have heard Me speak. For John baptized with water, but not many days from now you shall be baptized with (placed in, introduced into) the Holy Spirit" (Acts 1:4-5).

The promise of the Father was the outpouring of the Holy Spirit. Jesus said, "But you shall receive power (ability, efficiency, and might) when the Holy Spirit has come upon you, and you shall be My witnesses in Jerusalem and all Judea and Samaria and to the ends (the very bounds) of the earth" (Acts 1:8).

After Jesus said these things to His disciples, He was taken up and received into a cloud out of their sight (see v. 9).

These disciples were the same ones to whom He had appeared shortly after He was resurrected. At that time He breathed on them and said, "Receive the Holy Spirit!" (John 20:22). I believe it was at this time that they were born again. If they had already received the Holy Spirit, which they had, why then did they need to wait *to be baptized with the Holy Spirit* as Jesus instructed them to do immediately before He ascended into heaven?

It is possible to fill a glass with water without filling it to full capacity. Likewise, when we are born again we have the Holy Spirit *in* us, but we may not yet be totally filled with the Spirit. In Acts 1:8 Jesus promises that the Holy Spirit will also come *upon* us with His power (ability, efficiency, and might) to be Christ's witnesses to the ends of the earth. Acts 4:31 gives account that when people were filled with the Holy Spirit, they spoke the Word of God "with freedom and boldness and courage."

In the Old Testament, the Spirit of the Lord came upon His servants such as Gideon, Samson, David, Elijah, and Elisha, and miracles took place beyond their human ability that demonstrated God's power to the lost world. We live in the most exciting time of history, because the Holy Spirit is being poured out on all who will receive Him. Now we can enjoy the indwelling presence of God's Spirit through salvation and also be expectant of His power to fill us in order to demonstrate His glory to lost people around us.

In John 1:29-33 NKJV, John the Baptist said that he baptized with water but that the One who came after him would baptize with the Holy Spirit. In Matthew 28:19, Jesus told His followers to go and make disciples, baptizing them in the name of the Father, the Son, and the Holy Spirit.

Water baptism is an outward sign of an inner decision to follow Jesus and surrender one's life to Him. It signifies the burial of the old life and the resurrection of the new. The baptism of John spoken of in John 1:33 was a baptism of repentance. Those being baptized were in essence saying they wanted to turn away from sin and live a new life.

A person may have a desire to do something and yet

not have the power to perform it. I believe that power comes with the baptism of the Holy Spirit. For many years I was told what I should do, and I wanted to comply, but I just could not. It was only after I had been baptized or immersed in the Holy Spirit that I found the true desire to do God's will and the power to do it. There are varying levels of "want to." I had always wanted to obey God, but my desire was not strong enough to carry me through the hard parts of obedience. After I was filled with the Holy Spirit, my "want to" was strengthened to carry me through to the finish.

The Greek word translated *baptize* used by John in reference to water baptism in John 1:33 is the same Greek word used by Jesus in Acts 1:5 in reference to being baptized with the Holy Spirit: "For John baptized with water, but not many days from now you shall be baptized with (placed in, introduced into) the Holy Spirit." In both verses, in reference to both types of baptism, the meaning of *baptize* is "to immerse, submerge."[2]

If any born-again person is open to God, that individual can be immersed into and filled with the Holy Spirit.

In Acts 1:8 Jesus told the disciples that after they had received this power from on high, they would be enabled to *be* witnesses. The emphasis on *be* is mine; I placed it there to make the point clear that there is a difference between doing and being.

Before I was immersed in the Holy Spirit, I was going out once a week to *do* door-to-door evangelism, yet I did not have enough power in my everyday life to *be* what the Bible taught me to be. I wanted to, but I had no power to perform what I wanted. As far as having the power to successfully handle the events of daily life, there was not

much difference between me and any unbeliever I knew—
a little, perhaps, but not as much as there should have been.
Although I was born again, I needed something more.

ANOINTED WITH THE HOLY SPIRIT

When John baptized Jesus in water, the Holy Spirit
descended upon Him like a dove:

> Then Jesus came from Galilee to John at the Jor-
> dan to be baptized by him...Then Jesus, when He
> had been baptized, came up immediately from the
> water; and behold, the heavens were opened to Him,
> and He saw the Spirit of God descending like a dove
> and alighting upon Him. (Matthew 3:13,16 NKJV)

It is difficult, but necessary, to understand the teaching from Philippians 2:6-7 about the true nature of Jesus.
Although He possessed the fullness of the attributes of
God, was the Word of God, and was Himself God who
became flesh (see John 1:1-14), Jesus stripped Himself of
all His divine privileges to assume the guise of a servant
in that He became like men and was born a human being.
Then He demonstrated the steps He wanted us to follow.

Jesus was immersed not only in water but also in the
Holy Spirit. In other words, He was immersed in power,
which enabled Him to do the task His Father had sent Him
to do. Acts 10:38 NKJV tells "how God anointed Jesus of
Nazareth with the Holy Spirit and with power, who went
about doing good and healing all who were oppressed by
the devil, for God was with Him."

Before Jesus' public ministry began, He was anointed with the Holy Spirit and with power. When we are filled with the Holy Spirit, we are equipped for service in the kingdom of God because we are able to draw on the *power (ability, efficiency, and might)* (see Acts 1:8) of the Holy Spirit we received when He came upon us to be His witnesses. This power enables us to do what God wants us to do.

The John 1:32 description of the Holy Spirit's descent upon Jesus indicates that the Holy Spirit permanently remained with Him. The Spirit "dwelt on Him [never to depart]" or, in the *King James Version* wording, "abode upon him."

John the Baptist said, I have seen the Spirit descending as a dove out of heaven, and it dwelt on Him [never to depart]. And I did not know Him nor recognize Him, but He Who sent me to baptize in (with) water said to me, Upon Him Whom you shall see the Spirit descend and remain, that One is He Who baptizes with the Holy Spirit. And I have seen [that happen—I actually did see it] and my testimony is that this is the Son of God! (John 1:32-34)

For the Holy Spirit to reside with Jesus is significant because under the old covenant the Holy Spirit came upon people for specific tasks, but He did not permanently remain with them. After the Spirit descended and remained upon Jesus, the Spirit led Jesus in a more definite way.

The Holy Spirit led Him into the wilderness to be tempted of the devil forty days and nights (see Luke 4:1-2).

He passed every test and then began to preach, "Repent...
for the kingdom of heaven is at hand" (Matthew 4:17).
He began to do miracles, including casting out devils and
healing the sick (see Luke 4,5). It is important to see that
even Jesus did not do any miracles or other mighty acts
until after He had been empowered by the Holy Spirit. If
Jesus needed to be baptized in order to fulfill all righteousness (see Matthew 3:15 KJV) and be empowered by the
Holy Spirit, why wouldn't we need to be?

Paul was also filled with and empowered by the Holy
Spirit.

PAUL WAS FILLED WITH
THE HOLY SPIRIT

So Ananias left and went into the house. And he
laid his hands on Saul [Paul] and said, Brother Saul,
the Lord Jesus, Who appeared to you along the way
by which you came here, has sent me that you may
recover your sight and be filled with the Holy Spirit.
(Acts 9:17)

Many say that believers receive everything they will ever
get or need when they accept Jesus as Savior. That may
be the case with some believers, but certainly not with
all. Different people have different experiences. I am not
denying that some may be born again and baptized in the
Holy Spirit at the same time; but others are not, and Paul
was one of them.

As you probably know, Paul was formerly called
Saul and was a very religious man, a Pharisee among

Pharisees (see Acts 23:6). He was persecuting Christians and believing that he was doing God a service by doing so (see Philippians 3:5-6).

Acts 9:4 NKJV tells how, one day as he was traveling the road from Jerusalem to Damascus to bring back believers for trial and punishment, a light from heaven shone around Saul, and he fell to the ground. Then he "heard a voice saying to him, 'Saul, Saul, why are you persecuting Me?' "

Trembling, he said, "Lord, what do You want me to do?" (v. 6). This was the moment of Saul's conversion, the time of his surrender. He called Jesus "Lord" and then offered his will in surrender. He was told to arise and go into the city and wait there for further instructions.

Paul was blinded during this experience. His eyes were open, but he could see nothing. So his traveling companions led him by the hand into Damascus. For three days he was unable to see, and neither ate nor drank.

The Lord spoke to a disciple named Ananias in Damascus in a vision telling him where he would find Saul, noting that he would be praying. At the same time, Saul had a vision in which he saw a man named Ananias entering and laying his hands on him so that he would regain his sight. Ananias had heard of Saul and of how much evil he had brought on the saints. So, of course, he was reluctant to go. But the Lord said to him, "Go," and so he went. The Lord told Ananias that Saul was a chosen instrument of His to bear His name before the Gentiles and the descendants of Israel (see Acts 9:15).

Ananias went to the house where Saul was staying. There Ananias laid his hands on Saul and said (in so many words), "Brother Saul (the fact that he called him "brother" is another proof of Saul's conversion), the Lord has sent me to you to lay hands on you so that your eyes may be opened and you may be filled with the Holy Spirit" (see v. 17). Immediately, something similar to scales fell from Saul's eyes, and he arose and was baptized.

This seems to be quite clear. Saul was converted first, then three days later he was filled with the Holy Spirit and baptized in water. If Saul, who became the apostle Paul, needed to be filled with the Holy Spirit, then I believe we need to be also.

THE GENTILES WERE ALSO FILLED WITH THE HOLY SPIRIT

> While Peter was still speaking these words, the Holy Spirit fell on all who were listening to the message. (Acts 10:44)

In Acts 10 we read how once again God gave two different men visions that brought them together for His purpose.

Peter had a vision that he was to go and preach to the household of Cornelius, something he would have never done on his own because Cornelius was a Gentile, and Jews had absolutely nothing to do with Gentiles. Around the same time, Cornelius had a vision that he was to send for Peter. Through this supernatural occurrence, the two were brought together.

As Peter began speaking to the Gentiles gathered at the house of Cornelius, the Holy Spirit fell upon them as He had fallen on the Jewish believers at Pentecost. The Gentiles all began to speak in other tongues in the same

way the 120 disciples of Christ had done who had been
waiting in the Upper Room on the Day of Pentecost (see
Acts 1:13; 2:1-4). After those at the house of Cornelius
were filled with the Holy Spirit, Peter suggested that they
be baptized in water, and they were.

Prior to what took place in Cornelius's household,
Acts chapter 8 tells how Philip had preached the gospel
in Samaria. One of those who had believed and was baptized in water was a man named Simon, who had been
a noted magician. When the apostles in Jerusalem heard
that the Samaritans had received Jesus, they sent Peter
and John to pray for them that they might receive the Holy
Spirit. When Simon saw that this power was imparted to
people by the laying on of the apostles' hands, he was so
amazed that he offered to buy it and was severely rebuked
by Peter (see Acts 8:9,13-15,17-23).

Simon was a believer. He had been baptized in water
and had stayed close by Philip ever since, watching the
"signs and miracles of great power which were being
performed" (v. 13). So what was he seeing now that was
so impressive he wanted to buy it? Peter, of course, told
him that if he didn't ask God to forgive him for offering
money to buy this power, he would perish with his money
for thinking that the gift of God could be bought. But the
point is, Simon evidently saw something much more powerful than he was used to.

Jesus, Paul, and the Gentiles were empowered by the
infilling of the Holy Spirit. Why would we want to go
through life without being empowered as they were?

3

The Home of God

~~~~~~~~

More than anything else, I want to clearly hear God's voice and be aware of His abiding presence all the time. I know what God has called me to do, and I know that I cannot do it without knowing God is with me. I am desperate for the manifest presence of God in my life, and I know that I cannot live in the flesh and enjoy that intimate fellowship.

As I explained previously, for many years I believed in Jesus Christ as my Savior but did not enjoy close fellowship with God. I felt that I was always reaching for Him and coming short of my goal. One day, as I stood before a mirror combing my hair, I asked Him a simple question: "God, why do I consistently feel as though I am reaching for You and coming a little bit short of finding You?"

Immediately I heard these words inside my spirit, "Joyce, you are reaching *out,* and you need to be reaching *in.*"

God's Word says that He lives *in* us, but many people find this truth difficult to understand. Second Corinthians 4:6-9 says:

For God Who said, Let light shine out of darkness, has shone in our hearts so as [to beam forth] the Light for the illumination of the knowledge of the majesty and glory of God [as it is manifest in the Person and is revealed] in the face of Jesus Christ (the Messiah). However, we possess this precious treasure [the divine Light of the Gospel] in [frail, human] vessels of earth, that the grandeur and exceeding greatness of the power may be shown to be from God and not from ourselves. We are hedged in (pressed) on every side [troubled and oppressed in every way], but not cramped or crushed; we suffer embarrassments and are perplexed and unable to find a way out, but not driven to despair; we are pursued (persecuted and hard driven), but not deserted [to stand alone]; we are struck down to the ground, but never struck out and destroyed.

We have the treasure of God's presence within us; but just as earthen vessels can hold water without being filled and overflowing, so we can go through a prayer line, get baptized in the Holy Ghost, and receive the gift of speaking in tongues—but a single filling doesn't mean we are spiritual. To be spiritual is to be aware of the presence of God and to act accordingly.

The church in Corinth operated in all the gifts of the Holy Spirit, yet Paul told them they were still carnal (see 1 Corinthians 3:3 KJV). "How do I know you are carnal?" he asked. "Because you have jealousy, envy, and greed, and you gossip. None of this should be going on in you."

Jesus corrected a lot of religious people, telling them,

"Woe to you, teachers of the law and Pharisees, you hypocrites! You are like whitewashed tombs, which look beautiful on the outside but on the inside are full of dead men's bones and everything unclean. In the same way, on the outside you appear to people as righteous but on the inside you are full of hypocrisy and wickedness" (Matthew 23:27-28 NIV).

That Scripture gripped my heart. I didn't want to be a whitewashed tomb full of dead men's bones! Jesus had more trouble with the pretenders and the hypocrites than with anybody else.

One day I was dragging myself through the kitchen with my head hanging down—I was downcast! I was murmuring and complaining, saying, "God, I'm so tired of all this. When are You going to do something? When am I going to get a breakthrough? When am I going to get blessed?"

Just then I heard the voice of God say, "Joyce, don't you know that you have the life of almighty God on the inside of you? That ought to be enough to keep you jumping around in joy from now until Jesus comes to get you."

Ephesians 3:17 says, "May Christ through your faith [actually] dwell (settle down, abide, make His permanent home) in your hearts!" If you are born again, you know that Jesus is dwelling on the inside of you through the power of the Holy Spirit, but is God comfortable in you, and does He feel at home there within you? It took me a long time to understand that God lives in me with all the other stuff that's going on in my inner life.

God gave me an illustration of what it is like for Him to live in a heart where murmuring and complaining still reside. Suppose you go to the house of a friend who says to you, "Oh, come on in. I'll get you a cup of coffee. Sit down, make yourself at home." So you prop up your feet to get comfortable, and all of a sudden your friend starts yelling at her husband. They get into all kinds of strife while you sit there watching. Right in front of you, they rant and rave and carry on. How comfortable do you think you would feel in their home with all of that strife?

Or suppose you go to another friend's house to visit, and all of a sudden she starts talking ugly about another good friend of yours whom you dearly love. Would you feel at home in the midst of that kind of gossip and slander? Yet, how many times do Christians talk ugly about somebody else whom Jesus loves and to whom He is committed?

Because many Christians are not willing to submit to the inner promptings of the Holy Spirit, they are not full of peace. They keep their inner lives in a constant war zone. They don't sense the rest of the Lord within them because even though He in Himself is at rest, they resist His nudges to "let things go, and trust in Him." Their turmoil increases because they do not yield to His promptings, and they cannot be at rest if their inner life is not in harmony with Christ's nature.

If we want to be a comfortable home for the Lord, we must give up grumbling, complaining, faultfinding, and murmuring. Our words should be full of praise. We need to wake up in the morning and say, "Oh, good morning, Jesus. I want You to be comfortable in me today. Praise You, Father. I love You, Lord. Thank You for all the good things You're doing."

The Bible says that God inhabits the praises of His people (see Psalm 22:3 KJV). He is comfortable in the midst of our sweet praises, but He is not comfortable in the midst of our sour attitudes.

I am encouraging you to take inventory of your inner life because it is the dwelling place of God. When God used to dwell in a portable tabernacle that the children of Israel carried through the wilderness, they understood that the inner court was a holy place. But now in the mystery of God's plan, we are like a portable tabernacle; we move from place to place, and God dwells on the inside of us. There's still an outer court, a holy place, and a most holy place. The outer court is our body, the holy place is our soul, and the most holy place is our spirit.

When we examine our inner life, we are looking at holy ground where the Spirit of God wants to make His home. Our inner life is of more serious interest to God than our outer life. That's why we need to be more concerned about our inner life than our outer life. Our outer life reflects our reputation with people, but our inner life determines our reputation with God.

The Bible says, "On that day...as my Gospel proclaims, God by Jesus Christ will judge men in regard to the things which they conceal (their hidden thoughts)" (Romans 2:16). Everything we do will pass through the eyes of fire on the Day of Judgment, and everything that is not done out of a totally pure motive will get zapped! Fried! Gone!

> But the day of the Lord will come like a thief. The heavens will disappear with a roar; the elements will be destroyed by fire, and the earth and everything in it will be laid bare. Since everything will be destroyed in this way, what kind of people ought

you to be? You ought to live holy and godly lives as
you look forward to the day of God and speed its
coming. That day will bring about the destruction of
the heavens by fire, and the elements will melt in the
heat. But in keeping with his promise we are looking forward to a new heaven and a new earth, the
home of righteousness. So then, dear friends, since
you are looking forward to this, make every effort
to be found spotless, blameless and at peace with
him (2 Peter 3:10-14 NIV).

That passage should invoke reverential fear and awe in
us. It is a waste of time trying to impress people; what
matters is what God thinks of us. We should spend our
time doing things that have eternal value, things that are
inspired by right and pure motives.

WHAT'S INSIDE OF YOU?

Our lives can be like beautifully wrapped packages with
nothing inside of them. Our outer lives can look good, but
our inner lives can be dry and empty. We can look spiritual on the outside but be powerless within, if we don't
allow the Holy Spirit to make His home in our heart.

As we submit to Christ's lordship in our innermost
being, we will see His righteousness, peace, and joy in the
Holy Spirit rise up from within us to empower us for an
abundant life (see Romans 14:17).

Psalm 45:13 says, "The King's daughter in the inner
part [of the palace] is all glorious; her clothing is inwrought
with gold." God puts the Holy Spirit inside of us to work

on our inner life: our attitudes, our reactions, and our goals. Through His work in us, our inner life can be tested and refined into an environment in which the Lord is comfortable to reside.

When I didn't know much about my inner life, I wasn't a very happy Christian. But now the Holy Spirit acts somewhat like a traffic policeman inside of me. When I do the right things, I get a green light from Him, and when I do wrong things, I get a red light. If I am about to get myself in trouble, but I have not fully made a decision to proceed, I get a caution signal.

The more we stop and ask God for directions, the more sensitive we become to the signals within from the Holy Spirit. He doesn't scream and yell at us; He simply whispers, "Uh-uh-uh, I wouldn't do that if I were you." He will always lead us to life and inner peace, if we yield to Him.

Romans 7:6 explains it this way: "So now we serve not under [obedience to] the old code of written regulations, but [under obedience to the promptings] of the Spirit in newness [of life]."

From that day when God told me to look within, in the middle of an ordinary experience on an ordinary day, God began revealing a vital biblical truth to me. That truth is this: *We are the dwelling place of God.* I believe this truth is necessary for each of us to understand in order to enjoy close fellowship and intimacy with God.

The apostle Paul tells us in 1 Corinthians 6:19-20:

Do you not know that your body is the temple (the very sanctuary) of the Holy Spirit Who lives within you, Whom you have received [as a Gift] from God? You are not your own, you were bought with a price [purchased with a preciousness and paid for, made His own]. So then, honor God and bring glory to Him in your body.

Why would God want to live in us? And how can He? After all, He is holy, and we are weak human flesh with frailties, faults, and failures.

The answer is simply this: He loves us and *chooses* to make His home in us. He does that because He is God— He has the ability to do what He wants, and He elects or chooses to make His home in our hearts. This election or choice is not based on any good deeds we have done or ever could do, but solely on the grace (or power), mercy, and election (or choice) of God. We become the home of God by believing in Christ (as God tells us in the Bible to do) in order to become His dwelling place.

Jesus explained why some people never experience intimacy with God, saying, " 'You have never heard his voice nor seen his form, nor does his word dwell in you, for you do not believe the one he sent. You diligently study the Scriptures because you think that by them you possess eternal life. These are the Scriptures that testify about me, yet you refuse to come to me to have life' " (John 5:37-40 NIV).

We are to simply believe that Jesus' sacrifice for our sins was enough to allow us into the presence of God. God takes up residence within us when we give our life to Jesus by believing in Him as the only Savior and Lord. From that position He, by the power of the Holy Spirit, begins a wonderful work in us. This truth is so awesome that it is difficult for our finite minds to grasp and believe.

A NEW HEART AND A NEW SPIRIT

Ezekiel 36 contains God's promise through the mouth of the prophet that the day would come when He would give people a new heart and put His Spirit *within* them.

> A new heart will I give you and a new spirit will I put within you, and I will take away the stony heart out of your flesh and give you a heart of flesh. And I will put my Spirit within you and cause you to walk in My statutes, and you shall heed My ordinances and do them. (Ezekiel 36:26-27)

As we have seen, under the old covenant the Holy Spirit was with people and came upon people for special purposes, but He did not live inside them. God dwelled in a tabernacle made with human hands during that dispensation. But under the new covenant, signed and sealed in the blood of Jesus Christ (see Hebrews 13:20), He intends to dwell no longer in a tabernacle made by human hands but in the hearts of humans who have committed their lives to Him.[1]

No one could be born again and become a dwelling place for God's Spirit until Jesus died and rose from the dead. He is called "the firstborn among many brethren" (Romans 8:29). After Jesus was resurrected, He appeared first to His disciples, who were hiding behind closed doors for fear of the Jews. When He spoke peace to them and then breathed on them and said, "Receive the Holy Spirit!" (John 20:22), it was at this time that the disciples were born again or born of the Spirit. They had a spiritual awakening, so to speak.

This event marked a new beginning for them; but there still remained a work to be done in them to prepare them properly for service in God's kingdom. God's Word explains:

> But now put away and rid yourselves [completely] of all these things: anger, rage, bad feeling toward others, curses and slander, and foulmouthed abuse and shameful utterances from your lips! Do not lie to one another, for you have stripped off the old (unregenerate) self with its evil practices, and have clothed yourselves with the new [spiritual self], which is [ever in the process of being] renewed and remolded into [fuller and more perfect knowledge upon] knowledge after the image (the likeness) of Him Who created it. [In this new creation all distinctions vanish.] There is no room for and there can be neither Greek nor Jew, circumcised nor uncircumcised, [nor difference between nations whether alien] barbarians or Scythians [who are the most savage of all], nor slave or free man; but Christ is all and in all [everything and everywhere, to all men, without distinction of person]. (Colossians 3:8-11)

SANCTIFIED AND MADE HOLY

According to John 16:13-15, the Holy Spirit guides us into all truth. Everything that the Father has belongs to Jesus, and Jesus transmits that inheritance to us. The Holy Spirit receives from Jesus everything that belongs to Jesus and transmits it to us.

In 1 Peter 1:2 we are also told that we are sanctified by the Holy Spirit. To be sanctified is to be set apart for a sacred purpose. According to *Vine's Complete Expository Dictionary of Old and New Testament Words,* the word *sanctification* is defined as *"(a)* separation to God" and *"(b)* the course of life befitting those so separated." It is "that relationship with God into which men enter by faith in Christ...and to which their sole title is the death of Christ."

Vine goes on to explain, " 'Sanctification' is also used in NT [New Testament] of the separation of the believer from evil things and ways. This sanctification is God's will for the believer...and His purpose in calling him by the gospel...it must be learned from God...as He teaches it by His Word...and it must be pursued by the believer, earnestly and undeviatingly...For the holy character, *hagiosune*...is not vicarious, i.e., it cannot be transferred or imputed, it is an individual possession, built up, little by little, as the result of obedience to the Word of God, and of following the example of Christ...in the power of the Holy Spirit. The Holy Spirit is the Agent in sanctification."[2]

As Vine implies here, the word *sanctification* is synonymous with the word *holiness.*

When we receive Christ as Savior, Jesus comes to live in us by the power of the Holy Spirit, and our life begins to change. How? First John 3:9 says, "No one born (begotten) of God [deliberately, knowingly, and habitually] practices sin, for God's nature abides in him [His principle of life, the divine sperm, remains permanently within him]; and he cannot practice sinning because he is born (begotten) of God." Jesus comes as a Seed of everything that God the Father is. So when we become born again by accepting Jesus as our Savior, holiness is planted in us as a seed and continues to grow into fullness and bear fruit as we work with the Holy Spirit, who is constantly changing us into the image of Jesus Christ.

THE HOLY SPIRIT CHANGES US

And all of us, as with unveiled face, [because we] continued to behold [in the Word of God] as in a mirror the glory of the Lord, are constantly being transfigured into His very own image in ever increasing splendor and from one degree of glory to another; [for this comes] from the Lord [Who is] the Spirit. (2 Corinthians 3:18)

From this passage we learn that both the Word of God and the power of the Holy Spirit are required in order for believers to be changed into suitable representatives of Jesus Christ.

All of us who come to Christ need change. We can and should desire change, but we cannot change ourselves. We must lean entirely on the power of the Holy Spirit to effect the necessary change. There is, of course, a work of cooperation we believers must perform, but we must never forget that the Holy Spirit is the Agent in the sanctification process. In other words, holiness is impossible without the Holy Spirit.

I have to confess that, in ignorance, there were many years when I diligently sought God for His power. I wanted to see signs, wonders, and miracles and have authority over evil spirits and do great and mighty things in Jesus' name; but I was an "outer" Christian. I was a spirit-baptized Christian for at least ten years before I understood much at all about the inner life. Then God began to teach me that His kingdom is within me. As I allowed Jesus to rule over my inner life, I began to see more power in my outer life.

Jesus' disciples didn't understand a lot of what He was trying to say about His kingdom, either. They kept thinking He was going to set up a kingdom on earth and they would all be rulers in His new government.

"Once, having been asked by the Pharisees when the kingdom of God would come, Jesus replied, 'The kingdom of God does not come with your careful observation, nor will people say, "Here it is," or "There it is," because the kingdom of God is within you'" (Luke 17:20-21 NIV).

In Romans 14:17-19 NIV the apostle Paul explains the kingdom further, "For the kingdom of God is not a matter of eating and drinking, but of righteousness, peace and joy in the Holy Spirit, because anyone who serves Christ in this way is pleasing to God and approved by men. Let us therefore make every effort to do what leads to peace, and to mutual edification."

The kingdom of God is in us, and if we want to enjoy the presence of God, we must let Jesus be Lord over our inner life through the power of the Holy Spirit. If we make Jesus Lord of our life, we are to allow Him to rule over the entirety of that kingdom that is within us. His Spirit will always lead us to what brings peace and mutual edification to those around us.

The fact that the Holy Spirit lives inside us believers is itself proof of His willingness to always be available to help us when we need Him. Those of us desiring holiness will still experience temptation, but thank God, He has given us His Spirit to enable us to resist it and make right choices. We change gradually, little by little, or as 2 Corinthians 3:18 KJV states, "from glory to glory." While these changes are taking place, we still make mistakes, and God's forgiveness is always available to us through Jesus Christ. Receiving this forgiveness actually strengthens us and enables us to keep pressing on toward new levels of holiness or better behavior.

Forgiveness frees us and cleanses our heart of strife, selfishness, and discontent. When we become aware of the presence of the Lord in our heart, we no longer want to hold on to ungodly attitudes. God subdues the power of sin in us and works to change us as we set our minds on and seek after the things that gratify the Holy Spirit.

When we feel defeated and condemned by every mistake we make, it weakens us. Instead of using our spiritual energy to feel bad about ourselves, we should use it to press on to new levels in God. Any believer who has a right heart attitude toward God will continually press toward perfection, but none of us will totally arrive at perfection as long as we are in a flesh-and-bones body living in the present world.

Recently I was feeling bad about a wrong attitude I had displayed. I picked up a book I had been reading, and my eyes fell on these words: "There is a 100 percent chance that you will make a mistake today." Those words reminded me that Jesus died for people just like me, ones who have a heart to do what is right but who don't always succeed.

God, in His grace and mercy, has made provision for our sins (errors, faults, weaknesses, infirmities, and failures). That provision is forgiveness. When you fail, receive God's forgiveness, but don't stop trying to do better.

THE THREE PERSONS OF THE TRINITY

Jesus told His disciples that when He went away, the Father would send another Comforter, the Holy Spirit, who would live in them, counseling, teaching, helping, strengthening, interceding, performing the functions of an advocate, convicting of sin, and convincing of righteousness. The Holy Spirit would come into close fellowship with them, guide them into all truth, and transmit to them everything that was theirs as joint heirs with Jesus Christ (see John 16:7-15; Romans 8:17 KJV).

God would never expect us to do anything without providing us what we need to do it. We need the Holy Spirit, and God has provided Him. Every good thing comes from God, who is the Source of all good things (see James 1:17), through the sacrifice of His Son Jesus Christ, and is administered to us by the Holy Spirit.

The Holy Trinity, which is one God in three persons, is a concept that our finite minds cannot grasp easily. It does not work out mathematically; nonetheless, it is true. We serve one God, who is the only true God, but He ministers to us in three persons—God the Father, Jesus Christ the Son, and the Holy Spirit.

As we have seen, everything we need from God the Father comes through Jesus Christ the Son and is administered by the Holy Spirit. I am restating that point to emphasize how important it is not only to know God the Father and Jesus His Son, but also to know the Holy Spirit personally and to have close fellowship with Him.

Scriptural proof of the Trinity is found in many places in the Bible. For example, Genesis 1:26 tells us, "God said, Let Us [Father, Son, and Holy Spirit] make mankind in Our image, after Our likeness." In this verse, God does not refer to Himself as "Me" and "My," but as "Us" and "Our." We see the Trinity in Matthew 3:16-17 KJV at the baptism of Jesus, when the Holy Spirit descended like a dove, and at the same time a voice (the Father's) came out of heaven saying, "This is my beloved Son, in whom I am well pleased" (v. 17). In John 14:16 Jesus told His disciples, "And I will ask the Father, and He will give you another Comforter."

In Matthew 28:19 the disciples were told by Jesus to baptize in the name of the Father and the Son and the Holy Spirit. The apostolic benediction found in 2 Corinthians 13:14 NIV reads as follows: "May the grace of the Lord Jesus Christ, and the love of God, and the fellowship of the Holy Spirit be with you all."

When Jesus died on the cross, He was trusting in God to raise Him from the dead, which God did—by the power of the Holy Spirit. This truth is discussed in Romans 8:11.

Based on these and other supporting Scriptures, it is impossible to deny the concurrent existence of the three persons of the Holy Trinity. Yes, the Trinity is a scriptural fact, and it is time the Holy Spirit is given the place of honor in our lives that is due Him. He has been ignored for far too long and by far too many. May He forgive us for our ignorance and neglect of Him.

GET TO KNOW THE HOLY SPIRIT

It is the revelation and work of the person of the Holy Spirit that I am endeavoring to bring forth in this book. I approach the subject with fear and trembling, for what human flesh can accurately write on the subject of the Holy Spirit, unless the Holy Spirit Himself is the Leader of the project? Therefore, I ask for wisdom and guidance from the Helper (the Holy Spirit) and lean entirely on Him to bring revelation about Himself to you through this book.

It is my desire that you will understand the ministry of the Holy Spirit, so you can appreciate it, cooperate with it, and—through it—come into a new level of *intimacy with God,* one that will lead you into His good plan for your life.

Outer power only comes from inner purity, and that inner purification (or sanctification) is a work of the Holy Spirit living within. He wants to fill you with Himself, to give you the power to live the abundant life that is available through believing in Jesus Christ.

Be willing to take a serious inventory of what is going on in your inner life. Not what is going on in your circumstances at home, not what is going on in your bank account, not what is going on in your marriage or ministry, but what is going on inside of you. Allow the Holy Spirit to lead you to His perfect peace.

4

Live under the New Covenant

~

When Adam and Eve were in the Garden of Eden with God before they fell into sin, they had close fellowship and intimacy with Him; they were spiritually alive.[1] Their spirit, alert to the presence of God, was the leader of their body and soul.[2] They had been warned that if they disobeyed God, they would die (see Genesis 2:16-17). It was not physical death they had been warned of, but spiritual death.[3]

Once Adam and Eve experienced disobedience, they suddenly understood the magnitude of God's holiness. Ashamed of their own unholy nature, they hid from Him. They had known God as a friend; they had walked beside Him and talked with Him face to face. But now they were afraid of Him—as if He were a consuming fire.

Sin cannot survive in the presence of God's holiness, so when Adam and Eve heard the sound of the Lord walking in the garden, they instinctively tried to hide the shame of their nakedness. Even in their disobedience, God demonstrated His compassion for them by making them coats from animal skins to cover their shame, marking the first death and blood sacrifice to cover the consequence of sin (see Genesis 3:9-21).

It would have been tragic for Adam and Eve to hide from God for all eternity, so Genesis 3:22-24 explains that God drove them from Eden lest they eat from the tree of life and live forever in their current condition, separated from God by sin.

Adam and Eve's lives had been turned upside down. They became soul- and- body-ruled and spiritually dead, no longer sensitive to God's intimate presence.

We remain in a state of separation from God until we accept Jesus Christ's substitutionary work and through faith receive Him as our Savior. With our sins forgiven we are no longer separated from God's presence; we are free to enjoy an intimate friendship with our Creator as He originally planned. But now, God does not choose to meet us in our gardens at the end of each day. He does not choose to live on a nearby mountain where we can come visit Him by invitation only. He does not choose to live in a tent of meeting as He did with Moses when the children of Israel traveled through the wilderness. And He does not choose to live in a tabernacle made by our own hands.

When we accept Christ, the Holy Spirit comes to dwell *in* us (see John 14:20 KJV). God chooses to move into our spirit—into the center core of our lives—where He can be closer to us than any other living thing. When God's Holy Spirit moves into our human spirit, our spirit is prepared as a dwelling place for God (see 1 Corinthians 3:16-17) and is made holy because God is there.

This holy state into which we as believers are placed is then worked out in our soul and body to be seen in our everyday life. It occurs as a process, and the phases of change we go through actually become our testimony to those who know us.

Genesis chapter 3 tells us how Eve was deceived by Satan and how she enticed Adam to join her in disobedience. Their disobedient actions caused God, in His mercy, to immediately enact a plan for the redemption of His creation. He would buy back His people from slavery to sin and put them in a position to once again enjoy His presence and live holy lives (see Acts 20:28; 1 Corinthians 6:20).

Over thousands of years, God worked out His plan. While He was waiting for the appointed time of Jesus' arrival, the Holy Spirit was *with* man. Man knew right from wrong because God had given him the Law. The Law was holy and perfect, but man was not perfect and therefore could not keep the Law perfectly. During those years, when man had to make sacrifices for his sins, he could never be delivered from the consciousness of sin. He was always aware of being a sinner, which brought condemnation and guilt upon him.

The Law given to Moses made provision for mankind to cover up his sins through the sacrifices of the blood of bulls and goats, but his sins could never be completely removed (see Hebrews 10:1-14).

God never gave the Law expecting man to keep it, but rather to make him aware of his sinful, impotent position and of his desperate need of a Savior (see Romans 5:20). You see, we won't receive anything we don't believe we need. God had His Son prepared as a sacrifice to be received by faith by those who believe, but the Holy Spirit also needed to come and work in the lives of unbelievers to convict them of sin and their need of a Deliverer.

Before people accept Christ as Savior, they must be

convinced of their need for a Savior. Some people are convinced much sooner than others. Sad to say, some never get convinced, and many others waste much of their lives trying to save themselves before finally surrendering to Jesus.

The Holy Spirit works in the lives of unbelievers to make them conscious or aware of their sinful state and their need for salvation. Once they accept Jesus as their Savior, that facet of His job is completed. He then comes to live inside them to help them in every way that they need help. This help includes, but is not limited to, the process of sanctification, which means to be freed from sin and set apart for a special purpose.

When Jesus died, He was the perfect Lamb of God, the last sacrifice that would ever be needed (see John 1:29; Hebrews 7:26-27). From that time forward, all those who believed in Him and trusted Him for their salvation could have a righteous consciousness and enjoy the presence of God. They could have close fellowship and intimacy with God, as Adam and Eve did prior to sinning.

NO MORE SACRIFICE FOR SIN!

Whereas this One [Christ], after He had offered a single sacrifice for our sins [that shall avail] for all time, sat down at the right hand of God... Now where there is absolute remission (forgiveness and cancellation of the penalty) of these [sins and law-breaking], there is no longer any offering made to atone for sin. (Hebrews 10:12,18, emphasis mine)

What good news! No more sacrifices needed to atone for sins. Now we can turn to Jesus Christ, the final sacrifice good for all time, and *continuously* receive forgiveness and cancellation of the penalty of sin.

Under the old covenant, the high priest went once a year into the Holy of Holies where God met with him on the mercy seat. He took the blood of bulls and goats and sacrificed it to atone for his own sins and the sins of the people (see Hebrews 9:7).

But as soon as that ritual was performed, the account started adding up again for the next year. That would be like working all year to pay off last year's Christmas debts, and as soon as you pay the last bill, going back out and making debts for Christmas this year. You are only out of debt for a few minutes. It must have felt horrible never to be able to get away from the feeling of guilt and condemnation.

Those under the old covenant believed in the coming of a Messiah who would deliver them from all their sins, but they never actually saw the result of their faith except in their hearts.[4] They continually worked at trying to please God.

NEW COVENANT BELIEVERS WHO STILL LIVE UNDER THE OLD COVENANT

Do not be conformed to this world (this age), [fashioned after and adapted to its external, superficial customs], but be transformed (changed) by the [entire] renewal of your mind [by its new ideals and its new attitude], so that you may prove [for yourselves] what is the good and acceptable and

perfect will of God, even the thing which is good
and acceptable and perfect [in His sight for you].
(Romans 12:2)

Although a new and living way has been provided to
us by virtue of the sacrificial death of Jesus Christ and
His resurrection (see Hebrews 10:19-20 KJV), many
who believe in Christ still keep themselves under the old
covenant system. They still remain trapped in works of
the flesh, which is trying to reach God by virtue of good
works.

We no longer have to try to reach God. He has reached
us and taken hold of us through Jesus Christ. God cannot
get any closer to us than to offer to live inside of us, in our
spirit or our heart. I accepted Jesus Christ as my Savior
at the age of nine. I became aware of my sinful state and
sought forgiveness from God through Jesus. Although I
was born of the Spirit, I never knew it. I had no teaching on that subject, and therefore I remained in darkness
experientially even though the Light was living in me.

As a young adult I went to church faithfully, was
baptized, took confirmation classes, and did everything
I understood I needed to be doing, yet I never enjoyed
closeness and intimacy with God. I believe multitudes
are in that position today and have been throughout the
centuries.

*Jesus did not die to give us religion; He died to give us
a personal relationship with God through Him and by the
power of the Holy Spirit Whom He would send to dwell in
each believer.*

I was born of the Spirit but still lacked revelation of
what I had. People can be rich, but if they believe they

are poor, their experience will be no different from that of others whose lives are filled with poverty. If people have a great inheritance but do not know it, they cannot spend it.

Romans 12:2 informs us that God has a plan in mind for us. His will toward us is good and acceptable and perfect, but we must completely renew our minds before we will ever experience this good thing God has planned (see vv. 1-2). We renew our minds, get a new attitude and new ideals, by studying God's Word. His Word is truth (see John 17:17) and exposes all the lies of Satan we have believed and been deceived by.

Adam and Eve believed Satan's lie that there was something outside of God's provision that would satisfy them (see Genesis 3:1-7). We each make this same mistake until we learn that *nothing* can deeply satisfy us except the presence of almighty God.

Our contentment cannot be dependent on our spouse. Our joy cannot be derived from our kids, or our friends, or those who work with us. People will inevitably disappoint us, because God created us for His fellowship, and nothing will satisfy that longing but Him.

But Satan still whispers lies to us saying, "Oh, this will make you happy. This is what you need." Then we spend all of our energy entreating God for that *thing*. I couldn't even count the times I have thought, *Oh, that is what I need, God!* Then I would put all my spiritual energies, my prayer, and my study into receiving that thing.

Sometimes the desires of our heart can even seem noble. For years I wanted my ministry to grow. When it didn't, I became frustrated and dissatisfied. I fasted, prayed, and tried everything I knew to try to get more people to come to my meetings.

I remember complaining when God would not give me the increase I wanted, and it was keeping me upset most of the time. I would come to a meeting, and everybody would be late, nobody would be excited, and sometimes the attendance would be half of what it was the time before. Then I would leave the meeting questioning, "What am I doing wrong, God? Why aren't You blessing me? I'm fasting. I'm praying. I'm giving and believing. God, look at all my good works, and You're not moving on my behalf."

I was so frustrated I felt like I was going to explode. I asked, "God! Why are You doing this to me?"

He said, "Joyce, I am teaching you that man does not live by bread alone."

I knew God had spoken to me from the Bible, but at that time I wasn't familiar enough with it to know where that Scripture could be found. I knew He had spoken His Word, a *rhema* (a personal, individual message) to me. So I searched the Scriptures for more explanation, but I didn't like what I found. Deuteronomy 8:2-3 says:

> And you shall [earnestly] remember all the way which the Lord your God led you these forty years in the wilderness, to humble you and to prove you, to know what was in your [mind and] heart, whether you would keep His commandments or not. And He humbled you and allowed you to hunger and fed you with manna, which you did not know nor did your fathers know, that He might make you recognize and personally know that man does not live by bread only, but man lives by every word that proceeds out of the mouth of the Lord.

God wanted my desires to be purely for more of Him. The Lord said to me, "Anything that you have to have besides Me to be satisfied is something the devil can use against you."

It's not that we shouldn't want things; God just doesn't want us to put them before our desire for Him. He wants us to find a place in Him where we are living in His manifest presence and are satisfied with God Himself. He demands first place in our lives. Consider 1 John 5:21:

> Little children, keep yourselves from idols (false gods)—[from anything and everything that would occupy the place in your heart due to God, from any sort of substitute for Him that would take first place in your life].

THE NEW COVENANT HAS ALL YOU NEED

Colossians 3:1 tells us to "seek the [rich, eternal treasures] that are above, where Christ is." Verses 2 and 3 say, "And set your minds and keep them set on what is above (the higher things), not on the things that are on earth. For...your [new, real] life is hidden with Christ in God."

What do we have our minds on all day? What are we thinking about all the time? If we have our minds on our problems, then we are not seeking God. If we are trying to figure out how we can get God to do a particular thing for us, then we are not seeking Him with a pure heart.

Isaiah 49:8-10 prophesies God's promise to answer us and to quench our craving for Him:

Thus says the Lord, In an acceptable and favorable time I have heard and answered you, and in a day of salvation I have helped you; and I will preserve you and give you for a covenant to the people, to raise up and establish the land [from its present state of ruin] and to apportion and cause them to inherit the desolate [moral wastes of heathenism, their] heritages. Saying to those who are bound, Come forth, and to those who are in [spiritual] darkness, Show yourselves [come into the light of the Sun of righteousness]. They shall feed in all the ways [in which they go], and their pastures shall be [not in deserts, but] on all the bare [grass-covered] hills.

Verse 10 is very exciting:

They will not hunger or thirst, neither will mirage [mislead] or scorching wind or sun smite them; for He Who has mercy on them will lead them, and by springs of water will He guide them.

We actually thirst for more of God, but if we don't know He is what we are craving, we can be easily misled. Satan puts up a mirage much as he did with Adam and Eve. He says, "This is what you need; this will satisfy you." But if we set our minds on seeking God—if we give Him first place in our desires, thoughts, conversation, and choices—our thirst will truly be quenched, and we will not be misled.

David expressed his longing for the Lord in Psalm 42:1 NIV, saying, "As the deer pants for streams of water, so my soul pants for you, O God." Verse 2 in *The Amplified*

Bible says, "My inner self thirsts for God, for the living God. When shall I come and behold the face of God?"

We have needs, and God says, "Here I am. I have everything you need." We are to search after God like a thirsty man in the desert. What does a thirsty man think about? Nothing but water! He isn't concerned about anything else but finding what it takes to quench his thirst.

If we are looking for material things or improved circumstances instead of looking for God, Satan can set up a mirage to put us on the wrong track. But if we are seeking God, the devil can't mislead us, because God has promised that those who seek Him with their whole heart will find Him.

God says, "My people shall no longer be led by a mirage, but they will know to seek Me, the Living Water. Those who come to Me will never thirst again" (see John 4:10,14).

Until our desire for more of God takes first place in our life, the devil will have an edge over us. Once we see the truth, he will lose his advantage, and we will be in a position to begin making radical progress in our relationship and fellowship with God. Most of us will try almost everything else before we finally learn that what we need is not what God can give us, but God Himself. Those times often represent years of frustration and misery, but thank God, His Holy Spirit who lives in us teaches us and reveals truth to us as we continue to study, read, and listen to the Word of God.

So Jesus said to those Jews who had believed in Him, If you abide in My word [hold fast to My teachings and live in accordance with them], you are truly

My disciples. And you will know the Truth, and the Truth will set you free. (John 8:31-32)

If you are diligent to seek God, you will know Him in a deeper, more intimate way. God will reveal Himself to you; He will be found of you. When God wants to manifest Himself, He will, so don't get frustrated trying to *find* God. Just learn to wait on Him and pray, "God, reveal Yourself to me. Manifest Your presence to me."

God manifests His presence in many ways. Sometimes we can't see Him, but, like the wind, we can see the work He does in us. If I'm weary, tired, worn out, frustrated, or bothered about something, and I become refreshed after spending time with God, then I know that the wind of the Lord has blown upon me.

God wants to bring a refreshing into your life, like a mighty wind. Don't be poverty stricken in your soul when the answer is living on the inside of you. If you are too busy to spend time with God, then make some adjustments to your lifestyle. Don't be burned out, upset, weary, and stressed out when times of refreshing are available to you.

So repent (change your mind and purpose); turn around and return [to God], that your sins may be erased (blotted out, wiped clean), that times of refreshing (of recovering from the effects of heat, of reviving with fresh air) may come from the presence of the Lord. (Acts 3:19)

Learn to come apart from the busyness of life to spend time with God the way Jesus did. I tell people, "You'd better come apart before you come apart." You can't wait for everyone around you to approve of the time you need to spend with God. Somebody will always find something that they think you ought to be doing for them.

Don't try to substitute time spent working for God for time spent being with God. I was proud of myself because I had a job at a church, I went to all the prayer meetings, and I counseled people about God's ways. But I remember vividly exactly where I was the day when God said to me, "Joyce, you work *for* Me, but you don't spend any time *with* Me."

I decided then to set aside time each day to spend with God. When I first started to have this regular time with the Lord, my children weren't used to my spending time away from them.

They would come to me and complain, "Mom, you're always in this room."

"No," I would say, "I'm not *always* in this room. I'm in here for a certain period of time, and when I'm done, I'll come out."

"But why don't you come out and talk to us? Why don't you come make our breakfast?"

I would reply, "You can put cereal in a bowl and pour milk on it."

Now, I'm not saying that we're not to take care of our families and meet their needs. But at that time in my life I had a lot of problems, and I knew something had to be done about them. I wasn't acting too nice. I wasn't controlling my temper very well. I wasn't operating in the fruit of the Spirit, and I needed to seek God.

So I finally told my children, "Instead of trying to get me out of here, you'd better pray I stay in here! You'd better help me find ways to get in this room and spend time with God so I will be a nicer person. You ought to say, 'I'll do the dishes, Mom! You go to your room!'" I knew if I did not spend time with God, my family would not enjoy me very much.

The flesh cannot conquer the flesh. We need to turn to the Holy Ghost and confess, "I can't change myself, God, but You can change me. I'm going to seek You. I need You to blow on me like a mighty wind and bring a refreshing into my life."

God will be found of you when you seek Him with your whole heart. You will be refreshed beyond anything you can imagine. He will fill you with peace and joy. But I know by the Spirit of God that you will have to prune some things out of your life and make more room for God in your busy schedule.

You may be doing things that could be pruned away, things that you have no idea why you are even doing in the first place. You don't enjoy them; you may even resent having to do them. You may dread them because they drain you, frustrate you, and steal your joy—yet you keep doing them. It's time to live on purpose and to make choices that will help you know God more intimately.

Any person who accepts Christ as Savior begins a journey; that journey leads to an intimate friendship with God, and what an awesome journey it is.

INTIMACY LEVEL
2

~

God's Transforming Power

But we are citizens of the state (commonwealth, homeland) which is in heaven, and from it also we earnestly and patiently await [the coming of] the Lord Jesus Christ (the Messiah) [as] Savior, Who will transform and fashion anew the body of our humiliation to conform to and be like the body of His glory and majesty, by exerting that power which enables Him even to subject everything to Himself.

—PHILIPPIANS 3:20-21

5

"Not by Might, Nor by Power, but by My Spirit"

~

Not by might, nor by power, but by my spirit, saith the LORD of hosts. (Zechariah 4:6 KJV)

We will never have true success in anything in life except by the power of the Holy Spirit. Working to acquire possessions or fame will only frustrate and tire us. But allowing the Holy Spirit to do good works through us will bring contentment and deep joy to our own life.

In John 17:4-5 Jesus said, "Father, glorify me now for I have glorified You by completing the work that You have given me to do" (paraphrase). That passage gripped my heart one day, and I broke into tears. I thought, *Oh God, if only I can stand before You on the Last Day, look You in the eye, and not have to be ashamed, but be able to say, "Lord, I did it. With Your help I came through to the finish. I completed what you gave me to do."*

I realized that real joy comes from being an empty vessel for God's use and glory: letting Him choose where

He's going to take me, what He's going to do with me,
when He's going to do it—and not arguing about it. It's
one thing to be willing to do *everything* for the glory of
God (1 Corinthians 10:31); it's another thing entirely to be
willing to do *anything* for the glory of God.

The Holy Ghost lives inside of us and is working to
help us get our minds off ourselves and our own problems. We are to deposit our problems with God, since we
can't do anything about them anyway, and spend our time
doing something for those around us who are hurting or
who have needs that must be attended to. God's presence
in us will anoint us to do good things for others with ease.

> For it is by grace you have been saved, through
> faith—and this not from yourselves, it is the gift of
> God—not by works, so that no one can boast. For
> we are God's workmanship, created in Christ Jesus
> to do good works, which God prepared in advance
> for us to do. (Ephesians 2:8-10 NIV)

Years ago, when I first started walking more intimately with God, I used to wait for a word from God for
everything I wanted to do—until I learned that His Spirit
abides in me to do good works. In the early years of walking with God, it was in my heart to give a woman in need
ten dollars (which could buy more then than it can now).
I carried that desire around for three weeks until I finally
prayed, "God, is it really You telling me to give this person the money? I'll do this if it's *really* You!"

He answered so clearly, "Joyce, even if it isn't *really*
Me, I won't get mad at you if you bless somebody!"

One of the fruits of God's Spirit living within us is

goodness (see Galatians 5:22-23). Therefore we have a desire to be good to people. God told Abraham that He was going to bless him so that he could dispense blessings to others (see Genesis 12:2). Imagine how glorious it would be to get to the point where we just lived to love God and let good works flow out from us on a daily basis.

There is always someone, somewhere, who needs a word of encouragement. Somebody needs a babysitter. Somebody needs a ride. The world is full of people with needs. Abiding in the presence of God turns our minds away from our own problems and toward the needs of others; then He anoints us with power to do good works for His glory.

If we would simply ask God each day to show us how to bless someone for His glory, we would experience the joy, contentment, and peace we long for ourselves.

ARE YOU FULL OF YOURSELF?

God once said to me, "Joyce, people are unhappy because they're full of themselves." If we are full of ourselves, we're concerned about our own needs and desires all the time, instead of thinking about the needs and desires of others.

I often demonstrate in my meetings that when we are full of ourselves we appear to others like wind-up robots that march about repeating, "What about me? What about me? What about me?"

But if we are full of God, we will be so happy it won't make any difference what our circumstances are. If we stay full of God, His resurrection life will rise up inside of us and transform us into the likeness of Christ. The apostle Paul demonstrated that he desired to be full of God when he said:

> [For my determined purpose is] that I may know Him [that I may progressively become more deeply and intimately acquainted with Him, perceiving and recognizing and understanding the wonders of His Person more strongly and more clearly], and that I may in that same way come to know the power out-flowing from His resurrection [which it exerts over believers], and that I may so share His sufferings as to be continually transformed [in spirit into His likeness even] to His death, [in the hope] that if possible I may attain the [spiritual and moral] resurrection [that lifts me] out from among the dead [even while in the body]. (Philippians 3:10-11)

When we are full of ourselves, we are full of death and darkness. When we are full of God, we are full of life and light. We should pray like Paul, "Oh God, that I might know You and the power of Your resurrection that lifts me out from among the dead even while I'm in the body." Praying this way will keep us from trying to manipulate people into doing what we want them to do, and from throwing fits when things don't go our way.

Believe me, I was an expert on throwing fits, until God taught me to trust Him for everything. For example, one time I wanted to stop at a certain place to eat on the way to a meeting.

I told Dave, "I'd really like to stop at this place because it has good sandwiches, soup, salad, and coffee that I like.

I'm going to work hard all weekend, and I'd just like to get a good meal before I dive into it. I'd really enjoy doing that."

But Dave said, "I'd like to take you, but I don't see how it's going to work out. If I do, we're going to get there late, and I need to oversee the tape tables. There are a lot of other things I still need to do to get ready for the meeting."

God had been dealing with me about the importance of not being selfish and full of myself. So even though I was disappointed, I realized if I only thought about what I wanted and cared nothing for Dave's need and responsibility to get to the meeting early, I would be unhappy. I had a choice: to act according to the flesh or according to the Spirit. So I said, "That's okay, Dave. I understand that you've got a lot to do."

But two, three, four years before I would have thrown a fit about not stopping where I wanted to stop. I know that Dave's a lover of peace, so if I had nagged and pushed, he probably would have taken me where I wanted to eat. I might have won with Dave, but I would have lost with God. We must learn that getting our way about things may please the flesh, but it doesn't always please God. Giving someone else his or her way may be what will please God.

I used to think I was the only one who had anything to do when we came to our meetings. I didn't understand that Dave faced a time line, too. Dave finally got a little stern with me one day, when I was fussing about where we would eat. (Isn't it amazing the fits we throw about eating? Even those of us who don't eat very much can throw some pretty dandy fits about getting food when we want it, the way we want it!) That day, our whole team was going to go out to eat breakfast, but I had to stay behind and study, so I wanted them to bring something back for me. But Dave said, "I really don't think we're going to have time to do that. I'd like to, but I'm not going to get to the meeting in time to take care of the tapes if I do that. Couldn't you eat fruit this morning?"

Right away my little "fit thrower" kicked into power, and I said, "Well fine! Just leave me here in this hotel room and all the rest of you go out and have a good time. I'll just stay here and get ready for the meeting and starve!"

Have you ever thrown a fit about anything? We can throw silent fits, or we can throw out-loud fits. There are the pouting fits where we just close up inside. And there are the hang-the-head fits, the shut-the-mouth fits, and the Mr.- or Ms.-Stoneface fits. Or we may have a moaning fit to convince ourselves that nobody ever thinks about us, even though we do all kinds of nice things for others, and they don't even care if we get to eat or not.

So there I was, throwing my fit—until Dave got a little firm with me. (Sometimes we need somebody to get a bit firm with us.) Dave said, "Oh Joyce, everybody on this team does nothing but try to make things easy and right for you."

I knew Dave was right, but it was difficult for me to admit it.

So often when we want our way, we don't even think about what other people around us are going through. Everybody's got their own situations to handle. Everybody's got things they're going through. If we ever want to be truly happy, we have got to get beyond living in the midst of self, self, self.

LEARN TO TRUST GOD FOR ALL THINGS

We have a choice of (1) trying to get our own way by throwing fits to manipulate people, or (2) doing what God wants us to do, trusting Him to work out everything according to His perfect plan for us and for everyone else involved in our situation.

Dave used to say to me, "Will you stop trying to convince me? *You* are not going to convince me. Let God convince me if I need to be convinced."

I had a hard time letting God convince anybody of anything. I didn't have a problem trusting God to *try* to convince Dave, but I wasn't sure I could trust Dave to *listen*. It is hard to keep from trying to help God. We have our own little ways of trying to take care of our circumstances—and everyone involved in them.

But the reward is great for those who learn to lean on and trust in God to work out all things for their good (see Proverbs 3:5; Romans 8:28). Learning to trust God takes a while, so don't be discouraged if you can't give up self-care in the next twenty-four hours. However, I strongly encourage you to practice trusting yourself and all of your own needs to God's care. Trusting Him to work out your circumstances instead of using your own might and power will bring deep satisfying joy into your life. Once you take that initial step and trust things to God, you will soon realize it's fun to see what He will do.

In John 15:5 Jesus said, "Apart from Me [cut off from vital union with Me], you can do nothing." Hebrews 13:5 tells us He will never leave us or forsake us. In other words, He will always be with us (see Matthew 28:20;

John 14:18). The reason Jesus promises to be with us always is that He knows we need help in our everyday life.

It often takes a long time for us to humble ourselves and realize we need help with everything. We like to believe we can do whatever needs to be done independently and without anyone's assistance. However, the Lord sent us a Divine Helper; therefore, we must need help. Jesus Himself *continually* intercedes for us as He sits at the right hand of God (see Hebrews 7:25; Romans 8:34); therefore, we must *continually* need God's intervention in our lives. We are actually very needy and totally unable to handle life properly on our own.

Although we may seem to manage ourselves for a while, sooner or later we begin to fall apart in some way or another if we are not receiving divine help. Often we do fine until trouble comes.

It may be a broken marriage, the death of a loved one, some sickness or disease, financial lack, the loss of a job or of something else important to life. But sooner or later, we all come to a place of having to recognize our neediness. At least we must recognize it if we ever intend to live life the way it is meant to be lived—with righteousness, peace, and joy (see Romans 14:17).

On the outside, many people look as if they have it all together, while on the inside they are very unhappy. Some struggle all their life because they are too proud to humble themselves and ask for help. They may have other people convinced they are successful, but actually they are a failure. They may even have themselves convinced they are a self-made success, but sad to say, most of them end up with nothing but themselves—which is an empty and sad existence.

When I was what I refer to as a "religious believer," I only asked God for help when I was confronted with what I felt was a desperate situation or a serious problem that I could not find an answer for. I prayed in a general way each day—not much, but I did pray.

After I became what I call a "relational believer," I quickly learned that the Holy Spirit was living in me to help me and that I actually needed help with everything from getting my hair fixed properly, bowling with a good score, and choosing the right gift for someone, to making right decisions and getting through the desperate situations and serious problems of life. When I understood this truth and realized that Jesus did not die to give me a specific brand of religion but to bring me into a deep personal relationship with God, I made the transition from a "religious believer" to a "relational believer." My faith was no longer based on my works but on His works. I saw that His mercy and goodness opened up a way for me to be in close fellowship with God.

When Jesus died, the veil in the temple that separated the Holy Place from the Most Holy Place was torn from the top to the bottom (see Mark 15:37-38). That opened the way for anyone to go into God's presence. As we have seen, prior to Jesus' death, only the high priest could go into God's presence, and then only once a year with the blood of slain animals, to cover and atone for his sins and the sins of the people.

It is significant that the tear in the Veil of the temple was from top to bottom. The veil or curtain was so high and thick that no human could have torn it—it was torn supernaturally by the power of God, showing that He was opening up a new and living way for His people to approach Him.[1]

God has from the beginning desired fellowship with man; that was His purpose in making him. He never wanted to close people off from His presence, but He knew that His holiness was so powerful that it would destroy anything unholy that came near it. Therefore, the way for sinners to be completely cleansed had to be provided prior to man's having access to God's presence.

In Exodus 3:2-5 we read how God appeared to Moses in the burning bush and told him to take his shoes off of his feet because he was standing on holy ground. I believe the significance was that nothing that had touched earth could touch the holiness of God.

We are *in* the world, but we are not to be *of* it (John 17:14-16). Our worldliness and earthly ways separate us from the presence of God. Unless we are constantly receiving by faith the sacrifice of Jesus' blood to keep us clean, we cannot enjoy intimacy and come into proper fellowship with God.

HUMAN WEAKNESS RENDERS MAN DEPENDENT

O LORD, I know that the way of man is not in himself: it is not in man that walketh to direct his steps. (Jeremiah 10:23 KJV)

Jeremiah said it well in the verse quoted above: It really is impossible for man to properly run his own life. You and I need help, and a lot of it. Admitting that fact is a sign of spiritual maturity, not a sign of weakness. We are weak unless we find our strength in God, and the sooner we face that fact the better off we will be.

You may be like I once was—trying so hard to make things work out right and always failing. Your problem is not that you are a failure; your problem is simply that you have not gone to the right source for help.

God won't allow us to succeed without Him. Remember that true success is not just the ability to accumulate material wealth; it is the ability to truly enjoy life and everything God provides in it. Many people have position, wealth, power, fame, and other similar attributes, but they may not have what really matters—good relationships, right standing with God, peace, joy, contentment, satisfaction, good health, and the ability to enjoy life. Not everything that appears well *is* well!

According to Psalm 127:1, unless the Lord builds the house, those who build it labor in vain. We may be able to build, but what we build won't last if God is not involved in it. He is our Partner in life, and as such, He desires to be a part of everything we do. God is interested in every facet of our life. Believing that truth is the beginning of an exciting journey with Him. It makes it personal, not just global.

We know Jesus died for the world, but we must believe that He died for us personally and individually. We know that Jesus loves people, but we must believe that He loves each of us as a unique and imperfect individual. His love is unconditional; that means it is based on who He is, not on who we are or what we do.

I challenge you to take a step of faith and begin to approach God like a little child. At the time I am writing this book, I have an eighteen-month-old granddaughter, and she is certainly dependent on other people for literally everything. She is especially dependent on her parents. She will, of course, grow up and begin doing certain things for herself, and it is right that she does so. However, the principle that Jesus gave us in Mark 10:13-15 remains true: Unless we come to Him as a little child, we will in no way enter into the kingdom of God. How do we adults come to Him as a child? We come to Him with a childlike attitude.

We think we should be all grown up, and in some ways we may need to grow up. Yet at the same time, in other ways we need to become like a little child. Being childish is different from becoming childlike. Childishness is linked with immaturity, uncontrolled emotions and passions, and a self-centered attitude. Being childlike is linked with lowliness, humility, and a readiness to forgive.

A humble person has no difficulty asking for help. The apostle Paul certainly would be considered a great man, and yet in 2 Corinthians 3:5 he wrote: "Not that we are fit (qualified and sufficient in ability) of ourselves to form personal judgments or to claim or count anything as coming from us, but our power and ability and sufficiency are from God."

Paul knew where his ability and power came from, and he knew it was not from himself. He testified to human weaknesses, but he said that Christ's strength was made perfect in his weakness (see 2 Corinthians 12:9).

Jesus has come into our lives to help us and to strengthen us, enabling us to do with ease what we could never do without Him. *Grace* is said to stand for *God's Riches At Christ's Expense*. The grace of God comes to us as a free gift, to be received by faith (see Ephesians 2:8-9). However, we have to admit that we need it, or we will not be open to receive it.

DOING GOOD

> For I know that nothing good dwells within me, that
> is, in my flesh. I can will what is right, but I cannot
> perform it. [I have the intention and urge to do what
> is right, but no power to carry it out.] (Romans 7:18)

By virtue of the new birth, which occurs when we receive
Jesus as our Savior, we have a desire in us to be good and
do good, yet at the same time we seem to have no power
to do it. What is the problem?

When we become born again, God puts a new nature
in us (see 2 Corinthians 5:17) but leaves us in a fleshly
body with a soul that has inbred weaknesses. This is for
the sole purpose of rendering us needy. Remember, if we
don't need Jesus, we usually won't pay much attention to
Him, especially in the beginning of our walk with Him.

All good comes from God. Man is not good; God
is. Even Jesus said to someone who called Him "Good
Master" that there is none good but God (see Matthew
19:16-17 KJV). Although Jesus actually is God Himself,
the second person of the Trinity, in this instance He was
referring to His human side.

Remember that Jesus was both Son of God and Son of
man. In His human nature, He knew that the only good He
could ever do was what the Holy Spirit did through Him.
Luke chapter 1 tells us that His mother, Mary, became
pregnant by an act of the Holy Spirit (which will be discussed later). God was His Father. So Jesus was actually
God incarnate in man. He was in the same position that
we are in as born-again children of God. We are human

flesh with God living on the inside of us. This almost sounds too good to be true, but as we have seen, it can be proven again and again scripturally.

ARE YOU JUST GOING THROUGH THE MOTIONS?

> But the Comforter (Counselor, Helper, Intercessor, Advocate, Strengthener, Standby), the Holy Spirit, Whom the Father will send in My name [in My place, to represent Me and act on My behalf], He will teach you all things. And He will cause you to recall (will remind you of, bring to your remembrance) everything I have told you. (John 14:26)

I regret all the years I wasted being religious, just going through the motions, following formulas, and not having the revelation that Jesus was alive in me through the power of the Holy Spirit.

We ask people all the time if they have received Jesus, without ever really thinking about what that means. If we receive Him, then what do we do with Him? We certainly don't put Him in a little box marked "Sunday morning," go get Him out on that day, sing a few songs to Him, talk to Him a little, then put Him back in the box until the next Sunday. If we receive Him, then we have Him. Since He said He will never leave us or forsake us, He must be ours to keep.

I urge you to begin taking full advantage of your blood-bought relationship with God, through Jesus, by the power of the Holy Spirit. Don't tuck God away for emergencies and Sunday mornings. Allow Him to work in every area of your life through the power of the Holy Spirit. Why not lift your hands in worship to Him right now and sincerely say, "Welcome home, Holy Spirit"?

The Holy Spirit will help us do good things, but He will also help us by reminding us to give God the glory and not to try to keep it for ourselves. One of the ministries of the Holy Spirit is to remind us of what we need to know when we need to know it.

Countless times over the years the Holy Spirit has reminded me of where things are that I have misplaced and to do things I have forgotten to do. He has also kept me on the right track by reminding me of what God's Word says about certain issues at key times of decision in my life.

I learned I could trust God to help with big decisions by taking small needs to Him, too. One time we had some family members over and wanted to watch a movie, but we couldn't find the remote control. Everyone had gathered in the living room, but neither Dave nor I knew how to work the TV without the remote, so we were anxious to find it.

We searched everywhere for it. We looked in bedrooms, under couches, and under couch pillows. We called two of our other children who had been using the TV earlier that day to see if they remembered putting it somewhere, but nothing was producing the remote control.

I decided to pray. So silently in my heart I said, "Holy Spirit, show me where the remote control is, please." Immediately in my spirit I thought of the bathroom and, sure enough, that's where it was.

The same thing happened to me concerning my car keys. I was ready to leave. I was in a time crunch and couldn't find my keys. I searched frantically to no avail and then decided to pray. In my spirit I saw the keys in the front seat of my car, and that is exactly where they were.

One of the gifts of the Holy Spirit talked about in 1 Corinthians 12 is the word of knowledge. God gave me a word of knowledge about the remote control as well as the misplaced keys. These gifts are available to those who are filled with the Holy Spirit. They are supernatural endowments of power given to believers to help them live the natural life in a supernatural way. Yes, we can count on the Holy Spirit to remind us of things we need to be reminded of. If we needed no help, we would always perfectly remember everything and never need to be reminded; but if we are honest, we all know that is not the case. If the Lord cares enough to speak to us about remote controls and lost keys, think how eager He must be to talk to us about more intimate things.

Some people in business have no problem at all having a secretary to remind them of certain things, and they depend on that person to do so. Yet, these same people may have great difficulty leaning on God for the same kind of small details they lean on their secretary for. This happens for two reasons: (1) they don't even know it is proper to lean on God for such small details in life—they don't believe He is interested in those types of things; and (2) they won't humble themselves to display that type of need.

As prideful human beings, we do not like to appear needy. Remember, in John 15:5 Jesus said that apart from Him, we can do nothing. Nothing means nothing—the sooner we learn that fact, the better off we are, because the Bible tells us that God helps the humble but resists the proud (see James 4:6; 1 Peter 5:5).

It is not pleasing to God for people to leave Him out

of their daily lives, then work religious formulas to try to appease Him. Don't waste your time just going through the motions. Either have a real relationship with God that is alive and meaningful, or face the fact that you don't have one at all and do whatever is needed to get one.

Ask yourself these questions, and you will find out quickly enough where you are spiritually:

Are you growing daily in your knowledge of God and His ways?

Do you look forward to going to church, or is it something you do out of obligation? Is it interesting for you, or are you glad when it is over so you can go to lunch?

Do you feel close to God?

In your life are you manifesting the fruit of the Spirit—love, joy, peace, patience, kindness, goodness, faithfulness, gentleness (meekness, humility), and self-control (see Galatians 5:22-23)?

How much have you changed since you committed your life to Christ?

If you are not satisfied with your answers to these questions, throw your life entirely open to God and ask the Holy Spirit to get involved in every aspect of it. If you will do that in honesty and sincerity, He will begin to work in you in a powerful and exciting way.

Don't get stuck in old ways of doing things, which were right for a particular time but are no longer effective, because God wants you to use other methods to move beyond that state. Don't be afraid of new things; just make sure they are biblical. I believe God desires to take you to new heights in Him through the power of the Holy Spirit. He is knocking at the door of your heart. Will you open it wide and welcome Him?

If you have not been providing a good home for the Holy Spirit, He has been missing you, and whether you know it or not, you have been missing Him.

Much of the dissatisfaction that many people experience is due to a lack of fellowship and intimacy with God through the Holy Spirit. If you are one of those people, I believe that this book can be a turning point in your life. Why not make the turn quickly, so you can begin enjoying God more than ever before?

YOU CANNOT WIN YOUR BATTLES WITHOUT GOD'S HELP

The Lord says this to you: Be not afraid or dismayed at this great multitude; for the battle is not yours, but God's. (2 Chronicles 20:15)

Second Chronicles 20 describes a time of crisis in the life of the people of Judah. They were faced with a huge army that was out to destroy them. But the prophet of God told them not to be afraid because the battle was not theirs; it belonged to the Lord.

In verse 12 of that chapter we read a wise prayer that was offered to God by Jehoshaphat, king of Judah: "O our God, will You not exercise judgment upon them? For we have no might to stand against this great company that is coming against us. We do not know what to do, but our eyes are upon You."

I have studied this prayer many times over the years, and it has helped me get to the place where I can easily ask for help. Often we spin our wheels trying to do something we are not capable of doing, and acting as if we know something we don't know. I have discovered the hard way that it is much easier to just say, "I don't know what to do, and even if I did, I couldn't do it without help. Holy Spirit, help me!"

Pride is a hideous monster that prevents us from asking for help. We want to be self-sufficient and independent. However, God created us in such a way that although we do have strengths, we also have weaknesses and will always need help.

God wants us to lean entirely on Him; that is what faith really is. *The Amplified Bible* gives a definition of faith in Colossians 1:4 that I really love. It says that faith in Jesus is "the leaning of your entire personality on Him in absolute trust and confidence in His power, wisdom, and goodness."

We can lean on God to keep us in His will. It is too complicated to try to stay in His will under our own power. Which one of us can even say that we know 100 percent for sure what we're supposed to do every single day? Our mind plans our way, but God directs our steps (see Proverbs 16:9).

You can do everything that you know to do to make a right decision. You may be right, but there is a possibility you could be wrong. How can you know if you're right? You can't. You have to trust God to keep you in His will, straighten out any crooked paths in front of you, keep you on that narrow path that leads to life, and off of that broad path that leads to destruction (see Matthew 7:13 KJV).

We need to pray, "God, Your will be done in my life." Somewhere along the line, some folks have developed the theory that we should never pray "Your will be done." But Jesus prayed that way (see Luke 22:42), saying, "Here

I am, I have come to do Your will, O God" (see John 17:4-5).

I know some things about God's will for my life, but I don't know everything, so I have learned to stay in rest and peace by committing myself to God, praying for His will to be done, and trusting Him to keep me. I learned this when God was dealing with me to make a certain decision. I agonized, "But, oh God, what if I'm wrong? What if I make a mistake? What if I miss You, God!"

He said, "Joyce, if you miss Me, I'll find you."

Leaning is a good thing, as long as we are leaning on something or someone that won't cave in when we least expect it! God is a good choice to lean on. He has a proven record of faithfulness to those who commit their lives to Him.

6

The Divine Helper

~

> But the Comforter (Counselor, Helper, Intercessor, Advocate, Strengthener, Standby), the Holy Spirit, Whom the Father will send in My name [in My place, to represent Me and act on My behalf], He will teach you all things. (John 14:26)

There are countless things that we struggle with when we could be receiving help from the Divine Helper. The Holy Spirit is a Gentleman; He will not push His way into our life or our daily affairs. If given an invitation, He is quick to respond, but He must be invited.

As the third person of the Trinity, the Holy Spirit has a personality. He can be offended and grieved. He must be treated with great respect. Once we have the understanding that He lives inside those of us who believe, we should do everything we can to make Him feel at home.

The Holy Spirit is always available. *The Amplified Bible* calls Him the Standby. I love that particular trait because I like to think of Him just standing by me all the time in case I need help with anything at all. Just think about that for a while, and it gets pretty exciting. One of the most powerful prayers we can pray is, "Lord, help me!"

Not only is the Holy Spirit standing by to help in any situation that requires it, He is also available for counsel. How often do we run to our friends when we should be asking the Holy Spirit for advice? He desires to lead, guide, and direct our lives; it honors Him when we ask for His advice.

I feel honored when my grown children ask for my advice, and I especially feel honored when they take it. I always have their best interest in mind and would never tell them anything if I did not firmly believe it would help them. If we as humans can do that, how much more can the Holy Spirit do for us if we will turn to Him?

I think many people never find answers to their problems because they seek out wrong sources for advice and counsel.

HOW DOES THE HOLY SPIRIT COUNSEL US?

We have already seen in John 14:26 that the Holy Spirit is our Counselor. But you may be reluctant to go to Him for counsel because you don't know how to hear from Him. How does He speak to us?

One of the greatest ways that God leads His people is through the inner witness. In other words, we just know inside what is right or what is wrong. It is a deeper level of knowing than head knowledge. This type of knowing is in the spirit—we simply have peace or a lack of peace, and by that peace or lack of it, we know what we should do.

I once talked with a woman who needed to make a serious decision. Her family and friends were giving her advice, but she needed to know within herself what the right answer was because she was the one who would have to live with it. She had been in a certain business all of her life and was feeling that she wanted to get out of it and stay home with her children. Of course, this would mean severe financial changes as well as personal changes for her that might affect her emotionally. She needed to know from a Higher Source than other people what the right thing was for her to do.

This woman went to a retreat with a relative. Sometime during the course of that weekend as she sat praising and worshiping the Lord and listening to the speaker, a knowing and a peace came into her heart that she was indeed right in closing the business. She said a moment came when she simply knew what was right. Ever since that time she has had peace about it.

It is amazing how many people can tell us things that have no effect upon us, but when God tells us something, we feel totally different. Other people cannot always give us peace with their advice, but God can.

Another way God speaks to us is through His Word. We may be seeking Him for a certain answer, and as we read His Word, we come across a Scripture that speaks right to our heart so that we know what we should do.

There are many times when I ask the Holy Spirit to lead me in a conversation or a decision, and although I don't sense any specific leading, I believe that as I go through the situation, He is definitely leading me. My preaching and teaching is a good example. I always have a plan, but I also lean on God to lead me by His Spirit. I often open my mouth thinking I will say one thing and find myself going in a direction I had not planned at all. This is entirely scriptural, as we see in Proverbs 16:1: "The plans of the mind and orderly thinking belong to man, but from the Lord comes the [wise] answer of the tongue."

We often find it difficult to trust what we believe may be direction from the Lord. It is not that we distrust Him, but that we distrust our ability to hear from Him. I eventually found that I had to take a step of faith, and then I would find out by experience how to recognize the leadership of the Holy Spirit.

"Step out and find out" is what I always say. As we are learning to be led by the Holy Spirit, we are bound to make a few mistakes, but God always helps us get back on the right track, and we learn from our mistakes.

The process of learning to be led by God is no different from the process that babies go through in learning to walk. They all fall down in the process, but as long as they get up and try again, eventually they will end up not only walking but also running at full speed.

James chapter 1 begins by telling us how to handle the trials of life. There is a natural way of handling problems, but there is also a spiritual way to handle them:

> If any of you is deficient in wisdom, let him ask of the giving God [Who gives] to everyone liberally and ungrudgingly, without reproaching or faultfinding, and it will be given him. Only it must be in faith that he asks with no wavering (no hesitating, no doubting). For the one who wavers (hesitates, doubts) is like the billowing surge out at sea that is blown hither and thither and tossed by the wind. (James 1:5-6)

James is saying here, "If you are having trouble, ask God what you should do." You may not receive an answer immediately upon making your request, but you will find as you go about your business a wisdom operating through you that is divine and beyond your natural knowing.

In Psalm 23:2 the psalmist tells us that God leads His people into green pastures and beside still and restful waters. In other words, God will always lead us into a place of peace and safety if we seek Him.

Please notice that James says "ask." All too often we don't get any help because we don't ask for any. Remember: the Holy Spirit is a Gentleman and waits to be invited into our situations; otherwise, He would violate our free will. *We cannot assume and presume; we must ask!*

James 4:1-6 teaches us that strife and discord come from the evil or carnal desires that arise within us. We are jealous and covet what others have, and then our desires go unfulfilled because we try to get them fulfilled in the wrong way. James says that when people burn with envy and are not able to get the satisfaction they desire, they fight and war. James explains clearly, "You do not have, because you do not ask God" (v. 2, NIV). According to Strong's concordance, the meaning of the Greek word translated *ask* in this verse is "beg, call for, crave, desire, require."[1] If God gave us everything that we *casually* asked for, we would most likely beg Him to take some of it back! God responds to both our passion and the purity of our motive. Verse 3 of James 4 says about the things we desire, "[Or] you do ask [God for them] and yet fail to receive, because you ask with wrong purpose and evil, selfish motives. Your intention is [when you get what you desire] to spend it in sensual pleasures."

James concludes this discourse in verse 6 by saying that God "gives us more and more grace (power of the Holy Spirit, to meet this evil tendency and all others fully)." He tells us that "God sets Himself against the proud and haughty, but gives grace [continually] to the lowly (those who are humble enough to receive it)."

First Peter 5:5 states that God actually opposes, frustrates, and defeats those who are proud but gives grace (the help of the Holy Spirit) to the humble. Often we are trying to make something happen, and all we are getting is frustrated. That happens because we are leaning on ourselves or some other natural source, and the Holy Spirit is offended and grieved because we are not coming to Him. Therefore, He opposes us instead of helping us.

Consider the following Scriptures to help you gain understanding concerning the importance of seeking God for counsel:

> Blessed (happy, fortunate, prosperous, and enviable) is the man who walks and lives not in the counsel of the ungodly [following their advice, their plans and purposes]. (Psalm 1:1)
>
> The Lord brings the counsel of the nations to nought; He makes the thoughts and plans of the peoples of no effect. *The counsel of the Lord stands forever, the thoughts of His heart through all generations.* (Psalm 33:10-11, emphasis mine)
>
> They soon forgat his works; they waited not for his counsel: but lusted exceedingly in the wilderness, and tempted God in the desert. And he gave them their request; but sent leanness into their soul. (Psalm 106:13-15 KJV)

Multitudes of believers and unbelievers do what the Israelites did in the wilderness. They demand their own way and have no patience to wait for God's plans to develop. They don't want God to counsel them; they want to counsel God. They try to tell God what to do, and then they get impatient if He does not make it happen right away.

This very thing is what contributes to much of the unhappiness and discontent among people today. If God created us to need Him, and if we try to live as if we don't, how can we ever be fulfilled?

THE HOLY SPIRIT COMFORTS US

Blessed be the God and Father of our Lord Jesus Christ, the Father of sympathy (pity and mercy) and the God [Who is the Source] of every comfort (consolation and encouragement), Who comforts (consoles and encourages) us in every trouble (calamity and affliction), so that we may also be able to comfort (console and encourage) those who are in any kind of trouble or distress, with the comfort (consolation and encouragement) with which we ourselves are comforted (consoled and encouraged) by God. (2 Corinthians 1:3-4)

The Holy Spirit also wants to help us by comforting us when we need it. You and I may need to be comforted when we have been disappointed, hurt, or mistreated in some way or when we have experienced loss. We may also need to be comforted during changes in our life or even when we are just simply tired. Another time we may need to be comforted is when we have failed in some way.

As stated previously, the Holy Spirit is actually called the Comforter. His various names describe His character. They reveal what He does, or at least what He desires to do, for believers. He is willing to do a great deal for us if we are willing to receive His help.

For many years I regularly got angry with my husband because he wouldn't comfort me when I felt that I needed it. I am sure he was trying, but now I realize that God would not allow Dave to give me the comfort that I should have been going to Him for, which He would have given me by the Holy Spirit if I had only asked for it.

God will only allow people to do a certain amount and no more for us. Even those people who are extremely close to us cannot give us everything we need all the time. When we expect others to do for us what only God can do, we have our expectations in the wrong place, and we will always be disappointed.

There is no comfort that is as good as God's. Man can never give us what we really need, unless God Himself uses other people to reach us, which He often does.

People certainly can and should comfort one another, but God is the Source of all true comfort. I may ask God to comfort me in some situation, and He may have just the right person call me, but I am still aware that it was God who orchestrated the occurrence.

When we ask people to help us, they are often powerless to do so, but if we ask God for help, He can empower people and work through them.

God's Word comforts us. Many times when I need comfort, I run to the Bible. I have favorite passages that I read or meditate on when I need extra encouragement.

Psalm 23 is a good example that is a favorite of many

people. Yes, God's Word carries with it the ability to comfort. As long as we have His Word hidden in our heart, or as long as we have a Bible to refer to, we can always find comfort in times of affliction, as Paul tells us in Romans 15:4: "For whatever was thus written in former days was written for our instruction, that by [our steadfast and patient] endurance and the encouragement [drawn] from the Scriptures we might hold fast to and cherish hope.".

One time I went through a period of being judged adversely from several different sources. Sometimes when trouble comes, it comes in multiples. Whenever this happens to me, it always tips me off that Satan is attacking me. I know from experience to stand firm in my faith because, by doing so, I will simply outlast the devil. I have learned that if I will remain firm and stable, the enemy will quickly find he is wasting his time.

This does not mean that I wasn't hurting in that time of difficulty; in fact, I was hurting and needed comforting. During that period I went to specific Scriptures and read them. I also meditated on and thought about others.

In Psalm 20:6 David wrote, "Now I know that the Lord saves His anointed." I quoted that verse many times to myself during a two-day period while I was recovering from the shock of hearing that people had been saying adverse things about me. It should not have surprised me, because I know how the devil is and how people are, but I guess I always hope that sooner or later people will get enough of the love of God in them to stop judging others.

I always say that I have enough business of my own to mind that I don't need to get into other people's business. However, I was not always strong in this area. It was an area in which I had to grow. I might add that at one time

I was very critical and judgmental; therefore, I can truthfully say, "There, but for the grace of God, go I."

When someone is an authority figure of any kind or in the public eye, as I am in my ministry, they are always going to draw more judgment and criticism than those who are not in those positions. Judgment and criticism just seem to go with the territory, so to speak. These things still hurt, but Jesus went through them, and so will we.

I am so thankful for God's Word because I have experienced the power of it over and over in my life. It has the ability to provide comfort in every kind of affliction.

In Isaiah 61:2 it was prophesied that the coming Messiah would "comfort all who mourn." In the Sermon on the Mount, Jesus said those who mourn are blessed for they will be comforted (see Matthew 5:4). The comfort of God that is administered by His Holy Spirit is so awesome that it is almost worth having a problem just to be able to experience it. As with most things, it goes far beyond any kind of ordinary comfort.

Let God be your Source of comfort. In the future when you are hurting, just ask Him to comfort you. Then wait in His presence while He works in your heart and emotions. He will not fail you, if you will only give Him a chance to come to your aid.

THE HOLY SPIRIT STRENGTHENS US

The God of all grace [Who imparts all blessing and favor], Who has called you to His [own] eternal glory in Christ Jesus, will Himself complete and make you what you ought to be, establish and ground you securely, and strengthen, and settle you. (1 Peter 5:10)

The Holy Spirit also offers His help as our Strengthener. Just imagine having a well of strength inside you, a source you can draw on anytime you feel the need. When you feel weak or tired or discouraged to the point of giving up, just stop for a few minutes. Close your eyes, if possible, and ask the Holy Spirit to strengthen you. As you wait in His presence, you can often actually feel the strength of God coming to you.

It is not wise just to say we will do something without acknowledging God or even thinking it over. We often get committed to too many things and then find ourselves weak and worn out. God will strengthen us through His Spirit, but He won't strengthen us to do things that are out of His will. He won't strengthen us to be foolish! Once we commit to do something, God expects us to keep our word and be people of integrity, so His advice to us through His Word is "think before you speak" (see Acts 19:36).

I love the way *The Living Bible* translates Ecclesiastes 5:1:

As you enter the Temple, keep your ears open and your mouth shut! Don't be a fool who doesn't even realize it is sinful to make rash promises to God, for he is in heaven and you are only here on earth, so let your words be few. Just as being too busy gives you nightmares, so being a fool makes you a blabbermouth.

I had to learn to ask the Holy Spirit *before* I volunteered to do something in a moment of enthusiasm. I had the "loose mouth" disease that caused me to make promises in the midst of emotional excitement that I later wondered how I would have the energy to keep.

I would invite several people over for a barbecue; then I would spend my time murmuring and complaining about all the work I had to do in order to be prepared. Once I made several commitments and later found myself trying to find a way out of them because I no longer wanted to keep them.

God showed me an important truth, one that has greatly affected my life in a positive way. He said, "Joyce, if you want to carry My anointing and power, you must keep your word. Keep your promises and learn to think and pray and ponder before you make new commitments." He made it clear to me that once I made the commitment, He expected me to keep it and to follow through on it with a good attitude.

Ecclesiastes 5:4-7 TLB gives us clear instruction on the seriousness of seeking God before we make a vow:

> So when you talk to God and vow to him that you will do something, don't delay in doing it, for God has no pleasure in fools. Keep your promise to him. It is far better not to say you'll do something than to say you will and then not do it. In that case, your mouth is making you sin. Don't try to defend yourself by telling the messenger from God that it was all a mistake [to make the vow]. That would make God very angry; and he might destroy your prosperity. Dreaming instead of doing is foolishness, and there is ruin in a flood of empty words; fear God instead.

I frequently say that we wait in the doctor's office and at the drug prescription counter, so why not wait on God? He is the best Physician we could ever find. Make an appointment with Him, and don't break it. Wait in His presence, and you will find the results worth waiting for. One word from God can strengthen your faith and give you courage to do things that would otherwise be impossible.

Once when I had to have an operation, I was going through all the moments of doubt and fear that often occur before a serious surgery. Naturally, all my family members and everybody around me were telling me to trust God. I wanted to trust, but I found it more difficult sometimes than others. At times I would be feeling secure, and then suddenly a spirit of fear would attack me, and I would once again feel frightened.

This continued until one morning at about five o'clock, during a time when I could not sleep. The voice of the Lord spoke in my heart saying, "Joyce, trust Me; I'm going to take care of you." From that moment forward I did not have fear, because when God speaks to us in a personal way (when He gives us a *rhema* word), faith comes with what He says (see Romans 10:17).

If we knew we could go to the doctor and get a prescription for pills that would give us instant strength anytime we feel weak, we probably would not hesitate to do so. I am telling you from Scripture that this strength is available to you through the power of the Holy Spirit.

There is so much available to us in the Holy Spirit that we have missed because we have not been properly taught about His wonderful present-day ministry. We always talk about what Jesus did when He was here, but what about what He is doing now through the power of the Holy Spirit? Let us not live in the past, but rather let us fully enter into all that the present holds for us.

Let us be like Moses and the Israelites who knew the Source of their strength, as we see in Exodus 15:1-2:

> Then Moses and the Israelites sang this song to the Lord, saying, I will sing to the Lord, for He has triumphed gloriously; the horse and his rider or its chariot has He thrown into the sea. The Lord is my Strength and my Song, and He has become my Salvation; this is my God, and I will praise Him, my father's God, and I will exalt Him.

Actually, God does not want to just *give* us strength; He wants to *be* our strength. In 1 Samuel 15:29 He is referred to as the Strength of Israel. There was a time when Israel knew that God was their strength. When they forgot it, they always started to fail, and their lives began to be filled with destruction.

In 2 Samuel 22:33-34 KJV David wrote: "God is my strength and power: and he maketh my way perfect. He maketh my feet like hinds' feet: and setteth me upon my high places." David had many enemies, and throughout the Psalms he talks about the strength of God and about drawing on that strength.

It seems that many of the men and women we read about in the Bible knew that God was their strength. Had they not known it, they probably would have been forgotten like so many others have been and would not have become examples for our encouragement today.

The apostle Paul found the strength of God so wonderful that in 2 Corinthians 12:9-10 he actually said he would glory in his weaknesses, knowing that when he was weak, the strength of God would rest upon him and fill up his weaknesses. To put it in our language today, Paul was saying that he was glad when he was weak because then he got to experience the strength of God.

How do we receive strength from God? By faith. Hebrews 11:11 KJV teaches us that by faith Sara (Sarah) received strength to conceive a child when she was past childbearing age.

Start receiving the strength of God by faith. It will quicken your body as well as your spirit and soul. For example, if you have a weak back, it can be made strong. At our conferences, the Holy Spirit has strengthened weak knees, ankles, and backs as we have prayed for those who asked God for strength. His healing power came as we waited in His presence and received it from Him.

By faith you can receive strength to stay in a difficult marriage, raise a difficult child, or stick with a difficult job in which you have a difficult boss. You can receive strength to do great things even though you may have physical impairment yourself.

The strength of God really is amazing. David wrote in Psalm 18:29 that by his God he could run through a troop and leap over a wall. In 1 Kings 19:4-8 an angel came and ministered to Elijah who was tired and depressed, and he went forty days and nights in the strength that he received from that one visit.

Have you been trying to push through difficulties on your own? If so, make a change right now. Start getting strength from deep within you where the Holy Spirit dwells. If that divine strength does not yet dwell in you, all you need to do to receive it is admit your sins, repent of them, and ask Jesus to be your Savior and Lord. Surrender your life, all that you are and all that you are not, to Him.

Ask Him to baptize you in the Holy Spirit and to fill you through and through with the power of the Holy Spirit. This book will help you learn how to begin walking in the Spirit and living a life of victory rather than defeat.

Paul prayed for the Ephesians that they would be strengthened in the inner man by the power of the Holy Spirit indwelling their innermost being and personality. This particular Scripture in Ephesians 3:16 has truly ministered to me over the years. Thank God, I don't have to give up just because I feel weak or tired mentally, emotionally, physically, or even spiritually. I can ask God to strengthen me by the power of the Holy Spirit who dwells in me—and you can do the same thing!

THE HOLY SPIRIT IS OUR INTERCESSOR

But the Spirit itself maketh intercession for us. (Romans 8:26 KJV)

Why can't we just intercede ourselves? Why do we need the Holy Spirit to help us in this area? The answer is found in 1 Corinthians 2:11: "For what person perceives (knows and understands) what passes through a man's thoughts except the man's own spirit within him? Just so no one discerns (comes to know and comprehend) the thoughts of God except the Spirit of God." We need the help of the Holy Spirit because He is the only One who accurately knows the thoughts of God.

If you and I are to pray in the will of God, we must know what God is thinking and what He desires. Romans

8:26-28 tells us that we don't know how to pray as we should, so the Holy Spirit helps us:

> *So too the [Holy] Spirit comes to our aid and bears*
> *us up in our weakness; for we do not know what*
> *prayer to offer nor how to offer it worthily as we*
> *ought, but the Spirit Himself goes to meet our sup-*
> *plication and pleads in our behalf with unspeakable*
> *yearnings and groanings too deep for utterance.*
> And He Who searches the hearts of men knows what
> is in the mind of the [Holy] Spirit [what His intent
> is], because the Spirit intercedes and pleads [before
> God] in behalf of the saints according to and in har-
> mony with God's will. We are assured and know that
> [God being a partner in their labor] all things work
> together and are [fitting into a plan] for good to and
> for those who love God and are called according to
> [His] design and purpose. (Emphasis mine)

If we pray by the Holy Spirit, we can always be assured that all things will work out for good. God is great and mighty; there is no situation that He cannot use for good as we pray and trust Him. We dare not pray the way we want to, but as we are led by the Holy Spirit. Spirit-filled prayers are the only ones that receive a yes and amen from God (see 2 Corinthians 1:20).

THE HOLY SPIRIT IS OUR ADVOCATE

Who shall bring any charge against God's elect [when it is] God Who justifies [that is, Who puts us in right relation to Himself? Who shall come forward and accuse or impeach those whom God has chosen? Will God, Who acquits us?] (Romans 8:33)

In *Vine's Complete Expository Dictionary of Old and New Testament Words*, the Greek word *parakletos,* translated *advocate,* is defined under the heading COMFORTER. According to Vine, it means " 'called to one's side,' i.e., to one's aid."[2] Vine goes on to say, "It was used in a court of justice to denote a legal assistant, counsel for the defense...; one who pleads another's cause, an intercessor."[3]

This gives us much to think about. The Holy Spirit is One who is literally called to our side to give us aid in every way. When we need defense, He defends us, acting as a legal assistant would for a client. It is good to know that we don't have to defend ourselves when we are accused of something; we can ask for help from the Holy One and expect to receive it. He is our Advocate. That should bring us comfort just thinking about it.

Most of us spend a great deal of time and energy in life trying to defend ourselves, our reputation, our position, our actions, words, and decisions. We are truly wasting our time. When others are judgmental toward us, we may finally after much effort convince them of our purity of heart. But the problem lies in the fact that if they are judgmental in nature or character, they will quickly find something else to judge us for. It is best to pray and let God be our defense.

We notice in the Holy Scripture that Jesus basically never defended Himself. Philippians 2:7 KJV says that He "made himself of no reputation." He didn't try to make one, and therefore He did not have to worry about keeping it.

After years of trying to be well thought of, I discovered that it is much better to have a good reputation in heaven than on earth. I want to have a good reputation with people, and hopefully I live my life in such a way that I do. But I don't worry about it anymore. I do my best and let God take care of the rest.

Romans 8:33 says that it is God who justifies us; we don't have to justify ourselves, not even to God the Father. Why should we then have to try to justify ourselves before people? We don't have to—if we understand that the Holy Spirit is our Advocate.

7

The Seven Spirits of God

⁓

> John to the seven churches which are in Asia:
> Grace be unto you, and peace, from him which is,
> and which was, and which is to come; and from the
> seven Spirits which are before his throne. (Revela-
> tion 1:4 KJV)

The book of Revelation speaks of the seven Spirits that
are before God's throne. Revelation 3:1 and 4:5 KJV refer
to the "seven Spirits of God." We know there is only one
Holy Spirit, but the reference to seven Spirits shows us
that He has various ways of manifesting and expressing
Himself among men to bring fullness to their lives. Just
as the Trinity is one God in three persons, so the Holy
Spirit is one Spirit with different operations or modes of
expression.

In this chapter we will look at Scriptures that reveal
the seven different ways the Holy Spirit manifests Himself or expresses Himself in our everyday life. He operates in different modes as needed to meet different types
of needs, although ultimately He is everything we need.
Because this is a book about intimacy with God, it seems

worthwhile to be aware of the diverse ways that the Holy Spirit works in us and through us.

THE SPIRIT OF GRACE

Hebrews 10:29 tells us that it is "the [Holy] Spirit [Who imparts] grace (the unmerited favor and blessing of God)." Other versions or translations of the Bible (KJV, NIV, NASB) use the wording "the Spirit of grace," which is the Holy Spirit Himself.

Grace is the power of the Holy Spirit available to us to do with ease what we cannot do by striving. But first, it is the power that enables us to be right with God so that we will become His home, the home of the Holy Spirit. With the Holy Spirit inside us, we can reach *in* to draw on the power of the Spirit of Grace to do what we cannot do by striving in our own power.

For example, I spent years trying to change myself because I saw so many defects in my character. Most of the time I felt frustrated because all my effort and hard work was not producing any change. If I realized I was saying unkind things I shouldn't be saying, I would determine to stop. But no matter what I did, I couldn't change, and sometimes I seemed to get worse.

Finally, I cried out to God, admitting that I couldn't even try to change anymore. At that point I heard God speak into my heart, "Good. Now I can do something in your life."

In Galatians 3:3 the apostle Paul poses the question: "Having begun [your new life spiritually] with the [Holy] Spirit, are you now reaching perfection [by dependence] on the flesh?" Walking in the Holy Spirit is the only way to reach perfection. Understanding the work of grace is of major importance in learning to walk in His presence.

When God makes the changes, God gets the glory; therefore, He won't let us change ourselves. When we *try* to change or *try* to be nice, without leaning on God, we leave Him "out of the loop." Instead of trying to change ourselves, we simply need to ask Him to change us, and then let His Spirit of Grace do the work in us.

Many people feel that they need to earn their way to God by doing good things to win His acceptance. That is not true. We enter into relationship with God by receiving salvation as a free gift imparted to us by God's grace through our faith in His Son Jesus Christ. It is impossible for anyone to be right with God without knowing Jesus.

Grace is a wonderful thing. It is the power by which men are saved through their faith in Jesus Christ, as Paul tells us in Ephesians 2:8:

> For it is by free grace (God's unmerited favor) that you are saved (delivered from judgment and made partakers of Christ's salvation) through [your] faith. And this [salvation] is not of yourselves [of your own doing, it came not through your own striving], but it is the gift of God.

The Holy Spirit ministers grace to us from God the Father. Grace is actually the (Holy Spirit's) power flowing out from the throne of God toward men to save them and enable them to live holy lives and accomplish the will of God.

I had always heard that grace is God's unmerited favor, which it is; however, it is much more than that. When I learned that grace is the power of the Holy Spirit available to me to do with ease what I could not do by striving, I got excited about grace. I began to cry out to God for grace, grace, and more grace.

In Zechariah 4 we read of a group of people who were trying to rebuild the temple and who came up against much opposition. Satan always opposes the work of God. In verses 6 and 7 KJV the angel of the Lord told the prophet that the assigned task would be accomplished, "Not by might, nor by power, but by my spirit, saith the LORD of hosts." The people were promised that the grace of God would turn their mountains into molehills and that they would finish the temple, crying out, "Grace, grace unto it."

We usually try to push our mountains out of the way with our own strength when we should be calling on the Spirit of Grace to make it easy.

One of the symbols of the Holy Spirit is oil (see Zechariah 4:6). When I think of oil, I always think of ease. Oil makes things flow easily; actually, they can become downright slippery. Some people just need a little oil applied to their life; then everything won't be so difficult. If you are one of those people, I encourage you to go to God and tell Him you came for "an oil job"!

There is no rejoicing in life without grace. With the grace of God, life can be lived with an effortless ease that produces an abundance of peace and joy.

In Romans 5:2 we read: "Through Him also we have [our] access (entrance, introduction) by faith into this grace (state of God's favor) in which we [firmly and safely] stand. And let us rejoice and exult in our hope of experiencing and enjoying the glory of God." We enter into the grace of God through faith—the same way we receive all other things from the Lord. This grace causes us to rejoice and have hope of experiencing the glory of God.

Glory is the manifestation of God's excellence and goodness. We all want glory, but we can only hope to experience it because the Spirit of Grace lives inside of us as believers in Jesus Christ. That is what Paul is talking about in Colossians 1:27 when he says, "God was pleased to make known how great for the Gentiles are the riches of the glory of this mystery, which is Christ within and among you, the Hope of [realizing the] glory."

Christ must live in us; otherwise, there is no hope of our ever experiencing the glory of God. But because He does live in those of us who believe, because He is continually ministering grace to those who know how to ask for and receive it, we can look forward to new realms of glory on a continual basis.

When Paul and the other apostles greeted the churches of their day with, "May the grace of our Lord Jesus Christ be with you all," they were praying that the Spirit of Grace—the Holy Spirit of God the Father and of Jesus Christ the Son—would be with the people, helping them, and ministering to them the power they needed for everyday life.

I firmly believe we have missed the truth by not realizing that we need the power of God to live not only in times of difficulty or emergency, but in the course of our ordinary, everyday life—our Monday, Tuesday, Wednesday, Thursday, Friday, Saturday, and Sunday life.

Why not welcome the God of Grace into your life right now? Invite Him to invade your ordinary, everyday life with His power, which is the power of the Holy Spirit indwelling you. *You and I need a Holy Ghost invasion!*

Because grace is power, Paul encouraged believers

not to receive the grace of God in vain (see 2 Corinthians 6:1). In other words, Paul was saying, "Receive the Spirit of Grace into your life for a purpose—to help you live a holy life, to accomplish the will of God in you, and to enable you to live for the glory of God."

We cannot do that without God's grace. One of the spiritual laws of the kingdom of God is, "Use it or lose it." God expects us to use what He gives us. When we use the grace offered to us, then more and more grace is available. There is no power shortage in heaven, but sometimes we are not plugged in.

In Galatians 2:21 KJV Paul stated, "I do not frustrate the grace of God." What did he mean by that? To find out, let's look at what he said in the preceding verse in *The Amplified Bible:* "It is no longer I who live, but Christ (the Messiah) lives in me; and the life I now live in the body I live by faith in (by adherence to and reliance on and complete trust in) the Son of God, Who loved me and gave Himself up for me." Then he followed with his statement about not frustrating the grace of God. You see, it would have frustrated the grace of God if Paul had tried to live his life on his own, but he had learned to live by the power of Christ, which we have seen is the Holy Spirit.

I am sure most of us know how frustrating it is to try to help someone who keeps pushing us away. Imagine a drowning person who frantically fights and resists the lifeguard who is trying to save them. The best thing that person can possibly do is totally relax and allow the lifeguard to bring them to safety; otherwise, they may drown.

You and I are often like the drowning swimmer. The Holy Spirit is in us. As the Spirit of Grace, He tries to aid us in living our life with much greater ease, but we frantically fight to save ourselves and keep our independence.

According to Ephesians 3:2 KJV, we are living in "the dispensation of the grace of God." This refers to the time when the Holy Spirit has been poured out and is available to all flesh. But with the second coming of Jesus Christ, the dispensation of grace will come to an end and the Holy Spirit will no longer restrain the lawlessness of Satan (see 2 Thessalonians 2:6-7).

We are told in the Bible that the Spirit of God will not always strive with man (see Genesis 6:3). Let us be wise enough during this great dispensation of grace to take full advantage of all that is offered to us. Let us daily welcome the Holy Spirit into our life. By doing so, we will be letting Him know that we need Him and that we are very, very glad He has chosen us as His home.

THE SPIRIT OF GLORY

> If you are censured and suffer abuse [because you bear] the name of Christ, blessed [are you—happy, fortunate, to be envied, with life—joy, and satisfaction in God's favor and salvation, regardless of your outward condition], because the Spirit of glory, the Spirit of God, is resting upon you. (1 Peter 4:14)

Peter states that the Spirit of God, the Spirit of Glory, rests upon us when we are reproached for the name of Christ. Just imagine, we think it is awful when people mistreat us because we are Christians, but God sees it in an entirely different light. God never expects us to suffer for Him without His help. Therefore, we can firmly believe that anytime we are reproached or mistreated in any way because of our faith in Christ, God gives us an extra measure of His Spirit to counterbalance the attack.

The Holy Spirit often acts as a shock absorber. Automobiles have shock absorbers to soften the blow of an unexpected pothole in the road. There are potholes in the road of life, and I honestly doubt that we could endure a lifetime of them if God did not protect us.

I believe that is evidence of the fact that most people who are not serving God and trusting Him to meet their needs sometimes look and act like someone who has been in several bad car wrecks. What I mean is, they look worn out and often older than they really are. Their faces show the strain of the years they have lived without the Holy Spirit's help and protection. Their attitudes are sour due to a life of adversity. They often become bitter because life has seemed to them to be unfair. They don't realize that their life would have been very different had they been serving God and leaning on His Spirit to guide and protect them.

When we have the Spirit of God in our life, we can go through difficult circumstances and keep our peace and joy. Like Shadrach, Meshach, and Abednego in Daniel 3:20-27, we can go into the fiery furnace (into problems and struggles), and come out without even the smell of smoke upon us.

I was sexually abused from my earliest remembrance until the age of eighteen. I then married the first man who showed any interest in me because I felt that probably no one else would ever want me. That marriage ended in divorce after I had endured another five years of emotional and mental abuse, along with adultery and abandonment. I have been delivered from many physical

afflictions during the years of my life, including breast cancer. What I am trying to say, in a nutshell, is that by all stan-
dards of measurement, I have had a fairly rough life, and
yet I feel good physically. I don't look like a person who
has gone through that depth of difficulty. Why? Because I
learned to depend upon the Holy Spirit within me.

I was born again at the age of nine, and although I
didn't have revelation on what was really available to me,
God was with me and living in me from that time forward. I struggled for many years but eventually learned
about the power of the Holy Spirit that was available to
me. I have enjoyed close fellowship with God for years,
and He has taught me to follow His ways and serve Him.
Like everyone else, I still make mistakes, but He is patient
and has not given up on me.

God has restored me and actually made me better, I
believe, than I would have been had I enjoyed an easy life.
He has paid me back with His glory more than double for
anything Satan managed to steal from me, and He will do
the same for all those who consistently place their trust in
Him and walk in His ways.

Many times in my life I was reproached for the name of
Christ, but now I know that the Spirit of Glory was always
upon me. Right in the middle of attack and adversity, God
kept making my life better and better. He loves to take a
mess and make something glorious out of it.

If you ask Him to do so, He will take your mess and
turn it into your ministry. You can help others who are
facing the same kind of things God has helped you overcome. Your burden can become your blessing, and your
weakness can become your weapon.

When God's glory is manifested in your life, others

will look at you and say, "Wow, what a great God you serve," because the power of His goodness toward you is visually evident to them. God wants to "wow" you and them even more!

A portion of the definition of the word *glorify* in Vine's dictionary of Hebrew and Greek words says, "The glory of God is the revelation and manifestation of all that He has and is."[1] Therefore, when God's glory comes upon you, His excellent character and goodness begin to manifest in your life. Welcome the Spirit of Glory into your life and get excited about seeing the glory of God rise upon you.

THE SPIRIT OF LIFE

> Then the Lord God formed man from the dust of the ground and breathed into his nostrils the breath or spirit of life, and man became a living being. (Genesis 2:7)

When God created Adam, he lay on the ground a lifeless form until God breathed into him the breath of life, and he became a living soul. In 1 Corinthians 15:45 the apostle Paul says, "The first man Adam became a living being (an individual personality)." Adam walked beside God, talked to Him, and believed in Him. Scriptures say that Adam was earthly minded, and we can see in the events in Eden that he made a wrong choice when faced with temptation.

In verse 45 of 1 Corinthians 15, Paul continues to explain that "the last Adam (Christ) became a life-giving Spirit [restoring the dead to life]." In verse 46 he illustrates that God gives us a physical life first, and then a spiritual life: "But it is not the spiritual life which came first, but the physical and then the spiritual." This spiritual rebirth is given to those who place their trust in God, believing that Jesus paid the price for sin and that He died for those who sincerely repent of their sins, change their minds for the better, and amend their ways. We are all born earthly minded, as Adam was, but through Christ we can become heavenly minded:

> The first man [was] from out of earth, made of dust (earthly-minded); the second Man [is] the Lord from out of heaven. Now those who are made of the dust are like him who was first made of the dust (earthly-minded); and as is [the Man] from heaven, so also [are those] who are of heavenly (heavenly-minded.) And just as we have borne the image [of the man] of dust, so shall we and so let us also bear the image [of the Man] of heaven. (1 Corinthians 15:47-49)

Jesus resisted all temptation that tested His humanness and thus fulfilled the law of God that was required for a human to be righteous in the eyes of his Creator. Then Jesus offered Himself, and His righteousness, as an unblemished sacrifice to God, in exchange for the right to purify our conscience from dead works and lifeless observances (see Hebrews 9:14).

Because God's law required the shedding of blood for cleansing from the guilt of sin, man sacrificed the blood of goats and calves to atone for his sins; but Christ went once and for all in our behalf into the Holy of Holies and gave Himself as the payment for the wages of our sin in order to reconcile us to God.

Because there could not be a more perfect sacrifice

than Jesus, no other sacrifice was acceptable to God from that point on. Our good works are not an acceptable atonement for our sins. Our offerings or sacrifices are not more perfect than the blood of Jesus. That's why our good works cannot save us. The only acceptable atonement that reconciles us to God is our trust in the sacrifice of the One who *is* perfect. By our agreement with the Father that there is no more perfect sacrifice than Jesus, we are restored from death to life through our faith in Him.

Hebrews 9:22-28 NIV explains:

In fact, the law requires that nearly everything be cleansed with blood, and without the shedding of blood there is no forgiveness. It was necessary, then, for the copies of the heavenly things to be purified with these sacrifices, but the heavenly things themselves with better sacrifices than these. For Christ did not enter a man-made sanctuary that was only a copy of the true one; he entered heaven itself, now to appear for us in God's presence. Nor did he enter heaven to offer himself again and again, the way the high priest enters the Most Holy Place every year with blood that is not his own. Then Christ would have had to suffer many times since the creation of the world. But now he has appeared once for all at the end of the ages to do away with sin by the sacrifice of himself. Just as man is destined to die once, and after that to face judgment, so Christ was sacrificed once to take away the sins of many people; and he will appear a second time, not to bear sin, but to bring full salvation to those who are waiting for him.

When Christ entered the world, He said that God did not delight in sin offerings (see Hebrews 10:5-6). God delights when we stand before Him in fellowship with His Holy presence. Jesus fulfilled the law in order to establish the new covenant that allows us to enjoy life in the presence of the Father again.

Jesus said to the Father, " 'Here I am, I have come to do your will.' He [thus] sets aside the first [covenant] to establish the second [covenant]. And by that will, we have been made holy through the sacrifice of the body of Jesus Christ once for all" (Hebrews 10:9-10 NIV).

In John 10:10 Jesus said, "The thief comes only in order to steal and kill and destroy. I came that they may have and enjoy life, and have it in abundance (to the full, till it overflows)."

When Jesus said this, He was not speaking to dead people. He was speaking to people who were already alive. What then did He mean when He said He came to give them *life?* He was speaking of the life filled with the Spirit of God, or a heavenly minded life like the life He lived, which was certainly a much higher quality of life than the earthly minded life we receive at our physical birth. He must have been speaking of a higher kind of life that comes from being born of the Spirit.

John 1:12-13 NIV explains this second birth as being born of God: "Yet to all who received him, to those who believed in his name, he gave the right to become children of God—children born not of natural descent, nor of human decision or a husband's will, but born of God." Romans 8:8-11 NIV explains why we need Jesus to fill our human spirit with His Spirit:

Those controlled by the sinful nature cannot please God. You, however, are controlled not by the sinful nature but by the Spirit, if the Spirit of God lives in you. And if anyone does not have the Spirit of Christ, he does not belong to Christ. But if Christ is in you, your body is dead because of sin, yet your spirit is alive because of righteousness. And if the Spirit of him who raised Jesus from the dead is living in you, he who raised Christ from the dead will also give life to your mortal bodies through his Spirit, who lives in you.

That is exactly what happens to those of us who are born of the Spirit. When we accept Christ as our Savior, the Spirit of Life comes to dwell within us, and we are quickened and made alive in our spirit. We are not just breathing; we are being prepared to really and truly live life as it was meant to be lived.

John 1:4 says of Jesus, "In Him was Life, and the Life was the Light of men." What was in Jesus? The Holy Spirit was in Him; the Holy Spirit came upon Him with power the day of His water baptism. He demonstrated to us the life of a Spirit-filled man, empowered by the Holy Spirit, and He came to give us the same life that He had. We are instructed to imitate Him, to follow in His steps, to do what He did, and to receive His righteousness.

Remember how surprised John the Baptist was when Jesus came to him to be baptized in water?

John tried to deter him, saying, "I need to be baptized by you, and do you come to me?" Jesus replied, "Let it be so now; it is proper for us to do this to fulfill all righteousness." Then John consented. As soon as Jesus was baptized, he went up out of the water. At that moment heaven was opened, and he saw the Spirit of God descending like a dove and lighting on him. (Matthew 3:13-14 NIV)

Jesus was baptized so that we would see our need to be baptized also. It was at the baptism of Jesus that John saw the Holy Spirit come *upon* Jesus with power for the ministry that He demonstrated over the next brief years of His earthly life. That same power for life is available to us.

"The next day John saw Jesus coming toward him and said, 'Look, the Lamb of God, who takes away the sin of the world!'" (John 1:29-30 NIV). Second Corinthians 3:6 is one of my favorite Scriptures: "[It is He] Who has qualified us [making us to be fit and worthy and sufficient] as ministers and dispensers of a new covenant [of salvation through Christ], not [ministers] of the letter (of legally written code) but of the Spirit; for the code [of the Law] kills, but the [Holy] Spirit makes alive." The *King James Version* says that the Spirit giveth life.

Second Corinthians 3:17 states, "Where the Spirit of the Lord is, there is liberty (emancipation from bondage, freedom)." The picture is not that difficult to see. Wherever the Spirit of God goes, everything becomes free and alive. Without Him, things (even church) are dead and filled with bondage.

I have been to many dead church services in my life. I have also been to, and even had the privilege of leading, many that have been full of the life of God. Believe me, once you have experienced both, you definitely know the difference.

When we live under the old covenant—under the rituals and formulas, or the dead letter of the law (see 2 Corinthians 3:6 TEV), we don't really enjoy life or anything connected with it. When we live under grace, expecting glory, filled with the Holy Spirit, we are excited about life. We are filled with a holy expectancy that makes us want to get up in the morning and gladly greet another day. Everything seems to be filled with life—and that life makes things better, easier, and more enjoyable.

First John 5:12 says that if people don't have Christ in their life, they don't have life. Again, this statement was made to walking, talking, breathing people. They were alive by the normal standard of measurement, but not by God's standard. God wants us to be really alive—alive in Christ, filled with the Spirit of Life!

In Romans 8:2 NKJV Paul wrote: "For the law of the Spirit of Life in Christ Jesus has made me free from the law of sin and death."

The only thing that sets us free from the letter of the law, which produces death in us if we try to serve God under it, is the Spirit of Life found in Christ Jesus. When Jesus comes to make us His home, He brings the Spirit of Life with Him: "Jesus answered, If a person [really] loves Me, he will keep My word [obey My teaching]; and My Father will love him, and We will come to him and make Our home (abode, special dwelling place) with him" (John 14:23). When that happens to us, things begin to change—at least they do if we understand what we have and how to access it.

This is where the importance of teaching comes in. Those who have experience with God, and a gift to impart His Word to others, must teach the younger believers who may struggle all their life, even though they are saved, if they lack knowledge. In Hosea 4:6 God said, "My people are destroyed for lack of knowledge." As believers in Christ, we are joint heirs with Him. We have an inheritance; but if we don't know what is ours, we won't use it. Learning God's Word is vital to enjoying the Life Jesus wants us to have.

The Spirit of Life not only affects us spiritually, but He affects our souls, and even our bodies, if we allow Him to do so. How do we allow Him to do so? By believing! Paul explained this truth in Romans 8:11 when he said, "And if the Spirit of Him Who raised up Jesus from the dead dwells in you, [then] He Who raised up Christ Jesus from the dead will also restore to life your mortal (short-lived, perishable) bodies through His Spirit Who dwells in you."

Just imagine, the same Spirit who raised Christ from the dead dwells in us, if we are believers. I have to say it again:

"The same Spirit who raised Christ from the dead dwells in us!" Can it really be true? It must be, because it says so in Holy Scripture, which was inspired by God (see 2 Timothy 3:16 KJV).

When we enter into the reality of that truth by faith, we are quickened or made alive not only in our spirit and soul, but also in our body. The Holy Spirit ministers healing to us and to others through us. Healing is one of the gifts of the Spirit that we will discuss later.

The Holy Spirit will not be allowed to perform His full function in our life if we do not receive Him as the Spirit of Life. Welcome the life of God into you as a dwelling place, and death will be swallowed up in life, just as darkness is swallowed up by the light (see 1 Corinthians

15:54; 2 Corinthians 5:4). Think of going into a dark room and flipping on the light switch. The light swallows up the darkness. Jesus is the Light of the world, and His Spirit is the Spirit of Life that swallows up death and all that tries to defeat us (see John 8:12).

THE SPIRIT OF TRUTH

> But when He, the Spirit of Truth (the Truth-giving Spirit) comes, He will guide you into all the Truth (the whole, full Truth). (John 16:13)

In this passage Jesus refers to the Holy Spirit as the Spirit of Truth. Yet Jesus also said that He Himself is "the Way and the Truth and the Life" (John 14:6). If the Holy Spirit and Jesus are both the Truth, then They must be One.

The Holy Spirit was sent to guide us into all truth. Before Jesus' departure into heaven after His death, burial, and resurrection, He told His disciples He still had much He wanted to share with them, but they were not yet ready for it. In John 16:12 He said, "I have still many things to say to you, but you are not able to bear them or to take them upon you or to grasp them now." In verses 13 through 15 He told them the Holy Spirit would continue revealing things to them as they became ready to receive them.

This is the same way the Holy Spirit works in each of our lives. He gently works with each of us, showing us what we are able to handle at that time.

Truth is wonderful. In fact, according to what Jesus said in John 8:31-32, it is what sets us free. But as wonderful as truth is, we must be ready to face it. Truth is often harsh; it shocks us into a reality that we may not be prepared for if the timing is not right.

The Holy Spirit started bringing me into a great deal of truth, because this is His method of bringing us into wholeness. Most of us live in an unreal world that we have developed to protect ourselves.

For example, I had many difficulties in my life, but I blamed all of them on other people and my circumstances. I had a hard time developing and maintaining good relationships, and I was convinced that all of the people in my life needed to change so we could get along.

One day as I prayed for my husband to change, the Holy Spirit began speaking to my heart. He caused me to realize that I was the main problem, not my husband. In so doing, the Holy Spirit dropped a bomb of truth on me that left me devastated emotionally for three days. I was shocked and horrified as He gently unveiled to me the deception into which I had led myself by believing that everyone else except me was the problem. For three days the Holy Spirit showed me what it was like for the members of my family who had to live with me. He revealed to me that I was hard to get along with, impossible to keep happy, critical, selfish, dominating, controlling, manipulative, negative, nagging—and that was just the beginning of the list.

It was extremely difficult for me to face this truth, but as the Holy Spirit gave me the grace to do so, it was the beginning of much healing and freedom in my life. Many of the truths that I teach people today came out of that initial truth that the Spirit of Truth led me into in 1976. My life since then has been a series of new freedoms, each one preceded by a new truth.

Yes, the Holy Spirit is the Spirit of Truth, and He will guide us into all truth.

You and I live in a world today that is filled with people who are living false lives, wearing masks of pretense, and hiding things. That is wrong; it is very wrong. But the reason it happens is that people have not been taught to walk in the truth. Even those of us in the church have often failed for the same reason—we have not learned to do what we are told in Ephesians 4:15: "Rather, let our lives lovingly express truth [in all things, speaking truly, dealing truly, living truly]." This Scripture says it all. Those of us who are filled with the Spirit of Truth are to live a life of truth.

Most people today ask, "What is truth?" I am grateful that I have found truth; I welcome truth into my life daily. I don't want to live deceived.

Sometimes Satan deceives us, but at other times we are self-deceived. In other words, we fabricate lives that we are comfortable with instead of facing life as it really is and dealing with issues by the power of the Holy Spirit.

The Holy Spirit confronts issues in my life all the time, and He has also taught me to be a confronter, not a coward. Cowards hide from the truth; they are afraid of it.

If you are brave enough and wise enough to welcome the Spirit of Truth into every room in your house (and I am not talking about your home, but you personally), you are in for a journey that you will never forget.

It absolutely amazes me all the lies I believed for so many years that actually kept me in bondage. I was afraid of the truth, and yet it was the only thing that could set me free.

My father sexually abused me in my childhood. I grew up and got away from home and refused to think or talk about what had happened to me. I thought that because I had gotten away from it physically, the abuse was over. I failed to realize I still had the effects of the abuse in my soul (as well as in my mind, will, and emotions) and even in my body. The stress I lived under as a child had left me with physical damage that needed repair. I was hiding from what was in my past, but that did not make it go away. It sat in me like a big sore, growing more and more infected the longer I ignored it.

When the Holy Spirit began working in me, He put a book in my hands written by a woman who had also been sexually abused by her father. As I started reading that book and began to realize that the woman who wrote it had gone through the same experience I had, I started feeling some of the old emotional pain. I threw the book on the floor and said out loud, "I will not read this book." Yet, as I sat there I knew down deep inside that the Holy Spirit had led me to that place in my life and that I needed to take His hand and go through it.

The only way we ever get free from anything we have experienced in the past is by facing it with God and letting Him walk us out of it. I often say, "The only way out is through." We want to find a bypass, but that is usually not God's way.

When Dave and I are traveling by automobile and begin to approach a city, we are always glad if there is a bypass to take us around all the city traffic. This is good for road trips, but not for the journey of life. In life the best policy is plain, simple truth—facing everything head on and not bypassing anything.

You don't have to be afraid of truth. Jesus told His disciples they were not ready for some things; therefore, He did not try to reveal those things to them at that time. God won't bring revelation to you by His Spirit until He knows you are ready. When He does bring revelation to you, you need to believe that you are ready, whether you feel like it or not. We should trust God, not feelings.

THE SPIRIT OF SUPPLICATION

And I will pour out upon the house of David and upon the inhabitants of Jerusalem the Spirit of grace or unmerited favor and supplication. (Zechariah 12:10)

According to this verse, the Holy Spirit is the Spirit of Supplication. That means He is the Spirit of Prayer. Each time we sense a desire to pray, it is the Holy Spirit giving us that desire. We may not realize how often the Holy Spirit is leading us to pray. We may just wonder why we have a certain person or situation on our mind so much. We frequently think of someone and, instead of praying, we keep thinking.

Recognizing when we are being led by the Holy Spirit to pray is often a lesson that takes a long time to learn. We often attribute far too many things to coincidence or chance rather than realizing that God is attempting to lead us by His Spirit. Here is an example that should bring this point home.

One Monday I began thinking about my pastor. I love him and appreciate his ministry so much that thinking about him is not that unusual. But during a three-day period he kept coming to my mind, and I kept sensing a desire to talk to him. I consistently put off calling him because I was busy. (Does that sound familiar?)

On Wednesday I had an appointment at a place of business and as I walked into it, there was my pastor's secretary. I immediately asked her how he was doing. I learned that he had been sick himself and that while returning from his own doctor's appointment he had received a phone call telling him that his father had just been diagnosed with cancer that was spreading throughout his entire body.

I quickly realized why my pastor had been in my heart so much that week. I must admit that I had not taken the time to pray for him. I had *thought* about him, but I had never taken any action to call him or to pray for him.

Of course, I was sorry I had missed the leading of the Holy Spirit. I am sure God worked through someone else to prepare my pastor for the week he was facing. But had I immediately prayed on Monday, and perhaps made a phone call that day, I would have had the pleasure of knowing God used me to minister encouragement to my pastor in the Spirit before he even was aware of an upcoming problem.

God wants to use us as His ministers and representatives, but we must learn to be more sensitive to the Spirit of Supplication. We have all had experiences like the one I have just described; there is no condemnation, but we can and should learn from our mistakes.

The Holy Spirit not only leads us to pray, He helps us pray. He shows us how to pray when we don't know what to pray for (see Romans 8:26-27).

Welcome the Spirit of Supplication into your life and allow the ministry of prayer to be fulfilled through you. It is quite wonderful to watch the miraculous things that take place in response to prayer.

THE SPIRIT OF ADOPTION

> For [the Spirit which] you have now received [is]
> not a spirit of slavery to put you once more in bond-
> age to fear, but you have received the Spirit of adop-
> tion [the Spirit producing sonship] in [the bliss of]
> which we cry, Abba (Father)! Father! (Romans 8:15)

This verse teaches us that the Holy Spirit is the Spirit of
Adoption. The word adoption here means that we have been
brought into the family of God even though we were previously outsiders, unrelated to God in any way. We were sinners serving Satan, but God in His great mercy redeemed
us and purchased us with the blood of His own Son:

> But God—so rich is He in His mercy! Because of
> and in order to satisfy the great and wonderful and
> intense love with which He loved us, even when we
> were dead (slain) by [our own] shortcomings and
> trespasses, He made us alive together in fellowship
> and in union with Christ. (Ephesians 2:4-5)

We understand adoption in the natural sense. We know
that some children without parents are adopted by people
who purposely choose them and take them as their own.
In some ways this is better than being born into a family.
When children are born into a family, their birth is not
always the result of a choice their parents made; sometimes it is just something that happens. When children are
adopted, they are specifically picked out and chosen on
purpose.

Quite frequently people who have been adopted have difficulties due to feelings of rejection. They should be encouraged to look at the positive and not the negative in this situation. What an honor to have been chosen on purpose by those who wanted to pour out their love on them.

The following Scriptures describe God's attitude toward us:

> Even as [in His love] He chose us [actually picked us out for Himself as His own] in Christ before the foundation of the world, that we should be holy (consecrated and set apart for Him) and blameless in His sight, even above reproach, before Him in love. For He foreordained us (destined us, planned in love for us) to be adopted (revealed) as His own children through Jesus Christ, in accordance with the purpose of His will [because it pleased Him and was His kind intent]. (Ephesians 1:4-5)

I have often meditated on these Scriptures and sought revelation on the wonder of being adopted by God.

Psalm 27:10 is another wonderful verse on this subject. In it David says, "Although my father and my mother have forsaken me, yet the Lord will take me up [adopt me as His child]." I use this Scripture passage frequently to encourage those who feel unloved or rejected by their parents. It never fails to give them comfort.

When I met my husband Dave, I was twenty-three years old and had a nine-month-old baby from a marriage I had entered into at the age of eighteen. As I have said, that marriage ended in divorce due to my first husband's adultery and abandonment. When Dave asked me to marry him, I responded with these words, "Well, you know I have a son, and if you get me, you get him."

Dave said a wonderful thing to me: "I don't know your son that well, but I do know that I love you, and I will also love anything or anyone that is a part of you."

Dave adopted my son whom I had named David not having any idea that I would later meet and marry a man named David. God knows many things that we do not know, and He makes arrangements for us ahead of time.

This story closely corresponds to the reason God adopts us. As believers in Christ, we are part of Him—God the Father decided before the foundation of the world that anyone who loved Christ would be loved and accepted by Him. He decided He would adopt all those who accepted Jesus as their Savior (see Ephesians 1:3-6 KJV).

Through the new birth, we have been brought into the family of God. He has become our Father. We have become heirs of God and joint heirs with His Son Jesus Christ (see Romans 8:16-17 KJV). His Spirit dwells in us, just as surely as the Meyer spirit (my outlook and frame of mind) dwells in my children, and as surely as your spirit dwells in your children, if you have any children. They have inherited your traits. They have your blood coursing through their veins. They may look like you, have a body shaped like yours, or display mannerisms like yours.

One of my daughters looks a lot like me. Both of my girls have legs shaped like mine, and mine are like my mother's. My little toenails are shaped rather oddly, and my older son's are shaped the same way. He also has my personality. The daughter who looks like me has her father's personality.

It is really interesting when we begin to think along

these lines. Take these natural examples and begin to see the spiritual similarities in your relationship with God, and you will get excited.

We are to have ways and traits like God. His character is to be duplicated in us—His sons and daughters. In John 14:9 Jesus said, "If you have seen Me, you have seen the Father" (paraphrase). Should we not ultimately be able to say the same thing?

An adopted child may not look like the adoptive parent initially, just as we don't resemble God in any way prior to our adoption by Him. But even an adopted child begins to take on the traits of the adoptive parents.

People are absolutely amazed when they discover that our older son, David, is adopted by Dave. People continually tell him how much he looks like his dad, which, of course, is quite impossible because he has none of Dave's genes or blood in him.

When I was adopted into the family of God, I acted nothing like my heavenly Father, but over the years I have changed, and hopefully, people can now see Him in me. I pray that I act like Him in many ways.

The Spirit of Adoption, the wonderful Holy Spirit, patiently worked with me over the years to draw me into the family of God. It was He who worked in my heart, finally convincing me that I was a daughter of God, a legal joint heir with Christ. It is the knowledge of this family relationship that gives us boldness to go before the throne of God and let our requests be made known to Him (see Hebrews 4:16; Philippians 4:6 KJV). The Spirit of Adoption is the same Holy Spirit who worked in your heart bringing you into the family of God, or perhaps is working in your heart right now as you read these words.

Believe me, my children don't hesitate to make their requests known to their father and me. That is because they know full well that they are in the family and are greatly loved. This knowledge gives them boldness to approach us. We must learn to be the same way with our heavenly Father and the Holy Spirit. If we will allow Him to do so, the Spirit of Adoption will patiently work this truth in our heart.

THE SPIRIT OF HOLINESS

And [as to His divine nature] according to the Spirit of holiness was openly designated the Son of God in power. (Romans 1:4)

The Holy Spirit is called that because He is the holiness of God and because it is His job to work that holiness in all those who believe in Jesus Christ as Savior.

In 1 Peter 1:15-16 we are told: "But as the One Who called you is holy, you yourselves also be holy in all your conduct and manner of living. For it is written, You shall be holy, for I am holy."

God would never tell us to be holy without giving us the help we need to make us that way. An unholy spirit could never make us holy. So God sends His Holy Spirit into our heart to do a complete and thorough work in us.

In Philippians 1:6 the apostle Paul tells us that He who began a good work in us is well able to complete it and bring it to its finish. The Holy Spirit will continue to work in us as long as we are on this earth. God hates sin, and anytime He finds it in us, He quickly works to cleanse us of it.

This fact alone explains why we need the Holy Spirit

dwelling inside of us. He is there not only to lead and guide us through this life, but also to immediately work in cooperation with the Father to remove from us anything that is displeasing to Him.

The Holy Spirit continually seeks to glorify Jesus, and He is preparing us to do that very thing. In John 14:2-3 Jesus said, "I am going to prepare a place for you, so that where I am, there you may be also" (paraphrase). It is as if the Holy Spirit is saying to Him, "I will go and prepare them for the place."

Jesus is in heaven preparing a place for us, and His Holy Spirit is in us preparing us for the place.

In Isaiah 4:4 KJV we see the Holy Spirit as the Spirit of Judgment and the Spirit of Burning: "The Lord shall have washed away the filth of the daughters of Zion, and shall have purged the blood of Jerusalem from the midst thereof by the spirit of judgment, and by the spirit of burning."

The Holy Spirit as the Spirit of Judgment and of Burning relates to His being the Spirit of Holiness. He judges sin in us and burns it out of us. It is not a pleasant work as far as our feelings are concerned, but it eventually brings us into the state God desires us to be in so that we may glorify Him.

Are you permitting the Holy One of God to work in you, burning out all that is undesirable to Him? Hebrews 12:10 KJV says that God chastises us for our profit so that we may be partakers of His holiness. Don't be a compromising Christian who has one foot in the world and one foot in the kingdom of God. Don't be lukewarm, but rather be on fire for God, allowing His fire to burn in you daily. Welcome the chastisement of God, knowing that it is a sign of love and sonship:

For the Lord corrects and disciplines everyone whom He loves, and He punishes, even scourges, every son whom He accepts and welcomes to His heart and cherishes. You must submit to and endure [correction] for discipline; God is dealing with you as with sons. For what son is there whom his father does not [thus] train and correct and discipline? (Hebrews 12:6-7, emphasis mine)

The Virgin Mary became pregnant by the working of the Holy Spirit. When the angel appeared to her, telling her that she would have a son and call His name Jesus and that He would be called the Son of God, "Mary said to the angel, 'How can this be, since I have no [intimacy with any man as a] husband?'" The angel told her that the Holy Spirit would overshadow her, adding, "So the holy (pure, sinless) Thing (Offspring) which shall be born of you will be called the Son of God" (Luke 1:34-35).

The Holy Spirit came upon Mary and planted in her womb a "Holy Thing." The Spirit of Holiness was planted in Mary as a Seed. In her womb He grew into the Son of man and the Son of God who was necessary to deliver people from their sins.

When we are born again, this same thing happens in us. The "Holy Thing," the Spirit of Holiness, is planted in us as a Seed. As we water that Seed with God's Word and keep the "weeds of worldliness" from choking it out, it will grow into a giant tree of righteousness, "the planting of the Lord, that He may be glorified" (Isaiah 61:3).

We are taught in God's Word to "pursue holiness" (Hebrews 12:14). All those who set their heart on this great pursuit will be aided and helped by the Spirit of Holiness.

Those of us who desire holiness need to be completely filled with the Holy Spirit. For that to take place, we must permit Him access to every room in the house. Often we keep certain portions of our life closed off to God just as we might put something in a certain room in the house and close it off so that no one else can see it.

In our home, my husband and I have a packing room. It is where we pack and unpack for our road trips. It is full of suitcases and other travel bags as well as supplies that we take on the road with us. It is not a room that is decorated beautifully and not one I would want people to see; therefore, we keep the door to that room closed.

For many years of my life, even as a church-attending Christian, I kept many rooms in my heart and many areas of my life closed off to the Holy Spirit. I always say I had enough of Jesus to stay out of hell, but not enough to walk in victory. Then in 1976 I had an awesome experience with God that I later discovered was the baptism in the Holy Spirit. Prior to that experience, I had the Holy Spirit because I was born again, but He did not really have me. I only allowed Him to work where I wanted Him to and when I wanted Him to. I was not very happy and was actually very frustrated with Christianity and life in general. As I have described in chapter 2, one day I cried out to God in my automobile. He met me where I was, filled me to overflowing, and I have never been the same.

Acts 10:34 KJV says that God is no respecter of persons. That means He will do the same thing for you that He did for me, if you will allow Him to do so.

8

The Supernatural Realm

~

I was taught that the baptism in the Holy Spirit, speaking in tongues (which will be discussed later), and signs and wonders had passed away with the early church. Sadly, that is almost an accurate statement, but that was never God's will, nor His intention. He has always had a remnant of people somewhere on the earth who still believe in the full gospel, or in everything the Bible teaches, and it has been through that remnant that He has kept the truth alive.

If you have been one of the people who have not believed in these things, or even if you have been taught that such things are incorrect, I beg you not to put this book down but to read on and examine for yourself the Scriptures that I will share with you. After thoroughly searching the Word of God for yourself, I seriously doubt that you will be able to deny the availability of and need for the baptism in the Holy Spirit.

Most people are a little afraid of things they don't understand. We don't understand the supernatural realm, yet we are created by God in such a way that we hunger for it. We all have an interest in the supernatural, and if our need for it is not met by God, Satan will attempt to give us a counterfeit.

As I have stated previously, I was hungry for more spiritually. I was not getting what I needed in the religious arena in which I was participating, so I was searching in the only way I knew how.

I worked with a woman who was heavily involved in astrology, and she was getting me interested in it. It is not God's will for people to consult the stars for guidance, but since I was so hungry, Satan was hoping I would eat anything, even if it was poison. Based on the things the woman was telling me, the stars seemed to be able to tell her things that worked for her. Since I was not hearing anything that was working in my life, I was interested in what she had to say.

This is exactly how Satan deceives many people. They are searching for direction and solutions in their daily life, and if their church leaves them without sufficient answers, they are easy prey for the enemy. Why should we consult the stars for direction in life when we can consult the One who made the stars?

Satan has a counterfeit for everything good that God wants to give us. We must be very wise and know the Scriptures or we will be deceived in these last days in which we are living. The Bible warns us of a great deception in the final days before Jesus returns to earth to redeem His own (see Luke 21:8-11; 2 Timothy 3:13-14). We must pray for truth and seek God to protect us from being deceived.

Someone must have been praying for me, because God intervened and met my need before Satan could drag me into the pit he had dug for me.

After the baptism in the Holy Spirit, I experienced a closer fellowship and intimacy with God than any I had ever known before. I began to sense His leading in my life. He was speaking to me, and I knew it was His voice. In John 10:4-5 Jesus said, "My sheep know My voice, and the voice of a stranger they will not follow" (paraphrase). I was beginning to know His voice, and it thrilled me.

As Christians, we have a right to be spiritually excited. We get excited about all kinds of other things, so why shouldn't we be excited about our relationship with God?

People often say that any visible display in spiritual areas is just "emotionalism." I finally realized that it was God who gave us emotions and that although He does not want us to let them lead our life, He does give them to us for a purpose, part of which is enjoyment. If we are truly enjoying God, how can we not show some emotion about it? Why must our spiritual experience be dry and boring, dull and lifeless? Is Christianity supposed to be expressed by long faces, sad music, and somber church rituals? Certainly not!

In Psalm 122:1, David said he was glad when he was asked to go to the house of the Lord. David danced before the Lord (see 2 Samuel 6:14), played on the harp, and rejoiced greatly, yet he lived under the old covenant. Jesus and His disciples lived under the new covenant, and He told them to rejoice that their names were written in the Lamb's Book of Life, which applies to everyone who believes in Jesus (see Luke 10:20 NKJV; Revelation 21:27). Romans 15:13 tells us that we who believe in Christ are full of hope, joy, and peace (under the new covenant). That's reason enough to be excited and rejoice!

We have already seen that the old covenant is a covenant

of works, based on doing everything ourselves—struggling, striving, and laboring to be acceptable to God. That kind of covenant steals our joy and peace. But remember that the new covenant is a covenant of grace, which is based not on what we do but on what Christ has already done for us. Therefore, we are justified by our faith, not our works. That is so wonderful, because it takes the pressure off of us to perform. We can give up our outward efforts and allow God to work through us by the power of His Holy Spirit within us.

The bottom line is this: the old covenant brings bondage; the new covenant brings liberty. If David could rejoice under the old covenant, how much more should we be rejoicing under the new covenant?

HAVE YOU BEEN ROBBED OF THE POWER OF THE HOLY SPIRIT IN YOUR LIFE?

And afterward I will pour out My Spirit upon all flesh; and your sons and your daughters shall prophesy, your old men shall dream dreams, your young men shall see visions. Even upon the menservants and upon the maidservants in those days will I pour out My Spirit. (Joel 2:28-29)

Yes, the infilling with the Holy Spirit is different from anything else we may experience. It enables us to *be* what we are supposed to be *in* God and then to *do* what we are supposed to do *for* God.

Many Christians try to *do* something before they have

become something. This produces a type of Christianity that is dry and boring, dull and lifeless. Many preachers discourage others from seeking the baptism of the Holy Spirit because they have not experienced it themselves.

We should not tell people that something does not exist just because our experience says it does not. Instead, we should turn to the Word of God and the experience of multitudes who have gone before us and who have been baptized in the Holy Spirit and spoken with other tongues, those who have witnessed miracles of healing and seen devils cast out. We should talk to those who have seen lives radically transformed by the power of God.

I remember talking to one of the pastors of the first church I attended after Dave and I got married. I had experienced a visitation from God and was quite excited about it. Although I had been born again at the age of nine, I experienced a renewal of my faith one night in the kitchen while I was washing dishes. The Lord became very real to me, and suddenly I realized how He had led me all those years, even when I thought He was not there at all—or if He was there, He had forgotten about me. I was overwhelmed with wonder and awe at the faithfulness of God. I wanted to talk to someone I thought would understand such spiritual things, so I went to the pastor, who encouraged me to calm down and realize that my excitement would not last.

He may have meant well, but I believe he discouraged me because he had never experienced what I was describing; therefore, he rejected it as being nothing of any value. I was very disappointed and left his office deflated, like a balloon that has suddenly had the air let out of it.

It is a shame to throw water on the fire of a believer.

People are often afraid that an excited person may get into something wild. But, as one person said, "I would rather have a little wildfire than no fire at all."

Some people just go to church and park there, and that is the beginning and end of their spiritual experience. I found out a long time ago that if I wanted to get anywhere, I had to take the car out of park.

It is absolutely impossible to drive a car stuck in park. Take your life out of park and put God in the driver's seat—then buckle your seat belt and get ready for the ride of your life!

Ask God to do a new thing in your life. Don't insist that it fit inside the boundaries of your particular religious doctrine. According to the Bible, the power of God is shut down by the doctrines of men:

> For [although] they hold a form of piety (true religion), they deny and reject and are strangers to the power of it [their conduct belies the genuineness of their profession]. Avoid [all] such people [turn away from them]. (2 Timothy 3:5)
>
> If then you have died with Christ to material ways of looking at things and have escaped from the world's crude and elemental notions and teachings of externalism, why do you live as if you still belong to the world? [Why do you submit to rules and regulations? such as] Do not handle [this], Do not taste [that], Do not even touch [them], referring to things all of which perish with being used. To do this is to follow human precepts and doctrines. Such [practices] have indeed the outward appearance [that popularly passes] for wisdom, in promoting

self-imposed rigor of devotion and delight in self-humiliation and severity of discipline of the body, but they are of no value in checking the indulgence of the flesh (the lower nature). [Instead, they do not honor God but serve only to indulge the flesh.] (Colossians 2:20-23)

Man-made doctrines have robbed multiple thousands of believers of the power of the Holy Spirit in their lives. God is not interested in our man-made doctrines; He is only interested in what His Word says, and that should be our interest also.

When God baptized me in the Holy Spirit on that Friday in February 1976, He did not ask me about my religious doctrines or whether or not my church friends would approve. As it turned out, they did not approve. Not only was I asked to leave the church, but simultaneously I lost all of my so-called friends. It was a difficult time in my life, but through it I learned how Satan uses the pain of rejection to try to keep people from going forward with God.

I was, of course, tempted to forget the whole thing and just go back to being a "normal" Christian. But I knew that God had done something wonderful in my life. I had never felt like that before, and I made the decision that even if I never had any friends, I could not go back to what I used to be and have. It was not satisfying then, and it would never be.

I simply had to go on with God no matter what the cost!

I pray that you will feel the same way after reading this book. One of my main purposes in writing it is to stir up a hunger in those who love God but need more of the Holy Spirit in their life. If you are one of those people, I pray you will open every room in your life and let God take control. Remember that Jesus did not die for you so you could be religious but so you could have a deep, intimate, personal relationship with God through Him and could know the joy of being filled through and through with the Holy Spirit.

Sitting in church does not make one a Christian any more than sitting in a garage makes one a car. Our experience with God is to go far beyond church attendance. It always grieves me when I ask people if they are Christian, and they tell me what church they go to—it usually means they go to church but don't really know the Lord in a personal way.

OPEN EVERY ROOM IN THE HOUSE

Behold, I stand at the door and knock; if anyone hears and listens to and heeds My voice and opens the door, I will come in to him. (Revelation 3:20)

After I was baptized in the Holy Spirit, I found God in areas of my life in which He had not previously been welcome. He dealt with me about every area; there was nothing He was not involved in. I liked it, but I didn't like it, if you know what I mean. It was exciting, but frightening.

God got involved in how I talked to people and about them. He got involved in how I spent my money, how I dressed, who I had for friends, and what I did for entertainment. He got involved in my thought life and my attitudes. I realized He knew the deepest secrets of my heart and that nothing was hidden from Him. He was no longer in the "Sunday morning room" of my life, but it seemed as though He was running the entire house. He had the keys to every room, and He entered without notice—I might add, without even knocking or ringing the bell. In other words, I never knew when He might show up and voice an opinion about an issue, but it seemed to be happening more and more frequently. As I said, it was exciting, but I quickly realized that a lot of things were going to change.

We all want change, but when it comes, it is frightening. We want our lives to change, but not our lifestyle. We may not like what we have, but what if we like it more than what we get next? This is an example of the kind of questions we ask ourselves. It frightens us when we seem to be out of control and in the hands of another.

To be filled with the Holy Spirit means to live our life for God's glory and pleasure, not for our own. It means laying down the life we had planned and discovering and following His plan for us.

I know now that I was always called to be a teacher of God's Word. I can look back over my life and see the telltale signs all through it. I thought I was a professional career woman. I had a plan for my life, but suddenly on that Friday in February 1976 God interrupted my plan.

As we have seen, Proverbs 16:9 says that the mind of a man plans his way, but God directs his steps. Within three weeks following my baptism in the Holy Spirit, at God's direction I was making plans to teach a Bible study, and I have been teaching God's Word continually since then with the exception of one year.

When we give God the driver's seat in our life, things can change fast. That's why we should learn to pray first, and then make plans.

Most of my life I made plans and then prayed for God to make them work out. They were *my* plans, and I spent my life trying to push them through—and being disappointed and confused when they did not work out.

Will you let the Spirit of God have the run of your "house"? Will you welcome Him into your entire life and make Him feel at home and comfortable? I pray that you will, because I know you will never be fulfilled unless you do. You may run up against opposition, because with every opportunity there is always some opposition. The price may be high, but the benefits are certainly worth it. You were created to be the home of God. Will you allow Him full and free access to your life?

EVIDENCE OF THE BAPTISM IN THE HOLY SPIRIT

> Then the Spirit of the Lord will come upon you mightily, and you will show yourself to be a prophet with them; and you will be turned into another man. (1 Samuel 10:6)

The most important evidences of the Spirit-filled life are a change of character and the development of the fruit of the Holy Spirit described in Galatians 5:22-23. God baptizes people in the Holy Spirit to enable them to live for Him. If they are not doing that, then they are not showing forth the proper evidence of Holy Spirit baptism. Speaking in tongues was one of the evidences of the outpouring of the Holy Spirit at Pentecost, but the most important evidence was then, and always will be, changed men and women.

At the trial of Jesus, Peter denied Christ three times for fear of the Jews (see Luke 22:56-62); but after being filled with the Holy Spirit on the Day of Pentecost, he stood and preached an extremely bold message. The result of Peter's preaching that day was three thousand souls added to the kingdom of God (see Acts 2:14-41). The baptism in the Holy Spirit changed Peter; it turned him into another man. His fear suddenly disappeared, and he became bold.

The world is full of people who live daily with the torment of fear. Sadly, most of them don't even realize there is help available to them through the infilling of the Holy Spirit.

As a matter of fact, it was not just Peter who took a bold stand that day. All eleven of the remaining apostles did the same. They had all been hiding behind closed doors for fear of the Jews when Jesus came to them after His resurrection (see John 20:19-22). Suddenly, after being filled with the Holy Spirit, they all became fearless and bold.

The baptism in the Holy Spirit changed Saul; it changed Peter and the disciples; it changed me; and it continues to change earnest seekers the world over. Yes, changed men and women are the most important evidence, but it is not the only one we can expect to find. Speaking in tongues is also an evidence, and it is a very valuable gift.

THE EVIDENCE OF SPEAKING IN TONGUES

And when the Day of Pentecost had fully come, they were all assembled together in one place, when suddenly there came a sound from heaven like the rushing of a violent tempest blast, and it filled the whole house in which they were sitting. And there appeared to them tongues resembling fire, which were separated and distributed and which settled on each one of them. And they were all filled (diffused throughout their souls) with the Holy Spirit and began to speak in other (different, foreign) languages (tongues), as the Spirit kept giving them clear and loud expression. (Acts 2:1-4)

Some say that speaking in tongues may be for some people, but not for all. It is true that not all believers speak in tongues, but I believe all can if they are willing to do so.

In this passage the Bible says that on the Day of Pentecost *all* the disciples in the Upper Room spoke with other tongues. I believe that this first outpouring is a pattern for the church to follow. Had God's will been for only some believers to speak in tongues and for some not to do so, surely the Bible would say that 120 disciples waited in the Upper Room for the outpouring of the Holy Spirit, and suddenly they heard the sound of a mighty rushing wind and tongues of fire lit upon them, and eighty-five of them spoke with other tongues. Why would this Scripture in verse 4 say that *all spoke in tongues* if speaking in tongues is not for all?

I do believe many people are baptized in the Holy Spirit and don't speak in tongues, but I don't believe it is because they can't. I personally believe it is because they are afraid to do so because their church doctrine teaches them not to, or perhaps because they don't want the stigma that is often attached to people who are known to speak in tongues.

Some people even ask God for the gift of tongues, and

yet deep down inside they are afraid to receive it. It is rather unusual that the devil has chosen that one gift of all the many mentioned in the Bible to make such a fuss about. That in itself tells me there must be something very valuable in speaking in tongues; otherwise, Satan would not work so hard to discredit it.

Just think about it. People don't mind if we have wisdom, knowledge, discernment, faith, or any of the other gifts of the Holy Spirit, but they seem to get all upset if we speak in other tongues. Yet all these gifts are listed together in 1 Corinthians 12.

I have known some wonderful Christians who I believe were baptized in the Holy Spirit, and yet they did not speak in tongues. They had wonderful fruit in their lives, in many cases more fruit than others I have known who did speak in tongues. Sometimes Pentecostal people make too much of speaking in tongues. They act as if that is the one and only thing that makes a person spiritual, when, in fact, that is not the case at all.

As I have said, yes, I believe a person can be baptized in the Holy Spirit and not speak in tongues, but I don't believe that has to be the case for everyone. I encourage every person who wants to be filled with the Holy Spirit also to desire to speak in tongues and in faith to open their mouth and do what the 120 did at Pentecost—begin to speak with other tongues, as the Spirit gives the utterance (see Acts 2:4 KJV).

I do not believe we must be baptized in the Holy Spirit in order to be saved and go to heaven, but I do believe we need the baptism of the Holy Spirit and the power it brings in order to walk in victory in our daily lives. We need God's power to overcome the flesh and daily have the victory Jesus won at Calvary when He took authority over the enemy.

I am the type of person who wants everything God has to offer. I often say I am a "spiritual hog." Even though I could get to heaven without the baptism of the Holy Spirit, I don't know why I would want to do so. I could be baptized in the Holy Spirit and not speak in tongues, but why would I want to do that?

God must have sent these things and made them available to us because He wants us to have them, and since He sent them, I intend to receive them in all their fullness. *I don't intend to do without anything God has to offer just to appease people.* If God wants me to have something, I am open to receive it.

THE VALUE OF SPEAKING IN TONGUES

For one who speaks in an [unknown] tongue speaks not to men but to God, for no one understands or catches his meaning, because in the [Holy] Spirit he utters secret truths and hidden things [not obvious to the understanding].

For if I pray in an [unknown] tongue, my spirit [by the Holy Spirit within me] prays, but my mind is unproductive [it bears no fruit and helps nobody]. Then what am I to do? I will pray with my spirit [by the Holy Spirit within me], but I will also pray [intelligently] with my mind and understanding; I will sing with my spirit [by the Holy Spirit that is within me], but I will sing [intelligently] with my mind and understanding also. (1 Corinthians 14:2, 14-15)

When we speak in tongues, we speak secrets and mysteries unto God. We are speaking in a spiritual language that Satan cannot understand. We cannot even understand it. In verse 14 of this passage Paul said that when we pray in the Spirit, our understanding is unfruitful or our mind is unproductive. In other words, our mind does not understand, but our spirit is edified and built up. Jude v.20 says that when we pray in the Holy Spirit, we edify ourselves and build ourselves up in our most holy faith.[1]

Many times I have had the experience of feeling discouraged or physically tired, and yet I had work to do. Often I have needed to teach in one of my conferences, and I certainly did not feel like a woman of faith who was anointed by God, or filled with His power, to minister to others. At such times I have learned to pray in the Holy Spirit, or pray in other tongues. As I do so, I can literally feel the life and power of God rising up out of my "inner man" and ministering strength to my entire being (see Ephesians 3:16 KJV).

In John 7:38-39 NIV Jesus said, " 'Whoever believes in me, as the Scripture has said, streams of living water will flow from within him.' By this he meant the Spirit, whom those who believed in him were later to receive." As this passage indicates, Jesus was speaking of the Holy Spirit who was yet to be poured out. I believe speaking in tongues is the sound of those streams of living water as they flow out from within those who are filled with the Spirit.

When we speak in tongues, we are often prophesying great things over our own lives. If we knew what we were saying, the mystery would seem so great that we probably could not believe it; therefore, speaking in tongues is a great way to "call things that be not as if they are." Romans 4:17 tells us we serve a God who speaks of things that do not yet exist as if they already did, and I believe we should follow in His footsteps.

Praying in tongues is a way to pray accurately when we don't know how to pray "as we ought" (see Romans 8:26 KJV). Often these prayers may even seem inarticulate, just a sighing or groaning. *The Amplified Bible* version of Romans 8:26 says the Holy Spirit prays through us "with unspeakable yearnings and groanings too deep for utterance."

To be very honest, these things are hard to explain to anyone who has not experienced them, but once a person has experienced them, there is no denying the reality of this wonderful language of the Spirit.

Each person's prayer language is a bit different, and Satan is sure to tell nearly everyone initially that their particular language is just gibberish they are making up.

I did not receive my spiritual prayer language the day I was filled with the Holy Spirit. But shortly thereafter, while reading a book written by Pat Boone titled *A New Song*,[2] I was inspired to try speaking in tongues. Pat was describing what had happened to him when he received the baptism in the Holy Spirit and started speaking in tongues. Being the bold type that I am, I simply opened my mouth and spoke out the foreign-sounding words that came to my heart. I only received about four words. After a good speech from the devil, which was, of course, lies, I was convinced I had made up those four words. So I simply put a lid on the gift and went on about my business.

When we believe Satan's lies, we are deceived. I was deceived into believing that what I had received from God was not real.

Several days later as I was searching the dictionary to help my daughter with a homework assignment, I ran across some Latin words and realized that some of them were the words God had given me the day I spoke in tongues. From the dictionary I learned that the words I had received meant "Omnipotent heavenly Father." I just about came unglued. I knew God was speaking to me out of this dictionary, of all things, showing me beyond any doubt that I could not have made up those words. I did not know any Latin and would not have known how to put those words together to make such a statement. This was no coincidence—the Holy Spirit had given me the language and was then leading me into a discovery that would increase my faith and prevent Satan from stealing from me what God had so graciously given me.

One of the most important ways we can stop Satan from deceiving us is by living by faith. Faith goes beyond what we can see or feel. It concerns what we know deep inside our heart.

When I realized what had happened, I became very excited. My heart was full of faith because I knew for certain I had heard from God. Since that time, Satan has never been able to steal the gift from me again.

I began diligently using the four little words I had received, and soon God added more words to my spiritual prayer language. Now I pray in tongues regularly. It is part of my everyday life. I talk to God through the Holy Spirit, and I believe with all of my heart that what I am praying is the perfect prayer that needs to be prayed.

Faith is the only thing that brings us into the rest of God (see Hebrews 4:3). It eliminates all the questions and reasonings of life. We simply trust, and life becomes wonderful! Even when we have problems, life is still wonderful because we are filled with hope, believing that Someone greater than we is on our side (see Romans 8:31; 1 John 4:4).

In 1 Corinthians 14:13 we are told that we should pray that we may interpret our prayer language, and I believe we do interpret, but not always at the moment we pray. For example, I pray a lot in tongues on the days I minister. I believe the way I am led in the conferences, and the things I say and preach about that seem to really meet the needs of people are the interpretation of things I have prayed in the Spirit throughout the day.

Quite often people tell me they feel that I am speaking directly to them because I seem to know their problem. They say, "It is like you have been living in my house." Well, obviously I have not been living in their house, but the Holy Spirit has. He is ministering to them through me. Because He does know what their problems are, He can address them directly.

The praying in the Spirit that I do regularly helps prepare me to minister to the people. What I am saying to them seems perfectly normal to me, while at the same time it often seems extremely supernatural to them.

I firmly believe that God can lead us supernaturally in a natural way. All that is supernatural does not have to be "spooky" or "kooky." We can be solid citizens and still be filled with the Holy Spirit. We don't have to be "flaky" and "floating around on a cloud" somewhere half the time.

DON'T BE AFRAID OF THE UNKNOWN

> If you then, though you are evil, know how to give good gifts to your children, how much more will your Father in heaven give the Holy Spirit to those who ask him! (Luke 11:13 NIV)

I beg you not to be afraid of the Holy Spirit and His gifts just because you may not have experienced them. God will never give you a bad gift if you ask for a good one.

In a letter Paul wrote to the church in Corinth, he asked, "Do all possess extraordinary powers of healing? Do all speak with tongues? Do all interpret?" (1 Corinthians 12:30). The obvious answer is no. This is a Scripture that has been taken out of context by those who want to build a case against speaking in tongues. They contend that Paul was clearly saying that not all would speak with tongues. It is true Paul was saying that, but he was speaking of the gift of tongues exercised in a public meeting and needing interpretation. He was not speaking of the spiritual prayer language available to all born-again believers who have been baptized in the Holy Spirit, through which they can speak secrets and mysteries unto God. Not all believers possess the "gifts of healings," and yet the Bible says that all believers are encouraged to lay hands on the sick and see them recover.

THESE SIGNS SHALL FOLLOW THOSE WHO BELIEVE

> And these attesting signs will accompany those who believe: in My name they will drive out demons; they will speak in new languages; they will pick up serpents; and [even] if they drink anything deadly, it will not hurt them; they will lay their hands on the sick, and they will get well. (Mark 16:17-18)

In the book of Mark, this is the last recorded thing that Jesus said before His ascension into heaven. If these were His parting words, they must have been important.

Mark 16:15 records what we commonly call the Great Commission: "And He said to them, Go into all the world and preach and publish openly the good news (the gospel) to every creature [of the whole human race]." People from every Christian church accept and attempt to carry out this verse. Yet two verses later in verses 17 and 18, Jesus says believers will cast out demons, speak in new tongues, and lay hands on the sick. Some churches don't practice these things, and many teach against them.

I honestly believe that a few moments of sincere thought will reveal to the seeking soul that if Jesus meant for us to carry out Mark 16:15, then He also intended for us to carry out verses 17 and 18 as well. It is dangerous business to pick and choose among Scriptures. We cannot take the ones we are comfortable with and ignore the rest—at least not if we are going to follow the full gospel. We need the whole counsel of the Word of God, not just bits and pieces of it.

Satan has been very successful in removing the power of the gospel from many churches and, therefore, from the lives of many believers. He does not want people to be saved, but should that occur, he certainly does not want them to have and display any power in their lives. He knows that if believers manifest the power of God in their own lives, they are very likely to affect other people in a positive way and be used by God to bring many others into the kingdom of God.

Yes, Paul did indicate that not all would have the gifts of healings, not all would have the gift of speaking in tongues, and not all would have the gift of interpreting. But I want to stress again that Paul was not speaking of the manifestation of the Spirit available to every believer; he was speaking of the special supernatural endowment of power given to certain believers to operate in these gifts publicly for the good and profit of all.

Later in the book I will expound on the gifts of the Holy Spirit, which are dispensed by Him to all believers for them to use to help others and to make their own lives easier and more powerful. We are to "covet earnestly" (strongly desire) the gifts (see 1 Corinthians 12:31 KJV), and the Holy Spirit will let them flow through each of us as we have need and as He sees proper for the occasion.

PAUL SPOKE IN TONGUES

I thank God that I speak in [strange] tongues (languages) more than any of you or all of you put together. (1 Corinthians 14:18)

Paul was grateful for the ability to speak in other tongues, and apparently, judging by this Scripture, it was something he practiced often.

Once we are baptized in the Holy Spirit, we can speak in tongues whenever we want to. We don't have to wait for some special feeling to come over us and move us to do so. Just as we can pray in our native tongues whenever we choose, so we can pray in other tongues whenever we choose.

Paul instructed the Corinthians not to forbid anyone to speak in tongues: "So [to conclude], my brethren, earnestly desire and set your hearts on prophesying (on being inspired to preach and teach and to interpret God's will and purpose), and do not forbid or hinder speaking in [unknown] tongues" (1 Corinthians 14:39).

Although Paul specifically said not to forbid anyone to speak in tongues, there are spiritual leaders today who forbid those under their authority to speak in tongues. How can anyone justify such action and think that they are living in accordance with Scripture? As I have noted, I believe many people simply forbid others to have what they themselves have not experienced. This is wrong, and anyone under that kind of authority should confront it respectfully but boldly, sharing the Scriptures for confirmation of their beliefs.

Paul also clearly shows that praying with the spirit (by the Holy Spirit) is not the same as praying with the understanding, because in 1 Corinthians 14:14-15 he stated that he did both: "For if I pray in a tongue, my spirit prays, but my mind is unfruitful. So what shall I do? I will pray with my spirit, but I will also pray with my mind; I will sing with my spirit, but I will also sing with my mind" (NIV).

I am not saying that it is impossible to pray Spirit-led

prayers in one's native language. That, of course, is a valuable and right thing to do. But it is not what Paul was talking about in this passage. When Paul said he prayed with his spirit, he meant he prayed in other tongues.[3]

DID TONGUES PASS AWAY WITH THE EARLY CHURCH?

If tongues passed away with the early church, as many claim, then there are millions of people on the earth today who regularly practice, as did their spiritual ancestors before them, something that does not exist. I doubt that many people are making up languages and spending their time talking in gibberish just for the sake of thinking they are speaking in tongues.

I am a practical person. As such, I am not the least bit interested in wasting my time or doing anything foolish. I am a respectable woman with a good reputation. I have a husband, four grown children, eight grandchildren, and many friends—and I *speak in other tongues every day of my life*. In other words, I am an ordinary person, yet I regularly do this extraordinary thing.

Tongues did not pass away with the early church. In fact, they have never gone away; someone, somewhere, has always kept the flame alive. Down through the centuries, many have tried to put tongues away, but they have not succeeded.

Sometimes we blindly believe whatever someone tells us, never bothering to check it out for ourselves. I was doing that very thing, believing that tongues and the other gifts of the Spirit were not for today—until I was baptized in the Holy Spirit myself. Once people are fully immersed in the Spirit, it is difficult to convince them that they are not filled with the Spirit and that tongues and the other gifts of the Spirit are not for today.

Following God cost me a lot, just as Jesus said it would. In Matthew 16:25-26 He said that if we save our life here on earth, we will lose our heavenly life. I would rather lose my friends than lose my relationship with God. I would rather believe the Holy Scriptures than believe other people.

Those who are against speaking in tongues almost always use the following verses to support their argument:

> Love never fails [never fades out or becomes obsolete or comes to an end]. As for prophecy (the gift of interpreting the divine will and purpose), it will be fulfilled and pass away; as for tongues, they will be destroyed and cease; as for knowledge, it will pass away [it will lose its value and be superseded by truth]. For our knowledge is fragmentary (incomplete and imperfect), and our prophecy (our teaching) is fragmentary (incomplete and imperfect). But when the complete and perfect (total) comes, the incomplete and imperfect will vanish away (become antiquated, void, and superseded). (1 Corinthians 13:8-10)

According to this Scripture, there is coming a time when knowledge will pass away, and tongues will pass away.[4] I have never heard of anyone who believes that knowledge has passed away; in fact, knowledge is increasing rapidly in the world. Yet many of the same people who believe that knowledge has not passed away also believe and teach others that tongues have passed away. Why would one gift pass away and not the other if the basis for such belief is the Scripture quoted above?

Jesus is "the perfect and complete" spoken of in these passages of Scripture. At the appointed time He will return to establish His kingdom, a new heaven and a new earth. But for now we live in an imperfect world, one in which we need all the help we can get. The Holy Spirit and *all* of His gifts have been sent to us from God the Father and Jesus the Son to help us.

People try to explain away something they are uncomfortable with or want to get rid of, but their arguments usually don't even make any sense if we really examine them.

PROPER USE OF TONGUES

Another argument against speaking in tongues is based on the fact that many people abuse or misuse tongues. They get out of order with them, speaking out at wrong times or in front of the wrong people. The Corinthians were apparently doing the same thing, because Paul wrote a letter instructing them in what he considered the proper use of tongues and the operation of the gifts of the Spirit, described in 1 Corinthians 14:40 KJV as "decently and in order."

In verses 22 to 32 of that chapter Paul told them how many of them should speak in tongues in a service or gathering, instructing them that the tongues had to be interpreted so that everyone could understand. He said that if a person who is listening to someone else speak in tongues has an inspired revelation, the one who is speaking should yield the floor to that individual. He said that those who speak in tongues have control over their own spirit and can remain silent when necessary. He said that tongues are a sign to unbelievers, not to believers, and thus should be carefully handled so as not to confuse or mislead them.

Yes, Paul found excess in the exercise of the gift of tongues, and he dealt with it. But he did not suggest that tongues should be done away with in order to get rid of the excess.

We are making a big mistake if we would rather get rid of the gifts of God than learn how to use them properly.

Another reason some people are against speaking in tongues is that they have experienced people who do speak in tongues and who have a bad attitude, an "I'm-better-than-you, I'm-more-spiritual-than-you-are" attitude. This is wrong and is not the heart of God at all. God loves all of us equally, and speaking in tongues does not make us any better or any more pleasing to Him than other believers who do not speak in tongues. I do believe, however, that speaking in tongues opens a door to the supernatural realm that is available to all believers.

9

Receiving the Fullness of the Holy Spirit

◦──◦

[That you may really come] to know [practically, through experience for yourselves] the love of Christ, which far surpasses mere knowledge [without experience]; that you may be filled [through all your being] unto all the fullness of God [may have the richest measure of the divine Presence, and become a body wholly filled and flooded with God Himself]! (Ephesians 3:19)

All of this information about the baptism in the Holy Spirit will be of very little value to us unless we go on to receive the fullness of the Holy Spirit into our life, as we are instructed to do in Ephesians 3:19.

We must first be filled and then stay filled. To be filled, we must first have a desire.

If you remember, I had come to a place in my life where I knew I had to have something if I was to go on as a Christian. I was feeling rather desperate the day I was baptized in the Holy Spirit.

I personally believe that God often does not answer our first cries because He wants us to get desperate enough to be totally open to whatever He wants to do in our life.

I gave an example earlier of a drowning person who was fighting and resisting the lifeguard's attempt to save them until they were too tired to fight anymore. I was like that drowning person. I had fought with life so much I just did not have any "fight" left in me, but that actually worked to my advantage. I was at the bottom and had nowhere to go but up. I was ready for whatever the Great Physician said I needed.

If a person is dying from disease or is experiencing so much pain they cannot endure it one more second, they will do whatever their doctor tells them to do—and usually without question. We need to get to the same point in our walk with God. He wants to "doctor" our souls, and we should be willing to take whatever prescription He gives us.

God's prescription for me at that time was the baptism in the Holy Spirit, and I have been in a healing process ever since.

HAVE A DESIRE

> Thou openest thine hand, and satisfiest the desire of every living thing. (Psalm 145:16 KJV)

If you are hungry for more of God in your life, then you are a candidate to receive the baptism in the Holy Spirit.

Receiving the fullness of the Holy Spirit into our life is a holy thing, something to be reverenced and even feared in a respectful way. God does not endue us with His power just for fun and games. He is a God of purpose. Everything He does in our life is for a purpose. Finding God's purpose and allowing Him to equip us for it should be the primary quest of our life.

In my own life I have found that when I have a strong desire for something, I usually get it. That's because we are created in such a way that our determination usually rises to meet our desires, and we do whatever we need to do to reach the desired goal.

My husband, Dave, received the baptism in the Holy Spirit at the age of eighteen. The church he attended did not teach such things, but he had come to a point in his life where he knew that he was missing something. Like me, he did not know what it was. But his desire to have it had become so strong that one day at work he went into the rest room, entered one of the stalls, sat down, and told God that he was not going to move from that spot until He gave him whatever it was he was searching for. As he just sat there, God met him, and he was filled with the Holy Spirit. At the same time he received a healing in his eyes. He had previously needed glasses, but after that experience with God he did not have to wear them for many years.

Dave's strong desire let God know what was important to him.

Our desires tell a lot about who we really are. They are connected with the central part of us, our will. What we want speaks of our character. If we want more money, that may mean we are greedy. If we want more power, that could mean we seek control. But if we want more of God, that says something serious about our heart attitude.

I believe God always fulfills the desires of those of us who want more of Him—He will not leave us hungry (see Psalm 37:4)!

If you would like to have a desire for more of God, but in all honesty you cannot say that you do, then ask God to give you a desire. Tell Him your desire is to have more desire. I doubt that you are without desire. If you were not seeking more of God, you probably would not have read this far in the book.

God will meet you where you are. God met me in my automobile, and He met Dave in the rest room at work. That does not sound very religious, does it? Many people think God could not possibly touch them the way we have described in this book anywhere but in church. But God meets us where we are. Wherever He finds a hungry person, He comes to feed that individual.

God meets us in our imperfection and in our need, and He fills us with His Spirit to help us in every way to have a full and blessed life. I encourage you to cry out to God right now, right where you are. I believe He will meet you where you are and will help you get to where you need to be.

BE OPEN

Philip sought and found Nathanael and told him, We have found (discovered) the One Moses in the Law and also the Prophets wrote about—Jesus from Nazareth, the [legal] son of Joseph! Nathanael answered him, [Nazareth!] Can anything good come out of Nazareth? Philip replied, Come and see! (John 1:45-46)

Nathanael had an opinion, but at least he was open to being shown if he was wrong. I believe that is all God asks of any of us.

If you have had no information (or been fed a lot of negative information) about the baptism of the Holy Spirit, speaking in tongues, healing the sick, or other such things related to God, then naturally your opinion is probably, at the very least, cautious and perhaps even downright negative. All I ask is that you be open. Search the Scriptures for yourself and ask God to reveal the truth to you.

All the discussion in this book about the baptism of the Holy Spirit and speaking in other tongues may seem strange and foreign to you. Perhaps it is something you have never even heard of. I urge you to read the Scriptures on this subject. Look them up for yourself. Tell God you want to receive all that is rightfully yours as His heir and a joint heir with His Son Jesus Christ. Don't live in spiritual poverty any longer. Don't be satisfied with just enough of the Holy Spirit in your life to barely get you through each day. Welcome Him into your life in all His fullness.

Some people drive their car on fumes, barely getting from place to place. That is the way some Christians are spiritually. They have just enough of God's power to barely get through each day, and even that is a struggle. That is sad and unnecessary when there is so much more available.

If you need more of God's power, I urge you to be like Nathanael. No matter what you may have heard in the past, no matter what your opinion may be, at least come and see. Check it out for yourself!

As we have seen in Revelation 3:20, Jesus is knocking

at the door of many hearts right now, but we must remember that the doorknob is on our side. As I have said, the Holy Spirit is a Gentleman; He will not force His way into our life. We must welcome Him.

Be receptive to the Holy Spirit. Open the door of your heart to Him by stretching your faith a little. Be like Peter—the one person in the group who will get out of the boat and walk on the water. Peter probably had butterflies in his stomach when he got out of that boat, but as long as he kept his eyes on Jesus, he did all right (see Matthew 14:23-30).

Hardheaded people are narrow-minded. Their thinking is little, and they live little lives. God has a great big wonderful life planned for you and me, but if we are stiff-necked, as God called the Israelites (see Exodus 33:3), or hardheaded (as we say today), then we will miss what God has for us. Stubbornness sets us in our ways, and we never stop to ask ourselves if our ways are really right or not.

In the Old Testament book of Haggai, the people were living in lack and experiencing many problems, so God told them to consider their ways (see Haggai 1:5). Many times when people are not fulfilled in life, they look for the reason in everything and everyone except themselves. If you are not satisfied with your Life, do as God told the people of Judah: "Consider your ways." Like me, you may find that you need to make some changes.

I was stubborn, opinionated, hardheaded, proud, and everything else that kept me from making progress. But, thank God, He has changed me! I pray that He keeps on changing me, that He never stops changing me until I am just like Him—and that won't be until I get to heaven.

I want everything God wants me to have and nothing that He does not want me to have. I belong to Him, and so do you. God is your home, and you are His home. How could two be any closer than that? John 16:7 says that the Holy Spirit was sent by Jesus to be in "close fellowship" with believers. Answer that knock at your heart's door and allow the Holy Spirit to come into your life in all His fullness.

BE READY TO OBEY

If you [really] love Me, you will keep (obey) My commands. (John 14:15)

Proud people are not open people. They are closed up tight, tied up with pride. Their sense of pride won't let them step beyond their own opinions, their own way. They find it almost impossible to learn anything from anyone else because their pride won't let them admit they might need something other than what they have.

To receive the baptism in the Holy Spirit, one must be ready to obey the Holy Spirit, to lay aside a self-directed lifestyle. This is very difficult for a proud person to do. Obedience requires a willingness to humble oneself.

I can well remember how, after I received the baptism in the Holy Spirit, the Spirit of God began dealing with me about not staying angry, about forgiving people who had offended me or hurt me, and about apologizing to others I had hurt or offended. It took some definite obedience for me to do what He was telling me. I certainly did not want to; I did not feel like it or think it was right for me to have to apologize. At that time, no matter what happened in my life, I always thought it was the other person's fault.

It felt to me as if my flesh was screaming out against

these Holy Spirit orders. But I loved the Lord so much that I wanted to please Him. I guess I finally got to the place that I wanted to please Him more than I wanted to please myself.

When you ask for the baptism in the Holy Spirit, you should be ready for change, which always requires new levels of obedience. God may call you to do something special for Him that will require obedience. As the Holy Spirit leads you, you may have to separate yourself from influences that are poisoning your life, or change some behavior patterns that do not glorify God.

One thing is for sure—my life changed radically after that day in February 1976. Prior to that time, I had never really thought much about obedience to God. I went to church on Sundays, did church work, and enjoyed the social activities at the church. But I don't remember ever knowing that God lived inside me by His Spirit or that He wanted to lead, guide, and direct my life. I called on Him when things were going bad, I prayed some each day, I read a chapter in the Bible some days, and that was about it. I was doing all I knew to do, but I didn't realize that Christianity was not about what I was doing, but about what Jesus had done.

We do not show our love and appreciation for what Jesus has done for us by going to church on Sunday and doing our own thing the rest of the week. We show our love and appreciation by walking in obedience to the leadership of His Spirit who lives within us every day of the week.

As Jesus tells us in John 14:15, if we really love Him, we will obey His commands, just as He obeyed His Father's commands.

We have already seen how, immediately after Jesus was baptized in the Holy Spirit, He was led by the Spirit into the desert to be tempted by the devil for forty days and nights. That probably was not an enjoyable experience, and yet Jesus promptly obeyed. He trusted His Father, knowing that it would work out for His good in the end.

At the end of the forty days Jesus began His public ministry, as we see in Luke 4:14: "Then Jesus went back full of and under the power of the [Holy] Spirit into Galilee, and the fame of Him spread through the whole region round about." Jesus not only had to be willing to follow the Holy Spirit into power and fame, but also into difficult times, times of trial and testing.

We are always willing to follow the Holy Spirit into blessings, but we get hard of hearing if His leading means we are not going to get what we want.

Following his conversion and baptism in the Holy Spirit, Paul was told by the Spirit about the difficulties that he would be required to go through (see Acts 9:15-16). Paul went through many difficult situations, but he was also blessed in his lifetime. He was privileged to write a large portion of the New Testament through the inspiration of the Holy Spirit. Paul had spiritual experiences so magnificent that he could not even describe them. He was taken into the third heaven, saw visions, and was visited by angels, in addition to many other wonderful things. Yes, he was blessed—but he also had to follow the Spirit's leading whether it was convenient or inconvenient, comfortable or uncomfortable, to his advantage or not to his advantage.

In Philippians 4:11-12 KJV, Paul wrote that he had learned to be content whether he was abased or abounding.

In verse 13 he stated that he could do all things through Christ who strengthened him. Paul had learned to draw on the strength of God that was in him. He was strengthened for good times, to enjoy them and keep a right attitude in them, and for hard times, to endure them and keep a right attitude in them also.

Our attitude is very important to the Lord. It shows a lot about our character. Obeying God in hard times helps develop the character of God in each of us. I often say, "We will be called upon many times to do the right thing when we don't feel like it, and we will do it a long time before the right thing begins to happen to us."

We cannot do right just to get a reward or a blessing. We are to pursue God's presence, not His presents. We must do right because it is right, and because we love Jesus and know that our obedience honors Him. The Holy Spirit is sent to live in us to help us seek Him with a pure heart. He is given to us both for the easy times in life and especially for the difficult ones.

So many people today are wimpy and whiny all the time. They talk more about what they cannot do than what they can do. They give up easily and don't have enough determination to see anything through to the end.

I realized a long time ago that God gave me His Spirit to help me overcome any obstacle that got in the way of His plan for my life, whether that obstacle was a person, a circumstance, a demon, disappointment, disillusionment, or discouragement.

Are you ready to obey God? If so, then you are ready for the baptism in the Holy Spirit. If you have a willing heart, God will give you the fullness of His Spirit to enable you to follow through with action.

IT IS TIME TO ASK AND BELIEVE!

To the end that through [their receiving] Christ Jesus, the blessing [promised] to Abraham might come upon the Gentiles, so that we through faith might [all] receive [the realization of] the promise of the [Holy] Spirit. (Galatians 3:14)

If you have come this far, it is now time to ask. Remember: the Holy Spirit is a Gentleman. He will fill you, but only if invited to do so. In Luke 11:13 Jesus promises that God will give the Holy Spirit to those who ask Him. And James 4:2 KJV tells us we have not because we ask not.

Come boldly and ask. Ask expecting to receive. Don't be double-minded. Don't let doubt fill your heart. Ask in faith. Believe you receive, and you will receive. God is not a man, that He should lie (see Numbers 23:19). He is faithful to fulfill His Word, whenever anyone steps out on it in faith.

Galatians 3:14 says that we receive the promise of the Spirit through faith. Gifts cannot be forced onto anyone; they must be offered by the giver and then received by another. God makes the offer of His Spirit, and you must relax and receive by faith. You may feel something, or you may not feel a thing.

IT'S NOT ABOUT FEELINGS

I had a definite experience of feeling the Spirit being poured into me. Although I did not know I was being baptized in the Holy Spirit at the time, I did know that God was doing something wonderful in me.

Since that time, I have ministered the baptism in the Holy Spirit to literally thousands of people, and I have seen people react in every way from being extremely loud to being totally silent. I have seen tears, laughter, jumping up and down, falling down under the power of the Holy Spirit, and just about everything imaginable.

Many people who received the baptism in the Holy Spirit through my ministry expressed to me that they did not feel a thing. I have met some of these same people later and discovered that they were dramatically changed from that time forward.

We don't base our experience with God on feelings, but on faith. We don't have to experience emotional excitement in order to be filled with the Holy Spirit. As long as we see the fruit of the Spirit in our lives (see Galatians 5:22-23), we know we have received.

When you are filled with the Holy Spirit, you will experience a greater closeness and intimacy with God. You will notice a more direct and definite leading of the Spirit in your life. You will also experience more direct divine chastisement. In other words, God will start messing around in your business. Your business will become His business, and His business will become yours. You will feel that you have a Partner with you all the time, Someone you can talk to about *anything*.

RECEIVE THE BAPTISM IN THE HOLY SPIRIT

The Word of God teaches that though some people received the Holy Spirit through the laying on of hands, other times the Holy Spirit was simply poured out upon people. Acts 10:44 says, "While Peter was still speaking these words, the Holy Spirit fell on all who were listening to the message." The believers who came with Peter were amazed because they witnessed how the free gift of the Holy Spirit was poured out on the crowd, and they heard them talking in unknown tongues.

You can ask God to fill you and to baptize you in the Holy Spirit right now, right where you are, by simply praying. Here is a prayer you may want to use.

Father, in Jesus' name, I ask you to baptize me in the Holy Spirit with the evidence of speaking in tongues. Grant me boldness as you did those who were filled on the Day of Pentecost, and give me any other spiritual gifts that you desire me to have.

Now you may want to confirm your faith by saying out loud, "I believe I have received the baptism in the Holy Spirit, and I will never be the same again."

If you have prayed that prayer, wait on God quietly and believe that you have received what you have asked. If you don't believe you have received, then even if you have received, it will be to you as if you have not. You cannot act upon something you don't believe you have. I want to stress again the importance of "believing by faith" that you have received, and not making your decision based on feelings.

I think it is best to close your eyes when receiving; it helps to shut out everything that might be a distraction. Now offer your voice to God. Sit quietly, relax, and wait on Him. Don't try to make something happen; let God take the lead. Remember that the people "waited" in the Upper Room until they received the power from on high.

God loves you and wants His best for you. To speak in tongues, open your mouth, and as the Spirit gives you utterance, speak forth what you hear coming up on the inside of you. Remember that the words won't come from your head, but from your spirit. I suggest you turn your attention to what is taking place in your spirit; you will feel a stirring of life. God said that out of our bellies would flow a River of Life (see John 7:38 KJV).

The words may sound unusual or foreign to you; they may initially only be groanings or odd-sounding little syllables. Think of how odd a baby sounds when it first begins learning to talk. You may sound the same way to yourself as you begin speaking in other tongues. Don't be concerned about how you sound or get caught up in listening to yourself. Just give yourself completely to the Lord and trust Him as never before.

The more boldly you pray, the better. You have nothing to be afraid of or embarrassed about. You belong to God. He is your Father. He has filled you with His Spirit and has promised never to leave you or forsake you. If God instructs us to walk in the Spirit, why shouldn't we be able to talk in the Spirit, which is what speaking in tongues is.

Don't be in a hurry. Let God minister to you. There may be some unforgiveness in your heart He will want to speak to you about, or some sin of which you need to repent. Whatever He says to you, do it!

As you feel a stirring deep inside your spirit, you may feel like weeping or laughing, or you may feel a sense of deep peace or relief as if a burden has lifted from you. You may just feel downright good!

Don't compare your experience to anyone else's. We are all unique individuals, and God ministers to us as such. Know that He will meet you in whatever way is best for you. If you don't speak in tongues right away, don't become discouraged. Continue believing and confessing that God has filled you with His Holy Spirit because you asked Him to, and you will receive your prayer language.

Always remember these wonderful Scriptures:

> So I say to you, Ask and keep on asking and it shall be given you; seek and keep on seeking and you shall find; knock and keep on knocking and the door shall be opened to you. For everyone who asks and keeps on asking receives; and he who seeks and keeps on seeking finds; and to him who knocks and keeps on knocking, the door shall be opened. What father among you, if his son asks for a loaf of bread, will give him a stone; or if he asks for a fish, will instead of a fish give him a serpent? Or if he asks for an egg, will give him a scorpion? If you then, evil as you are, know how to give good gifts [gifts that are to their advantage] to your children, how much more will your heavenly Father give the Holy Spirit to those who ask and continue to ask Him! (Luke 11:9-13)

NOW WHAT?

Lord, what do You desire me to do? (Acts 9:6)

Once you are baptized in the Holy Spirit, what should you do? Many people make a mistake by trying to tell everyone what has happened to them. This is, of course, a natural thing to want to do; you will probably be excited and want to share your enthusiasm with others. However, that may not be the wisest thing to do; not everyone will be excited for you. You cannot allow that to bother you.

First of all, other people may not understand your enthusiasm. Second, they may feel threatened if you seem to give the impression that you have something they are missing and must now try to get. You may mean well, but aggressive enthusiasm can frighten or offend other people. If you do feel led by the Spirit of God to share with someone, you may also want to give them a copy of this book so they can have full understanding of this provision from God.

My husband and I made a lot of mistakes with friends and relatives when we received the baptism in the Holy Spirit. To be honest, it took years in some instances to recover the relationships we lost. That, of course, was not totally our fault, but had we been wise enough to handle ourselves differently in the beginning, things could have been somewhat better.

It is sometimes better to say less and show more. Just wait and let people see the changes in you, and then they will ask what has happened to you. When they do, their heart will be open to receive. That is much better than causing them to feel that you are trying to force something on them they don't want to hear anything about.

We Christians frequently do a lot of preaching, but we need to be like the kids in school who participate in "Show and Tell." During this activity they show something special and then tell about it; they don't tell about it and show nothing. Living proof is always better than empty words.

As I have said, I was baptized in the Holy Spirit on a Friday afternoon. Dave and I bowled in a league every week on Fridays, and I must have been acting obviously different that evening, although I was not aware of it. I didn't know how to explain what had happened to me, so I was not yet trying to tell anyone about it. As the evening wore on, one of the men we regularly bowled with looked at me and said, "Meyer, what is with you tonight? You look like you're off on another planet."

I actually felt drunk on the love of God. What I mean by "drunk" is that I was so full of God it was affecting how I acted. I was extremely peaceful. Nothing bothered me. Actually, everything just seemed wonderful to me.

As the weeks went by, people at work began asking me what had happened to me. After a few had asked me that question, I started realizing that what God had done in me must be showing.

By then God had led me to read some books and hear some testimonies, so I realized that what had happened to me was happening to other people also, and that it even had a name. I realized that I had received the baptism of the Holy Spirit. In the 1970s there was an outpouring of the Holy Spirit on people worldwide. People from every denomination were receiving the Holy Spirit and speaking in tongues. Actually, several people at my church had already received it, and God led me to them for fellowship and encouragement.

It was really amazing to me how God led me after that Friday in 1976 when I received that special touch from Him in my automobile. For example, I had never listened to the radio as I drove home from work, but I suddenly felt the urge to turn on the radio. The station I "just happened" to turn to also "just happened" to be airing testimonies from people sharing their experience of being baptized in or filled with the Holy Spirit. Their testimonies helped me to have confidence in what God had done for me.

I now know those things didn't just happen but they were ordained and arranged by God. As soon as I released my life to Him, He took over. I began to see wonderful things take place in my life, things that increased my faith and excited me, things like His leading me to turn to that radio station so I would hear just what I needed at that time in my life.

As people asked me what had happened to me, because they could plainly see that I was different, I found them quite receptive since they had brought it up themselves.

When people are hungry for more of God in their life, they are very open to hearing about God in the life of another. If they are not hungry, it is hard to force-feed them; they keep spitting out whatever they are given.

Just be patient, and God will open doors for you to share your faith and excitement. He will start giving you "divine connections." He will link you up with people who have had the same thing happen to them. You will find a wonderful, rich fellowship that is different from any other friendships you have ever had. Actually, when you meet another believer who is baptized in the Holy Spirit, it will be like meeting a relative you have never seen. You will instantly feel connected in some special way. This is a spiritual connection that does not always make sense to the natural mind.

Get some good books on the subject of the Holy Spirit, such as *Nine O'clock in the Morning* by Dennis J. Bennett, *Aglow with the Spirit* by Robert C. Frost, and *They Speak with Other Tongues* by John L. Sherrill, and learn more about the baptism of the Holy Spirit and how it has changed the lives of many other people. The more you read, the better. Look up these verses and study them: Acts 1:8; Acts 2:1-18; Acts 8:12-17; Acts 10:42-48; Acts 19:1-6.

Search the Holy Scriptures, and go over all the references I have shared in this book. Pray for God to lead you to the place He wants you to be. If you have the opportunity, go to a Spirit-filled Bible study or church service. Come to one of our conferences, if we are in your area, or take a vacation and come to wherever we are holding a conference that month.

If you haven't already been baptized in water since you believed on Christ, I encourage you to search out a church that will lead you through this scriptural demonstration of your faith. The importance of both the water baptism and the baptism of the Holy Spirit is demonstrated in the following two examples.

The Lord sent Philip to meet an Ethiopian eunuch who was reading the prophecy from Isaiah, proclaiming the coming of a Savior. When Philip proclaimed the good news that the Savior had come and that He was Jesus, the eunuch was so excited he asked to be baptized in water right away.

In Acts 8:37, Philip said, "If you believe with all your heart [if you have a conviction, full of joyful trust, that

Jesus is the Messiah and accept Him as the Author of your salvation in the kingdom of God, giving Him your obedience, then] you may." And the eunuch replied, "I do believe that Jesus Christ is the Son of God." So he was baptized immediately.

But the believers listening to Peter, who received the baptism of the Holy Spirit with the evidence of speaking in tongues, had not been previously baptized in water. So Peter asked, "Can anyone forbid or refuse water for baptizing these people, seeing that they have received the Holy Sprit just as we have? And he ordered that they be baptized in the name of Jesus Christ (the Messiah)"(Acts 10:47-48).

God has many things to teach you, enough to require your attention on Him every remaining day of your life. But let me encourage you again—just be patient, and God will lead you. Spend special time with Him each day. Get to know Him better and better. Read the Bible; it will be easier for you to understand after receiving the fullness of the Holy Spirit.

You have embarked upon a great journey. Sometimes you will make fast progress, and at other times it will seem as if you aren't making any progress at all. But it all works together, so remember: *Be patient!*

If you have received the baptism of the Holy Spirit as a result of reading this book, please contact us. We want to share in your joy and pray for you as you begin your new journey with God. If you have questions, we will be glad to assist you in any way we can. You may call or write my office, and someone will be glad to help you. Our telephone number and address are listed at the back of this book.

INTIMACY LEVEL
3

∼

God's Reflective Glory

And if we are [His] children, then we are [His] heirs also: heirs of God and fellow heirs with Christ [sharing His inheritance with Him]; only we must share His suffering if we are to share His glory. [But what of that?] For I consider that the sufferings of this present time (this present life) are not worth being compared with the glory that is about to be revealed to us and in us and for us and conferred on us! For [even the whole] creation (all nature) waits expectantly and longs earnestly for God's sons to be made known [waits for the revealing, the disclosing of their sonship].

—ROMANS 8:17-19

10

"Ever Be Filled" with the Holy Spirit

And do not get drunk with wine, for that is debauchery; but ever be filled and stimulated with the [Holy] Spirit. (Ephesians 5:18)

If you are already filled with the Spirit, or if you have just received the Spirit as a result of reading this book, it is important for you to know that you must be instructed in God's Word in order to "ever be filled" with the Spirit— that is, to be filled at all times.

To "ever be filled" with the Holy Spirit, it is necessary to give Him first place in our life. Often this requires discipline, because many other things demand our time and attention. There are many things we want and need, but none of them is more important than God.

The Holy Spirit never goes away; He always comes to remain and stay. He does not change addresses; once He takes up occupancy, He settles in and refuses to leave. But it is important that we keep ourselves stirred up in spiritual things. Anything that is hot can grow cold if the fire goes out.

I once went through a six-month period of time when God forbade me to ask for anything except more of Him. It was a great discipline in drawing near to Him in a deeper level of intimacy than I had known before. I would start to say, "God, I need—," then I would stop myself as I remembered His instruction to me. I would finish my petition with "more of You."

During that time, I had a craving for homemade zucchini bread, but I spoke nothing about it to anyone. Of course I was too busy to try to bake any myself. Then after a meeting, a woman handed me a box saying, "The Lord put it in my heart to give you this."

Looking at the box with the picture of a kitchen appliance on it, I couldn't imagine why God would tell her to give it to me. But when I opened the box, inside it was a freshly baked loaf of zucchini bread.

Through this example, God was proving to me that if I delight in Him, He will give me the desires and secret petitions of my heart. If I would seek Him first and foremost, He would take care of providing the other things I desired, even small things that might seem insignificant but would mean a lot to me (see Psalm 37:4).

STIR UP THE GIFT

That is why I would remind you to stir up (rekindle the embers of, fan the flame of, and keep burning) the [gracious] gift of God, [the inner fire] that is in you by means of the laying on of my hands [with those of the elders at your ordination]. (2 Timothy 1:6)

In spiritual things either we are aggressively going forward on purpose, or we are starting to slip backward. Either we grow, or we start to die. There is no such thing as dormant Christianity. We cannot put our Christian walk on hold, or in cold storage, until next year. It is vital to keep pressing on. That's why in this passage Timothy was instructed by Paul to stir up the gift that was in him through the laying on of hands by the elders at his ordination. He was told to fan the flame and rekindle the fire that once burned in him.

Evidently, Timothy had begun to slip backward. Judging by 2 Timothy 1:7, he must have gotten into fear,[1] because Paul wrote to tell him: "For God did not give us a spirit of timidity (of cowardice, of craven and cringing and fawning fear), but [He has given us a spirit] of power and of love and of calm and well-balanced mind and discipline and self-control."

Anytime we get into fear, we begin to become immobile instead of active. Fear freezes us in place, so to speak; it prevents progress.

Timothy may have become afraid because of the extreme persecution of Christians in those days, and he may have temporarily lost his boldness. After all, his mentor Paul had been thrown in prison. What if the same thing happened to him?

It is certainly easy to understand why Timothy may have lost his courage and confidence. Yet Paul strongly encouraged him to stir himself up, get back on track, remember the call on his life, resist fear, and remember that God had not given him "the spirit of fear; but of power, and of love, and of a sound mind," as the *King James Version* puts it.

That is exactly what we get when we receive the fullness of the Holy Spirit: power, love, and a sound mind.
According to Romans 5:5 KJV, it is the Holy Spirit who
sheds abroad the love of God in our hearts. He is the Spirit
of Power, the Spirit of Love, and the Spirit who keeps our
mind sound and strong.

Timothy needed some encouragement, and there will
be times when each of us will need some also. Timothy
had probably been thinking and talking all wrong, and the
more he thought and talked, the worse he felt. If we intend
to stay stirred up in the Holy Spirit, we must choose our
thoughts and words carefully.

HAVE A HAPPY HEART

Speak out to one another in psalms and hymns and
spiritual songs, offering praise with voices [and
instruments] and making melody with all your
heart to the Lord. (Ephesians 5:19)

The *King James Version* translates this verse, "Speaking to
yourselves in psalms and hymns and spiritual songs, singing and making melody in your heart to the Lord." I like to
apply this Scripture both ways. It is important what kind of
"self-talk" I do, as well as how I talk to other people.

It is easy to fall into the trap of talking about negative
things, the problems of life, all of our disappointments,
and so on. But none of that helps us to "ever be filled"
with the Spirit. Why not? Because the Holy Spirit is not
negative in any way. His silence during such times is our
signal that He is not pleased with our conversation.

When I feel the Holy Spirit being stirred up in me, I know He is pleased; when I feel Him receding, I consider that He may not be pleased.

The Holy Spirit is very fond of "right" music—music that is encouraging, uplifting, positive, and joy-filled—music that has a good message. In the last part of Ephesians 5:19, the *King James Version* says that we are to make melody in our heart to the Lord. That literally means that we are to go through the day with a song in our heart. We can do that without spending the day singing loudly.

When I have a happy heart, I find myself whistling, humming, or quietly singing throughout the day. A song can make an otherwise unpleasant task pleasant. It can lighten our load in life and brighten the darkest day. In fact, it is also spiritual warfare.

Satan is opposed to joy and will do all in his power to prevent us from having it. According to Nehemiah 8:10 KJV, the joy of the Lord is our strength. Satan wants us weak, but music stirs up our joy and, therefore, our strength. The more we sing and make melody in our heart, the better off we are.

The Bible is filled with powerful Scriptures that make reference to music, especially praise and worship. Repeatedly the Scriptures say to "sing unto the Lord a new song."

Some people have been singing the same old sad song all their life. They need a new song, a happy song. A new song can be one nobody has ever heard, one that rises up out of the heart because of admiration for the Lord.

Listen to music. Learn songs by listening, and then open your mouth and sing. You may not be a great singer, but Psalm 98:4 KJV encourages us to "make a joyful noise unto the Lord." That is one of the best ways to stir up the flame of the Holy Spirit within you.

BE THANKFUL AND SAY SO

At all times and for everything giving thanks in the name of our Lord Jesus Christ to God the Father. (Ephesians 5:20)

Grouped in with Scriptures that teach us to "ever be filled" with the Holy Spirit, we find this instruction to give thanks at all times and for everything. That means we are to remain in an attitude of thankfulness no matter what our current circumstances may be.

This requires the power of the Holy Spirit because it is natural for us humans to experience fluctuating emotions when we are going through fluctuating circumstances. We may be tempted to act naturally, but in the power of the Holy Spirit we can always act supernaturally. We already have the "natural," but the Holy Spirit comes into our life to bring the "super." When we add His "super" to our "natural," we have the supernatural.

If we are to "ever be filled" with the Holy Spirit, we must realize that we have the Holy Spirit always standing by to help us with whatever difficulties may arise. You and I can do the right thing in every situation if we draw upon the power that dwells in us by the Holy Spirit. It is right to remain thankful, because no matter what is going on in our life currently, God is still good. And if we look at our entire life, we realize we have plenty to be thankful for.

When times are hard, and we get discouraged, it is

easy to become negative and see everything through eyes clouded by the current problem. But we have all experienced the faithfulness of God many times in our lifetime. God's providential care is absolutely amazing.

For example, how many times do you suppose God has saved us from a serious accident, kept us from injury, or protected us from harm? We get into the habit of looking at the negative things that happen to us and complaining about them, but what about all the negative things that could have happened to us if God had not prevented them? Can we not, and should we not, be extremely thankful for those times?

Being thankful and saying so helps us to "ever be filled and stimulated" with the Holy Spirit, as we are told to do in Ephesians 5:18. In that verse we are encouraged not to get drunk with wine for stimulation, but instead to be filled with the Holy Spirit.

Let's think about what it feels like to be stimulated. Webster's dictionary says that the verb *stimulate* means "to rouse to activity or heightened action, as by goading: EXCITE... To act or serve as a stimulant or stimulus."[2]

When we are thankful, it stirs up the Holy Spirit within us, and we can actually feel His joy. Many times when we are depressed or unhappy, it is because the Holy Spirit in us has been grieved or offended by our behavior. When the Holy Spirit approves of our actions, we feel good inside; when He doesn't approve, we don't feel good inside.

Singing, the right kind of self-talk, right conversation with others, right thoughts, a thankful attitude—all of these things are stimulants that stir up the Holy Spirit and help us to "ever be filled" with Him.

Some people use alcohol as a stimulant. It helps them forget the things that bother them and makes them feel good—at least until the next morning. We must realize the irony of the Holy Spirit using this example in God's Word. Don't get drunk with wine; you don't need that for a stimulant. Instead, "ever be filled" with the Holy Spirit. That is the only stimulant you will ever need.

For thirty-six years my brother was in bondage to drugs and alcohol. Since his conversion and baptism in the Holy Spirit, he has commented many times that there was no feeling he ever had from drugs or alcohol that even came close to being as good as the feeling he experienced by being filled with the Holy Spirit.

PHYSICAL ENERGY

He gives power to the faint and weary, and to him who has no might He increases strength [causing it to multiply and making it to abound]. (Isaiah 40:29)

Being filled with the Holy Spirit actually gives us physical energy.

Many times I have been quickened by the Holy Spirit and have suddenly gone from being extremely tired to feeling as if I could run around the city. This is another good reason to keep ourselves ever filled; we need all the energy we can get. I firmly believe we can make ourselves feel drained by the way we think and talk. Likewise, we can help ourselves feel energetic by following biblical guidelines for everyday living.

It seems that most people in the world today are tired.

Part of their fatigue comes from being too busy, but another large part of it is due to the way they live—how they think, talk, and act toward other people.

The Holy Spirit will not energize us to be mean, hateful, selfish, or self-centered.

THE SPIRIT OF LOVE

> God's love has been poured out in our hearts through the Holy Spirit Who has been given to us. (Romans 5:5)

When the Holy Spirit comes to live in us, love comes to live in us. God is love (1 John 4:8), and when He comes, love comes.

First John 4:12 is one of my favorite Scriptures. I love to read it and just take time to think about it: "No man has at any time [yet] seen God. But if we love one another, God abides (lives and remains) in us and His love (that love which is essentially His) is brought to completion (to its full maturity, runs its full course, is perfected) in us!"

This Scripture helps me understand why I felt as if I had been filled with liquid love at the time of my baptism in the Holy Spirit. At that time, an extra measure of God's love was poured into my heart. I had to receive that love for myself; then I could begin returning it to God; and then, finally, I could start letting it flow out of me toward others.

We cannot give away what we don't have. It is useless to try to love someone else if we have never received God's love for ourselves. We should love ourselves in a balanced way, not a selfish, self-centered way. I teach that we should love ourselves but not be "in love" with ourselves.

In other words, believe in the love that God has for you; know that it is everlasting and unconditional. Let His love affirm you and make you feel secure, but don't begin to think more highly of yourself than you ought to (see Romans 12:3 KJV). I believe loving ourselves in a balanced way is what prepares us to let love flow through us to others around us. Without receiving God's love for ourselves in a balanced way, we may have some kind of feelings for another individual, a humanistic type of love; but we certainly cannot love people unconditionally unless God is provoking that love.

It is the Holy Spirit who purifies our heart so we can allow the sincere love of God to flow through us to others, as we are told in 1 Peter 1:22: "Since by your obedience to the Truth through the [Holy] Spirit you have purified your hearts for the sincere affection of the brethren, [see that you] love one another fervently from a pure heart." The aim of the Holy Spirit is to get us to the place where the sincere love of God can flow through us. This helps us to "ever be filled" with the Holy Spirit.

Walking in love is the ultimate goal of Christianity. That should be the primary thing we all strive for. We are told in the Scriptures to keep our love red-hot. We are to have fervent love for one another. Jesus gave the command for us to love one another as He loves us. He said that was one new commandment that He was giving and that in the commandments to love God and one another all the other commandments were summed up (see John 13:34; Matthew 22:37-40).

When I think of what I can do for myself or how I can get others to bless me, I am filled with *me*. When I think of other people and how I can bless them, I find myself filled with the Holy Spirit, who is the Spirit of Love.

KNOWN BY OUR FRUITS

If I [can] speak in the tongues of men and [even] of angels, but have not love (that reasoning, intentional, spiritual devotion such as is inspired by God's love for and in us), I am only a noisy gong or a clanging cymbal. And if I have prophetic powers (the gift of interpreting the divine will and purpose), and understand all the secret truths and mysteries and possess all knowledge, and if I have [sufficient] faith so that I can remove mountains, but have not love (God's love in me) I am nothing (a useless nobody). Even if I dole out all that I have [to the poor in providing] food, and if I surrender my body to be burned or in order that I may glory, but have not love (God's love in me), I gain nothing. (1 Corinthians 13:1-3, emphasis mine)

First Corinthians 13:1-3 begins a discourse on love. It tells us clearly that no matter how many gifts of the Spirit we may operate in, if we are not operating in love, all of it is useless. If we speak in tongues, but have not love, we are just a big noise. If we have prophetic power, and power to understand and interpret secrets and mysteries, if we have all knowledge and so much faith we can move mountains, but have not love, according to the apostle Paul, we are useless nobodies. Even if we give away all that we have to feed the poor and even surrender our very lives, but do it with wrong motives and not out of love, we gain nothing.

These Scriptures are not to be ignored. On the day when Christ hands out rewards for works done on earth, there will be many disappointed people when they discover they lost their reward because their motives were impure.

First Peter 1:22 says that love must come through a pure heart and that affection must be sincere. And Romans 12:9 reminds us to let our love be sincere, a real thing.

In 1 Corinthians 12 the apostle Paul gives in-depth teaching about the gifts of the Holy Spirit and concludes in verse 31 by saying: "But earnestly desire and zealously cultivate the greatest and best gifts and graces (the higher gifts and the choicest graces). And yet I will show you a still more excellent way [one that is better by far and the highest of them all—love]."

After I was baptized in the Holy Spirit and began fellowshipping with other people who were baptized in the Spirit, I heard much talk about the gifts of the Spirit. It seemed that all anyone was concerned about was what their gift was and being able to exercise that gift. I attended many seminars and read lots of books about the gifts of the Holy Spirit. I heard much more about gifts than about fruit.

There are nine gifts of the Spirit listed in 1 Corinthians 12 and several others in Romans 12. There are nine fruits listed in Galatians 5. The gifts of the Spirit are extremely important, and as I have said before, we should covet (deeply desire) them. We are instructed to learn about them, not to be misinformed about them, and to nurture the gifts we have and learn how to operate in them properly.

In 1 Corinthians 12:4 Paul reminded the Corinthians

that there are many varieties of gifts, but they all come from the same Holy Spirit. I think we can interpret that to mean, "Don't get so caught up in the gifts that you forget the Giver."

Let us concentrate on the Holy Spirit and be assured that He will distribute His gifts to individuals in the right way. Let us be sure the gifts we have are well balanced with the fruit of the Holy Spirit.

In Matthew 7:16-18, Jesus said, "You will know them by their fruits" (paraphrase). He did not say Christians would be recognized by their gifts. There are people who have a gift that can take them somewhere, but not enough character to keep them there. We see many gifted people fall into sin and lose their position in life because they never bothered to develop the fruit of the Spirit and godly character.

A woman once came to one of my conferences and shared with me that she never stopped thinking and talking about her problems even though she was being taught differently. She knew what she needed to do, but she seemed to have no power to do it. She was lacking power to perform because she kept thinking and talking about wrong things. She met several other ladies who had also been abused just as she had.

As they talked over lunch she realized that God had told her everything He had told them, but they had obeyed while she had disobeyed. They had renewed their minds with the Word of God while she had kept driving her problems deeper into her soul by refusing to get them off of her mind.

What we have on our mind eventually comes out of our mouth. Because she refused to obey God and stop thinking and talking about her problems, she was in a prison she could not get out of. We seek things by thinking and speaking about them. She could have sought God in this way; instead, she actually was seeking more of the very problems she was trying to overcome.

PUT LOVE FIRST

Let people recognize that you are a Christian by your loving attitude toward them.

> For by the grace (unmerited favor of God) given to me I warn everyone among you not to estimate and think of himself more highly than he ought [not to have an exaggerated opinion of his own importance], but to rate his ability with sober judgment, each according to the degree of faith apportioned by God to him. For as in one physical body we have many parts (organs, members) and all of these parts do not have the same function or use, so we, numerous as we are, are one body in Christ (the Messiah) and individually we are parts one of another [mutually dependent on one another]. Having gifts (faculties, talents, qualities) that differ according to the grace given us, let us use them. (Romans 12:3-6)

Gifted people who are lacking the fruit of the Spirit can quickly become puffed up with pride. Pride is very dangerous. It is the opposite of humility, which is a fruit of the Holy Spirit. Pride is a fruit of the devil and should be avoided at all costs.

The flesh has a natural tendency toward pride, and for this very reason we must remind ourselves regularly that whatever we do, we do by the power and goodness of God. It is God who gives gifts to us, and not we ourselves who obtain them (see Ephesians 2:8,9; James 1:17). He not only gives us gifts, He also gives us the grace to function in them. Remember: grace is the power of the Holy Spirit available to you and me to do with ease what we could not do by striving.

Romans 12:6 says that we are to use our gifts according to the endowment of grace that is upon us.

Two people can be gifted to teach, yet one may be a stronger teacher than the other because they have more grace from God for their particular calling. One pastor may be anointed by the Holy Spirit to lead a church of five hundred people, while another pastor may be anointed and given grace to lead a church of five thousand. Why? Because the Holy Spirit distributes the gifts to whomever He wills (see 1 Corinthians 12:11 KJV). He has His reasons for what He does, and it is not our place to question. We are to be thankful for what He gives us and not allow pride to cause us to become jealous or envious of someone else's gift. We cannot walk in love with someone and be jealous of that person at the same time.

My husband could be jealous of the fact that God has given me a preaching gift but has not given him that gift. Dave realized long ago that he would not be happy if he tried to operate beyond the grace given to him. If he tried to be what I am, he would lose his joy. Dave is anointed in administration and finances, and his part in our ministry is just as important as mine.

If you want to be really happy, give yourself to whatever

you are called to do (see Romans 12:6-8). Don't be jealous of others. Don't compare yourself with them. Avoid pride. When we allow negative emotions such as pride to rule in our life, it grieves the Holy Spirit. The only answer to all these things is to walk in love.

Actually, for several years I was caught up in a teaching that overly emphasized the gifts of the Spirit. It was not until the Holy Spirit confronted me in my heart about it that I began to gain a more balanced attitude. He seriously began to deal with me about the fruit of the Spirit and walking in love. The more I studied these two important aspects of the Christian walk, the more I realized that the Bible has a lot more to say about them than it does about the gifts of the Spirit. It was only when I began concentrating on walking in love that I started feeling that I could "ever be filled" with the Holy Spirit.

When we get excited about the right thing, the Holy Spirit gets excited—we sense His excitement in us, and it energizes our life in a way that nothing else can.

The gifts of the Spirit are important, but they are not as important as the fruit of love. Actually, a person with gifts (talents and abilities) but without love (God's love for others) can become a real problem.

In saying these things, I am not in any way making light of or devaluing the gifts of the Holy Spirit. In fact, I am writing this book to encourage you to be open to them. But it is also important that I share these truths in a way that will not cause you to become lopsided in your search for what God wants you to have. To learn more about the fruit of the Spirit, I recommend my book titled *Secrets to Exceptional Living*.

I believe speaking in tongues is very important, but

not as important as love. I believe words of wisdom and knowledge are definitely important, but not if they cause us to be puffed up with pride because of what we know. Love is meek and humble, not proud and arrogant.

I believe the gift of faith, the gifts of healings, and the working of miracles are all important. But 1 Corinthians 13 tells us plainly that if we have all these things and have not love, then they are useless to us, and heaven sees us as someone who is just a big noise.

I believe that interpretation of tongues, prophecy, and discerning of spirits are excellent gifts, but they are not as important as love. We must put love first and let all other things come in order after that.

Paul told the Romans that they were free, but if they exercised their freedom at the expense of hurting someone else, they were not walking in love (see Romans 14:15). Everything always comes back to love; that must be the goal and the deciding factor in all of our actions.

11

Do Not Grieve the Holy Spirit

And do not grieve the Holy Spirit of God. (Ephesians 4:30)

The above Scripture always sounded so somber and serious to me. I knew I did not want to grieve the Holy Spirit, but I was not sure exactly how to avoid doing it.

We can usually determine how to interpret a Scripture by studying the verses before and after the one in question. Reading the verses surrounding Ephesians 4:30 makes it clear that one thing that grieves the Holy Spirit is for people to mistreat one another.

Ephesians 4:29 encourages us to make sure the words of our mouth are edifying and beneficial to the spiritual progress of others. Ephesians 4:31 exhorts us not to be bitter, angry, and contentious and to beware of slander, spite, and ill will of any kind. Verse 32 of that chapter tells us to be kind to one another, forgiving readily and freely, as God in Christ has forgiven us.

THE HOLY SPIRIT AND THE LOVE WALK ARE CONNECTED

> And walk in love, [esteeming and delighting in one another] as Christ loved us and gave Himself up for us. (Ephesians 5:2)

From these and other similar Scriptures we learn that the love walk and the Holy Spirit are directly connected, that it is by Him that the love of God is shed abroad in our hearts. It is He who teaches us, convicting us of wrong conduct when we mistreat others. It is He who works in us to give us a tender heart.

It is not God's will that we be hard-hearted, as He says in Ezekiel 11:19: "And I will give them one heart [a new heart] and I will put a new spirit within them; and I will take the stony [unnaturally hardened] heart out of their flesh, and will give them a heart of flesh [sensitive and responsive to the touch of their God]."

I had a hard heart because I had been abused as a child and abandoned by my first husband. It seemed that, all my life, people had taken advantage of me and used me for their own selfish purposes. My response was to become hardhearted in an attempt to block any more emotional pain.

Once our heart becomes hard, it is nearly impossible to change it by decision alone. That type of change requires a supernatural working of the Holy Spirit. He is the only One who can get inside our soul and heal the wounds and bruises there. He alone can restore us to the condition we were in prior to our injury.

Don't ever allow yourself to remain hard-hearted. It is impossible to walk in love with others if you are not sensitive to their needs. Pray for God to soften your heart and give you a tender conscience, one that is responsive to His touch. Ask Him to allow you to feel what He feels and to work His character in you.

When I realized that it grieved the Holy Spirit when I was sharp or hateful with someone, or when I stayed angry at someone, I began to take that kind of behavior more seriously. I loved God, and I certainly didn't want to grieve His Spirit.

When you and I do grieve the Holy Spirit, we also feel grieved. Even though we may not realize what is wrong with us, we know that we feel sad or depressed, or that something is just not right.

I have come to believe that much of the sadness, depression, and heaviness that we experience is most likely linked to our own behavior with other people. Galatians 6:7 says that whatever you and I sow, we will reap. If we sow words and actions that sadden others, we will reap sadness. But if we sow happiness in the lives of others, we will reap happiness in our own life.

Actually, I have found the secret to being happy all the time—it is to walk in love.

"WHY CAN'T I SENSE GOD'S PRESENCE?"

Keep on asking and it will be given you; keep on seeking and you will find; keep on knocking [reverently] and [the door] will be opened to you. (Matthew 7:7)

Throughout my years in ministry, I have frequently been asked, "Why can't I sense God's presence?" At times, I have asked myself the same thing.

We know from Scripture that the Holy Spirit does not run away and leave us every time we do something that displeases Him (see Hebrews 13:5). Actually, He is committed to stick with us and help us work through our problems, not just abandon us in them with no help.

No, the Holy Spirit never leaves us, but He does sometimes "hide." I like to say that sometimes God plays hide-and-seek with His children. Sometimes He hides from us until eventually, when we miss Him enough, we begin to seek Him. God has repeatedly told us in His Word to seek Him—to seek His face, His will, His purpose for our life, etc. And we are told to seek Him early, earnestly, and diligently (see Proverbs 8:17; Hebrews 11:6). If we don't seek Him, we will live a disappointing life.

Seeking God is central to our walk with Him; it is vital for spiritual progress. As evidence of this truth, consider these Scriptures, beginning with the one we studied earlier:

> One thing have I asked of the Lord, that will I seek, inquire for, and [insistently] require: that I may dwell in the house of the Lord [in His presence] all the days of my life, to behold and gaze upon the beauty [the sweet attractiveness and the delightful loveliness] of the Lord and to meditate, consider, and inquire in His temple. (Psalm 27:4)
>
> Know the God of your father [have personal knowledge of Him, be acquainted with, and understand Him; appreciate, heed, and cherish Him] and serve Him with a blameless heart and a willing mind. For the Lord

searches all hearts and minds and understands all the wanderings of the thoughts. If you seek Him [inquiring for and of Him and requiring Him as your first and vital necessity] you will find Him; but if you forsake Him, He will cast you off forever! (1 Chronicles 28:9)

Let all those that seek and require You rejoice and be glad in You. (Psalm 40:16)

Evil men understand not judgment: but they that seek the Lord understand all things. (Proverbs 28:5 KJV)

Seek ye the Lord while he may be found, call ye upon him while he is near. (Isaiah 55:6 KJV)

I will go and return to my place, till they acknowledge their offense, and seek my face: in their affliction they will seek me early. (Hosea 5:15 KJV)

He [God] is a rewarder of them that diligently seek him. (Hebrews 11:6 KJV)

The Bible is filled with Scriptures encouraging us to seek God. But what exactly does it mean to seek God? *Vine's Complete Expository Dictionary of Old and New Testament Words* shares some wonderful insight concerning this word as it applies to our relationship with God. It says that we " 'seek' by thinking."[1]

We need to think about God a lot. We should think about His Word, His ways, what He has done for us, how good He is, how much we love Him, and so on. What we think about, we end up talking about, and one of the best things we can talk about is God. He is the Answer to all the dilemmas we face in life. So why talk about the problem all the time, when we can talk about the Answer?

Malachi 3:16 tells us that God records the conversations

of those who talk about Him and think on His name: "Then those who feared the Lord talked often one to another; and the Lord listened and heard it, and a book of remembrance was written before Him of those who reverenced and worshipfully feared the Lord and who thought on His name."

Another way we seek the Lord, according to Vine, is by our desires.[2] Our desires say a lot about us. They clarify what we really want.

God wants to be first in our life. He is a jealous God, and although He wants to bless us with things, we must always desire Him more than anything (see Exodus 34:14). We must be careful of falling into the trap of using God to get the things we desire.

In the Old Testament, David was loved and honored by God even though he made some serious mistakes in his life. As we saw in Psalm 27:4, he revealed that his number-one desire and goal was to dwell in God's presence and behold His beauty all the days of his life.

This Scripture became important to me personally during a time when God was helping me make a transition from seeking Him for what He could do for me to seeking Him for who He is.

I believe that as new believers we all begin our relationship with God very much in need. He establishes His relationship with us as a loving Father who is always available to meet our needs and do the things for us that we cannot do without Him. This is good and healthy as a beginning, but the time always comes when we must make a transition. We must let go of those beginnings and go on to maturity.

As children are growing up, their parents are glad to take care of them. But the day comes when the parents want their children to do some things for them.

My husband and I have four adult children. When they were small, we spent our time taking care of them. Of course, we still do many things for them and help them in any way we can, but I can tell you from experience that I also want them to do some things for me. I want them to come to visit me or call me just because they love me, not because they need or want something. In other words, I want them to desire *me*—not what I can give them or do for them.

It grieves the Holy Spirit when we do not seek God or when we seek Him for the wrong reason, with the motive of just getting something from Him. It is important for us to seek God. When we don't seek Him, often He hides from us, hoping to encourage us to seek Him.

When I finally made the transition and began seeking God on a regular basis, I almost always felt that I was enjoying His presence. Prior to that time, it seemed I was always wondering why I could not feel or sense God's presence as others seemed to do.

When we seek God regularly, it pleases Him, and when He is pleased, we feel pleasure because His Spirit dwells in us. If He is grieved, we feel grieved.

If you are always feeling depressed or sad, this lesson may help you discover the root cause of your frequent depression or sadness.

DISOBEDIENCE GRIEVES THE HOLY SPIRIT

Though I formerly blasphemed and persecuted and was shamefully and outrageously and aggressively insulting [to Him], nevertheless, I obtained mercy because I had acted out of ignorance in unbelief. (1 Timothy 1:13)

All disobedience is sin, and sin grieves the Holy Spirit. Disobedience especially grieves the Holy Spirit when it is known disobedience. There are times in our life when we disobey God, but it is done in ignorance of His commands; and there are times when we disobey God, knowing that our behavior goes against His commands.

The apostle Paul once persecuted Christians zealously, but he did it thinking He was doing God a favor. He was a very religious man who sincerely believed that Christians were evil. As we saw earlier, the Lord confronted him, and he was immediately converted and later baptized in the Holy Spirit. Paul later made the statement that he received mercy from God because he had acted in ignorance.

Anyone who wishes to live a life filled with peace and joy must decide to live a life of obedience to God. *Disobedience is the root cause of all unhappiness.*

The writer of the book of Ecclesiastes said it well in chapter 12, verse 13: "All has been heard; the end of the matter is: Fear God [revere and worship Him, knowing that He is] and keep His commandments, for this is the whole of man [the full, original purpose of his creation, the object of God's providence, the root of character, the foundation of all happiness, the adjustment to all inharmonious circumstances and conditions under the sun] and the whole [duty] for every man."

The writer of Ecclesiastes was a man who literally tried everything to be happy. He had much wealth, great power, and many wives. He restrained himself from no earthly pleasure. Anything his eyes desired, he took. He ate, drank, and made merry. He had tremendous knowledge, wisdom, and respect, yet he hated life. Everything began to appear useless to him. He tried to figure out what life was all about and became more and more confused.

Finally, he realized what his problem had been all along. He had not been obeying God's commandments. He was unhappy because of it and made the statement that the foundation of all happiness is obedience.

There are many, many sad, grieved individuals walking around blaming their unhappy lives on people and circumstances, failing to realize that the reason for their dissatisfaction is their disobedience to God. The truth sets people free, but for it to do so, it must be faced and accepted.

One of the ways we disobey God is by rebelling against the authority figures He has placed in our life. It may be our spouse, a boss, a teacher, a spiritual leader, the government, or the owner of the grocery store where we shop. Actually we are confronted with authority all day long. God tells us to submit with a good attitude to the authority we are under, yet the world today is filled with the spirit of rebellion.

I was a rebellious person, partially because I had been abused by an authority figure in my life, but also because I walked in the flesh. After I was filled with the Holy Spirit, He began to deal with me about my rebellious attitude, especially toward my husband.

I remember as I prayed one morning for my ministry to grow that the Lord said to me, "Joyce, I cannot do anything else in your ministry until you obey what I have told you concerning your attitude toward your husband." At that time I was disrespectful, argumentative, and quickly angered if I did not get my own way about things.

My flesh suffered, but through the power of the Holy Spirit I was finally able to submit to God by submitting to Dave. Submission does not mean that we cannot have any opinions or that we must let people abuse us, but it does mean that we will not get our way all the time. We will have to keep some of our opinions to ourselves and have a godly attitude when we are asked to do things we would prefer not to do.

Even as I am writing this book I have encountered a situation just like what I am talking about. Dave wants me to go to a meeting with him a few days from now, which I really don't want to go to because I feel he can handle it alone. I have told him all the other things I have to do myself, but he feels it will be an important example to others for me to be there. I have decided to disagree agreeably and submit to his request. Believe me, this is a big change from the way I would have handled the situation years ago. My rebellion would have grieved the Holy Spirit, but my obedience pleases Him.

OBEYING GOD IN RELATIONSHIPS

And do not grieve the Holy Spirit of God [do not offend or vex or sadden Him], by Whom you were sealed (marked, branded as God's own, secured) for the day of redemption (of final deliverance through Christ from evil and the consequences of sin). (Ephesians 4:30)

As we have seen, close examination of Ephesians 4:30 and the Scriptures surrounding it, which instruct us not to grieve the Holy Spirit, reveals that the way we handle our relationships with other people is of great importance to God.

Many times we develop a habit of mistreating those close to us when we are not feeling well, have had a rough day at work, have suffered a disappointment, etc. But we are to treat one another with respect at all times, not just when we feel like it.

I used to ask myself why I acted badly with my husband or children, but not with other people. The Holy Spirit quickly showed me that I controlled my negative emotions and attitudes when I was around people I wanted to impress. But when I was with my own family, those with whom I already had a relationship, I took liberties that clearly showed my character flaws and spiritual immaturity. I had myself convinced that I really could not help myself, that when I became angry, grouchy, or hard to get along with, I just could not discipline myself. I felt so frustrated that it seemed I had to explode at someone for something.

Most of the time when I became angry with Dave or one of the children over a small, insignificant issue, it really was not that particular issue that was bothering me, but something unresolved within me. It may have been fretting over a lack of finances, driving in heavy traffic, having a headache, or being corrected at work. It really did not matter what it was; the truth is, I was angry and difficult to get along with. I was a troublemaker, not a peacemaker—and I was in disobedience!

Relationships are one of our greatest assets, and God

wants us to value them. When we value something, we treat it carefully. We are cautious in handling it. We actually go to great extremes to make sure it is safe from harm. We certainly don't damage it ourselves by displaying a casual attitude toward it.

Have you ever damaged a relationship by your own thoughtless, insensitive actions? I am sure we would all have to answer yes to that question, but part of the good news of the gospel is that we can change by and through the power of God that dwells within us.

If we have a possession that is extremely valuable to us, one that we cherish and admire, it would deeply grieve us if we saw another person carelessly tossing it around, leaving it out in bad weather or not using caution to make sure it was not damaged.

God feels the same way about His possessions as we do about ours. People belong to God. They are His creation, and it grieves Him when He sees them being mistreated. When God is grieved, His Spirit is grieved. And since that same Spirit dwells inside all believers, naturally those who are mistreated also feel grieved.

God is an Equal Opportunity Employer who has assignments for every individual. Not everyone shares the *same* call on their life, but everybody has the same inheritance. Every born-again person is an heir of God and a joint heir with Christ. Every individual has a right to peace, righteousness, and joy. Every individual has the right to have their needs met, to be used by God, to see the anointing flow through them.

Everyone has an equal opportunity to see fruit in their ministry, but their willingness to love others has a lot to do with how much fruit they are going to see. God told me a long time ago, "One of the main reasons people don't walk in love is because it's an effort. Anytime they walk in love, it's going to cost them something."

Love requires us to withhold some things we would like to say. Love demands that we not do some things we would like to do and give away some things we would like to keep.

When God first started dealing with me about loving people, He showed me how King David was not willing to give God something that had cost him nothing (see 2 Samuel 24:24). I had given some of my older clothes to women who worked with me, but God showed me that I needed to give away some things that had cost me something. I remember a pretty red dress that I bought that was one size too big for me, but it was new. I found the perfect earrings to go with it and put them away for a special event.

The dress had hung in my closet for a while, when one day the Lord put it on my heart to give the dress to a woman who worked for us. I hesitated. "But Lord, I haven't even worn that dress yet!" The prompting within me only intensified, so I added, "And besides, I have the perfect earrings to go with it."

So the Lord said, "Joyce, I was going to let you keep the earrings, but since they mean more to you than they should, I want you to give them to her, too."

I have learned that love will tell you to give time to somebody that you would rather keep for yourself. It will tell you to take someone somewhere you would rather not go—even to go out of your way to get them there when you don't want to do it.

Love will tell you to forgive someone when they don't

deserve it. Forgiveness is better than holding a grudge; unforgiveness is like taking poison and hoping your enemy will die. Without argument, love is an effort. Love will cost you something. Many people never see fruit in their works because they aren't willing to pay the price and love people. Once I learned these things, I began being much more careful about how I treated people. I love God and certainly don't want to grieve Him. Realizing that my treatment of people at certain times was grieving Him provoked me to change my behavior.

John 16:8 tells us that the Holy Spirit has the job of convicting us of sin and convincing us of righteousness, which is uprightness of heart and right standing with God. He always convicts me quickly if I act rudely, show disrespect, use the words of my mouth to hurt others instead of helping them, think unkind thoughts about someone, judge others critically, or if I am not longsuffering and patient.

God desires for us to be toward one another the same way He is toward us. He is merciful, kind, patient, tender, compassionate, exhortative, and many other such good things. Let us, therefore, live before the Lord with a clean conscience, void of offense toward God and toward man. That is what the apostle Paul said he strove to do (see Acts 24:16). Let us pray for a tender conscience, one that is promptly convicted of wrong behavior toward another person, especially a child of God. We can learn a lot about what pleases or grieves God simply by looking at what pleases or grieves us.

One of the ways we honor God is by honoring His people. I can relate to that because I know how I like it when people honor my children just because they are my children.

At our ministry I expect our employees to honor our children the same as they honor Dave and me.

I recall having an employee once who was very rude to one of our sons, who at that time was about fifteen years old. This employee became impatient with our son and was talking to him in an angry tone of voice. It offended me because I expected my son to be treated with respect.

You may ask if my son had done anything to deserve the treatment he received. The answer is yes, he probably did. But it still was not that employee's place to talk to him in that manner. I would not have minded a loving correction delivered with a proper tone of voice and facial expression, but I did aggressively dislike the angry, impatient attitude displayed by this employee toward my son. Likewise, we as believers are all the property of God. As such, He is committed to take good care of us, and He does not like it when we are mistreated.

In Matthew 18:6 KJV Jesus Himself said that it would be better for a person to have a millstone hung around their neck and be thrown into the depths of the sea than to hurt "one of these little ones." The example being used was that of a little child, but I think it can also be expanded to include a child of God.

Make a decision to talk nicer to people. Speak to them in a tone of voice that is comforting, not harsh. Think nicer thoughts about them. Show them respect. Don't be rude. If you have had a bad day or don't feel good, don't take it out on other people. Realize the value of every human being. Be like God; don't be a respecter of persons; that is, don't show partiality (see Acts 10:34). Do all you can to avoid grieving the Holy Spirit in these areas.

12

Do Not Quench the Holy Spirit

~

Do not quench (suppress or subdue) the [Holy] Spirit. (1 Thessalonians 5:19)

In this verse we are told not to quench, suppress, or subdue the Holy Spirit. According to Webster, to *quench* means to "put out," to *suppress* means "to check or stop (a natural flow)" and to *subdue* means "to make less intense."[1] If we quench a fire, we put it out or extinguish it. We do not want to quench the Holy Spirit; instead, we want to make sure we do everything we can to increase His activity and flow in our life.

What can we do as individuals to increase the activity and flow of the Holy Spirit in our daily life? First Thessalonians 5 gives us some rich insight on this subject.

In verse 12 of that chapter we are instructed to get to know those who labor among us—to acknowledge, appreciate, and respect them. Although this verse seems to be directed toward getting to know our leaders, I believe Jesus would want us to apply the same principle to anyone working alongside us for a common cause.

Verses 13 and 14 teach us to remain at peace and to

correct those who get out of line, but at the same time to be very patient with everybody, always keeping our temper.

In verse 15 we are told to repay no one with evil for evil, but to always aim to show kindness and to seek to do good to one another and to everybody we come in contact with.

In verses 16 through 20 we are instructed to be happy in our faith, to always rejoice and be glad-hearted, to be unceasing in prayer, to thank God in everything no matter what the circumstances may be, and not to spurn the gifts and utterances of the prophets or despise instruction, exhortation, or warning.

From these Scriptures, it appears that our attitude is once again being highlighted as something that either increases or decreases the flow of the Holy Spirit in our personal life.

ATTITUDE DETERMINES DESTINY

> Keep and guard your heart with all vigilance and above all that you guard, for out of it flow the springs of life. (Proverbs 4:23)

Attitude is very important; it is all about how we act, the behavior patterns we display. Our attitude involves our character, and our character begins with our thoughts.

I heard someone say, "Sow a thought, reap an action; sow an action, reap a habit; sow a habit, reap a character; sow a character, reap a destiny."

Destiny is the outcome of life; character is who we

are; habits are subconscious patterns of behavior. Our destiny, or the outcome of our life, actually comes from our thoughts. That is where the entire process begins. No wonder the Bible teaches us to entirely renew our minds, developing new attitudes and ideals (see Romans 12:2; Ephesians 4:23). We are to be good students of God's Word and by it develop new thinking patterns, which will ultimately change our entire destiny (the outcome of our life).

It hinders the Holy Spirit when we have a bad attitude such as bitterness, anger, unforgiveness, spitefulness, disrespect, vengefulness, a lack of appreciation, and the list could go on and on. The Holy Spirit flows through a godly attitude, not an ungodly one.

Regularly examine your attitude, and guard it with all vigilance as Proverbs 4:23 says. Don't think that you cannot change your attitude; all you need to do is change your thoughts.

Many people are deceived into believing they cannot help what they think, but we can choose our own thoughts. We need to consider what we have been thinking about. When we do that, it does not take very long to discover the root cause of our bad attitude.

Satan will always try to fill our minds with wrong thinking, but we do not have to receive everything he tries to give us. I would not take a spoonful of poison just because someone offered it to me, and neither would you. If we are smart enough not to swallow poison, we should also be intelligent enough not to allow Satan to poison our mind, attitude, and ultimately our life.

I wrote a powerful book on this subject titled *The Battlefield of the Mind*. If you have not read it, I highly recommend it.

LOOK BEYOND THE SURFACE

And walk in love, [esteeming and delighting in one another] as Christ loved us and gave Himself up for us. (Ephesians 5:2)

We are instructed to walk in love, esteeming and delighting in one another. To esteem and delight ourselves in one another, we have to first get to know one another, which is an act of love.

It takes time and effort to look beyond the surface of any human being. We are tempted to judge according to the flesh, and we judge hastily. The Word of God condemns both of these practices:

Be honest in your judgment and do not decide at a glance (superficially and by appearances); but judge fairly and righteously. (John 7:24)

So do not make any hasty or premature judgments before the time when the Lord comes [again], for He will both bring to light the secret things that are [now hidden] in darkness and disclose and expose the [secret] aims (motives and purposes) of hearts. Then every man will receive his [due] commendation from God. (1 Corinthians 4:5)

I was always the kind of person who makes snap judgments. God dealt with me about it several times, and I finally realized the danger of judging hastily and by appearance.

Before we judge an individual, we must take time to

get to know the real person, what 1 Peter 3:4 KJV calls "the hidden man of the heart."

Otherwise, we can make a mistake in either one of two ways: 1) we can approve of someone because they appear to be something they are not; or, 2) we can disapprove of someone because of some outward appearance or action, when actually that individual is a wonderful person inside.

I have found that we all have our little quirks, our little oddball actions, behaviors, and ways that are not easily understood by others. God Himself does not judge by appearance, and we should follow His example.

David would never have been chosen by man to be king. Even his own family disregarded him. They did not even include him in the selection process (see 1 Samuel 16:1-13). God saw David's heart, the heart of a shepherd. God saw a worshiper, someone who had a heart for Him, someone who was pliable and moldable in His hand. These are qualities God is looking for.

I often think of the geodes, which are rocks that are ugly and crude looking on the outside but on the inside are absolutely gorgeous. Inside, they look like gemstones, and some actually are, but on the outside they are rough and crusted over.

Like those rocks, we are often rough, crude, and crusty on the outside, but God knows He has placed beautiful things inside us. Just as the gold miner knows he must be patient when digging for nuggets, God knows He must be patient with us as His Holy Spirit continues working with us, digging in our lives, and eventually bringing forth what is inside us.

What we sow into the lives of other people, we will

surely reap in our own. If we sow hasty, harsh judgment, that is exactly what we will reap. We don't like it at all when people sit in judgment of us, when they decide about us at a glance without getting to know us. We should do what Matthew 7:12 KJV says and do unto others as we desire them to do unto us.

AVOID STRIFE

Do nothing from factional motives [through contentiousness, strife, selfishness, or for unworthy ends] or prompted by conceit and empty arrogance. Instead, in the true spirit of humility (lowliness of mind) let each regard the others as better than and superior to himself [thinking more highly of one another than you do of yourselves]. (Philippians 2:3)

Don't quench the Holy Spirit in your life by allowing or being a party to strife.

In 2 Timothy 2:24 the apostle Paul teaches us that the servants of the Lord must not strive, explaining that they "must not be quarrelsome (fighting and contending)." Instead, they must be kind and good to everyone. In other words, they must be peacemakers, not troublemakers.

Many Christian homes and churches are filled with strife. Strife kills the anointing; it hinders the flow of it—it quenches it. Where there is no anointing, no bondages are broken. Satan knows this and, therefore, works diligently to stir up strife anywhere he can. It pleases the Holy Spirit when we refuse to get involved in strife, and even more so when we actively try to stop it:

Strive [or make an effort] to live in peace with everybody and pursue that consecration and holiness without which no one will [ever] see the Lord. Exercise foresight and be on the watch to look [after one another], to see that no one falls back from and fails to secure God's grace (His unmerited favor and spiritual blessing), in order that no root of resentment (rancor, bitterness, or hatred) shoots forth and causes trouble and bitter torment, and the many become contaminated and defiled by it. (Hebrews 12:14-15)

As we see in this passage, to strive can also involve positive behavior. These verses teach us to watch out for each other and to be sure to help people avoid anything that steals peace. We are to avoid resentment, bitterness, and hatred, all of which contribute to strife and cause torment.

I would like to call to your attention that the Bible says *many* will be contaminated and defiled by strife. That is why it is imperative that we stop it anywhere we find it. Strife spreads like a disease and contaminates all it touches.

It's easy to keep strife stirred up if we are not willing to trust God with the desires of our heart. Dave and I were at the mall once, and I saw a certain picture that I wanted to buy in one of the shops. Dave didn't think we needed it, and so I threw one of my silent "temper tantrums." I got real quiet because I was angry.

He asked, "You okay?"

"Yeah, I'm fine, fine, just fine. Everything's fine." It was one of those times when my lips were smiling, but my eyes didn't reflect pleasure, and inside I was thinking, *Oh, you've always got to try to tell me what to do. Why can't you just leave me alone and let me do what I want to do? You always act like I don't know what I'm doing. Well, you go out and play golf if you want to; why can't I buy that picture if I want it? Neh, neh, neh———*

And so I pouted for about an hour as we walked up and down the mall. I was trying to manipulate Dave. I knew that with his peaceful, phlegmatic personality, Dave would rather let me have my way than fight with me. I was too immature in the Lord to understand that is ungodly behavior. I have since learned the hard way that demanding my own way results in strife instead of true satisfaction.

But that day, I was pushing Dave to give in and stop at the shop to buy the picture. Because he is such a lover of peace, Dave said, "Come on, come on, we'll go get the picture. Come on, let's go get the picture."

Of course I said, "No, no, no, I don't want the picture now. I don't want it."

"Come on, you're going to get that picture. I want you to have it. Get the picture—I want you to have the picture."

So we bought the picture, and as I placed it in my home the Holy Ghost said to me, "You know, you really didn't win. You got your picture, but you're still the loser because you didn't do it My way."

We must avoid strife on the job, in the neighborhood, among relatives, in our immediate family, in the church, and even between the Lord and ourselves. He never gets in strife with us, but there are times when we get angry with Him. It is not right, but it happens.

Also, I would be remiss if I did not mention the importance of not being in strife with ourselves. Many people don't get along with themselves very well. Life is difficult if you don't get along with and accept yourself. After all, you are one person you never get away from—you are everywhere you go! If you don't get along with yourself, you won't get along with others either.

If a church is filled with strife, the entire fellowship can be consumed by it. I once watched a church die, and it was not a comforting experience. However, it taught me about the dangers of strife. I learned that I need to avoid it if at all possible.

For the whole Law [concerning human relationships] is complied with in the one precept, You shall love your neighbor as [you do] yourself. But if you bite and devour one another [in partisan strife], be careful that you [and your whole fellowship] are not consumed by one another. But I say, walk and live [habitually] in the [Holy] Spirit [responsive to and controlled and guided by the Spirit]. (Galatians 5:14-16)

The Holy Spirit always guides us into peace. Even if He leads us into confrontation, it is so that we may ultimately live in peace.

We must be guided and led by the Spirit. We must love people, not devour them with gossip and judgment. That kind of negative behavior is ungodly and does not promote the will of God. It quenches the Holy Spirit in our life, and we want His power to increase and flow, not decrease and be quenched.

DESPISE NOT PROPHESYING

> Do not spurn the gifts and utterances of the prophets
> [do not depreciate prophetic revelations nor despise
> inspired instruction or exhortation or warning]. (1
> Thessalonians 5:20)

Following the instruction in 1 Thessalonians 5:19 not
to quench the Holy Spirit, we have an instruction not to
despise prophesying. Let's look at what this word means
in the original text.

According to Vine, the Greek word translated *prophecy* "signifies 'the speaking forth of the mind and counsel
of God,'" and also refers to "the exercise of the gift or of
that which is 'prophesied.'"[2]

Vine then goes on to say: "'Though much of OT [Old
Testament] prophecy was purely predictive,...prophecy
is not necessarily, nor even primarily, fore-telling. It is
the declaration of that which cannot be known by natural
means,...it is the forth-telling of the will of God, whether
with reference to the past, the present, or the future.'"[3]

In the New Testament, God gave spiritual gifts to
men, one of which was the prophet. According to Vine,
"'The purpose of their ministry was to edify, to comfort,
and to encourage the believers,...while its effect upon
unbelievers was to show that the secrets of a man's heart
are known to God, to convict of sin, and to constrain to
worship.'"[4]

The Old Testament prophets were the mouthpiece of
God. He spoke to the people through them. Even kings
listened closely to the prophets. If they did not, they gen-

erally lost their kingdom. Some wicked kings refused to listen to the prophets. Their reigns brought great ruin and destruction and opened the door for much evil to enter the land.

There are, of course, modern-day prophets, but not everyone who prophesies is called to stand in the office of a prophet. In 1 Corinthians 12:10 *The Amplified Bible* version states that prophecy is "the gift of interpreting the divine will and purpose" of God. I believe anointed teachers of God's Word prophesy every time they teach. They interpret, or tell forth, the divine will and counsel of God.

Receiving a divine word from God does not make one a prophet. Many people today call themselves prophets, but they are not. They try to tell people how to live their lives. They prophesy lies and tell forth their own will, calling it the will of God. Many innocent and undiscerning people have been confused and even led astray by such false prophets as these. We are told in 1 John 4:1 that we are to prove (or test) the spirits to see if they are from God, and in 1 Thessalonians 5:21 we are told to test and prove everything until we are sure it is good. Don't believe everyone who tells you something; make sure their ministry is in line with God's Word.

What does the Bible mean when it says if we despise prophesying we will quench the Holy Spirit?

First, I believe it means that we must love the preaching of God's Word, or we will quench the progress the Holy Spirit desires for us to make. It is impossible to grow spiritually without God's Word. His Word is to our spirit what food is to our body; we must have it regularly to be healthy.

Second, I believe it means that we should not have a

judgmental or otherwise bad attitude toward the gift of prophecy or any of the gifts of the Spirit. We should have respect for all the ways God chooses to work through men and women. We should cherish the gifts and honor those through whom they flow. Their gifts were given to them by the Holy Spirit for our benefit, to help us grow and mature.

GOD USES A VARIETY OF PEOPLE

And His gifts were [varied; He Himself appointed and gave men to us] some to be apostles (special messengers), some prophets (inspired preachers and expounders), some evangelists (preachers of the Gospel, traveling missionaries), some pastors (shepherds of His flock) and teachers. His intention was the perfecting and the full equipping of the saints (His consecrated people), [that they should do] the work of ministering toward building up Christ's body (the church), [that it might develop] until we all attain oneness in the faith and in the comprehension of the [full and accurate] knowledge of the Son of God, that [we might arrive] at really mature manhood (the completeness of personality which is nothing less than the standard height of Christ's own perfection), the measure of the stature of the fullness of the Christ and the completeness found in Him. (Ephesians 4:11-13)

Although my gift of teaching has been a great blessing to my own life, it was actually put in me by God for the benefit of other people. However, there are people who decide for whatever reason they either don't like me or don't believe God called me. When they do that, they are quenching the work the Holy Spirit would do in their life through the gift He placed in me.

This is the case with all ministers. There are always some people who will open their hearts and receive from them, and others who will not. We should learn to receive from a variety of people because God uses a variety of people. It is a mistake to look too much at the vessel God decides to use—sometimes we don't like the looks of the "pot," so we reject what is in it.

What if someone deposited ten thousand dollars in the bank for you, but when you drove up to the bank, you did not like the looks of the building and refused to go in and withdraw your money? This, of course, would be very unwise, and if poverty ensued, it would be deserved.

Often we keep our problems and bondages because we don't approve of the help God sends us. We reject it as being a counterfeit without really testing it to find out for sure.

It seems that some people swallow everything hook, line, and sinker, as they say, without ever checking anything out. Then there are others who are so critical and overly cautious they cannot receive from anyone unless the person is exactly like what they are accustomed to. The only problem with this is that what they are accustomed to, in all probability, has not been meeting their need, so why would more of the same be of any benefit?

Don't cry out to God for change, and then be afraid of it when it comes.

I recall one gentleman who told me he would never

236   KNOWING GOD INTIMATELY

have listened to me had he known I was a woman, because
he didn't believe in women preachers. At that time I was
only on radio, and since my voice is deeper than most
women's, I am often mistaken for a man when people hear
me without seeing me. This man actually told me that by
the time he figured out I was a woman, his life had been
changed so drastically by the Word I was preaching and
teaching that he could not deny that I must be from God.

Those who oppose women in the ministry make the
mistake of basing their beliefs and practices on the two
places in the Bible where Paul wrote that women should
keep silent in the church, and that if they wanted to learn
anything, they should ask their own husbands at home
(see 1 Timothy 2:11-12; 1 Corinthians 14:34-35). These
Scriptures have been misunderstood for centuries.

Proper study of history and the Greek text shows
that in the day in which these words were written, men
and women sat on opposite sides of the church.[5] At that
time, most women were uneducated and, in general, not
informed about what was going on.[6] The gifts of the Spirit
and even Christianity itself were new, so naturally women
as well as men were very curious. From other accounts, it
seems that in the meetings women would frequently call
out across the room to their husbands for explanations
of what was taking place. This was causing confusion.
When asked how to handle this situation, Paul responded
that a woman should keep quiet in the church, and that
if she wanted to know anything she should ask her own
husband at home.[7]

In the Scriptures in which Paul said that women were
to keep silent in the church and not teach or "usurp"
authority over men, some scholars have said that the same

Greek word translated *men* is also translated *husband* in other places, and in the same way, the usage of the Greek word for *woman* in 1 Timothy 2:12 can be translated as *a wife*.[8] What if these Scriptures were translated to read that a woman (or a wife) was not to teach her husband or to "usurp" authority over him? That would change the entire context.

We have biblical texts and study books available to us, so we can dig a little deeper and gain revelation in matters that concern us. Scripture must be interpreted in light of other Scripture.

There are many other places in the Bible where God used women. Deborah was a prophetess and certainly gave instructive words from God to men and women alike (see Judges 4-5). Joel prophesied that in the last days God would pour out His Spirit upon men and women, and that they would both prophesy (see Joel 2:28-29). A woman certainly cannot prophesy and keep quiet at the same time. The apostle Peter quoted this same Scripture on the Day of Pentecost (see Acts 2:16-18).

If the Scriptures Paul wrote about women were taken without any deeper study, we would have to assume that women could not teach men at all, in any way. Therefore, they could not be schoolteachers, Sunday school teachers, driving instructors, doctors, lawyers, etc. They basically could not hold *any* position in which they would have to instruct men. Of course, we know that kind of thinking is foolish.

If no women had ever been Sunday school teachers, I really don't know where the church would be today. Actually, it appears that women do more of the work in church than men. I have never attended a prayer meeting in which there were more men participating than women. In fact, the only thing I have ever seen at church that was predominantly male was the "men's club"; in everything else the women always outnumbered the men. I don't believe it should be that way, especially since the Bible teaches us that a man should be the spiritual head of his home. But I can tell you for sure that God is not prejudiced. In Galatians 3:28 Paul himself wrote, "There is no more male nor female, but we are all one in Christ" (paraphrase). When God calls a person into ministry, He does not see gender; He sees availability and heart attitude.

In obedience to Scripture I submit to my husband, and I do not consider myself to be his teacher (see Ephesians 5:22; Colossians 3:18). He has listened to me preach thousands of times, and I am sure he has learned some things as I have taught. But neither one of us sees me as his teacher; I am his wife. I know my place in the pulpit and at home. When people ask Dave if he is Joyce Meyer's husband, he always says, "No, Joyce Meyer is my wife." This is his fun-loving way of asserting and maintaining his position as the head of our marriage and home.

Most of the men who ask me what I think I am doing by teaching and preaching are the ones doing nothing. We must look at the fruit of a person's life and ministry before we decide what God can and cannot call them to do. One thing is for sure, there is absolutely no way I could have done what I have done since 1976 and have been as successful at it as I have been if God had not been fully behind me.

Yes, we quench the Holy Spirit when we spurn the gifts of the prophets or, for that matter, any of the gifts. Let us learn from one another in submission, having humble hearts.

13

The Gifts of the Spirit

~

> Now about the spiritual gifts (the special endowments of supernatural energy), brethren, I do not want you to be misinformed. (1 Corinthians 12:1)

Much has been written about the gifts of the Spirit since the past century's great outpouring of the Holy Spirit, which began in the early 1900s.[1]

The Bible teaches us the importance of the gifts of the Holy Spirit. It also teaches us how important it is that we not be ignorant of them, as the *King James Version* of this passage says. Yet, in spite of all the information available today on the subject, many people are totally ignorant of these gifts. I, for one, attended church for many years and never heard one sermon or lesson of any kind on the gifts of the Spirit. I did not even know what they were, let alone that they were available to me.

There are many varieties of "gifts" or "endowments," as they are called in *The Amplified Bible,* which also refers to them as "extraordinary powers distinguishing certain Christians" (1 Corinthians 12:4). The gifts vary, but they are all from the same Holy Spirit. We find a list of some of the gifts described in 1 Corinthians 12:8-10. In the *King James Version* they are listed as:

- the word of wisdom
- the word of knowledge
- faith
- the gifts of healing
- the working of miracles
- prophecy
- discerning of spirits
- divers kinds of tongues
- the interpretation of tongues

These are all abilities, gifts, achievements, and endowments of supernatural power by which the believer is enabled to accomplish something beyond the ordinary.

Let's look at each of these important gifts separately.

WORD OF WISDOM

To one is given in and through the [Holy] Spirit [the power to speak] a message of wisdom. (1 Corinthians 12:8)

First Corinthians 1:30 KJV says that Jesus is made unto us wisdom from God. And the writer of the book of Proverbs repeatedly tells us to seek wisdom and do all we can to gain it. Wisdom is made available to all people, but the word of wisdom that functions as a gift of the Holy Spirit is a different or higher type.

All wisdom is from God, but there is a wisdom that

can be learned from experience and attained intellectually. That is not the word of wisdom spoken of in 1 Corinthians 12:8. The word of wisdom is a form of spiritual guidance. When it is operating, an individual is made to know supernaturally by the Holy Spirit how to handle a certain issue in an exceptionally wise way, one that is beyond their natural learning or experience and which lines up with God's purpose.[2]

We frequently operate in this gift without even being aware of it. We may say something to someone that seems ordinary to us, but to the listener it is a tremendous word of wisdom for his or her situation.

Actually, I firmly believe the Lord wants us to operate naturally in these supernatural gifts. I have seen many people try to be so superspiritual concerning the operation of the gifts of the Spirit that they become difficult to be around. For example, a special announcement does not have to be made each time someone is operating in a gift of the Spirit. We are not to draw attention to ourselves, but to Jesus. The Holy Spirit came to glorify Jesus, not man.

We cannot force the operation of the word of wisdom. We can covet (sincerely desire) all the gifts, but it is totally up to the Holy Spirit when and through whom they operate.

I have received words of wisdom from children I knew for sure did not even have a clue to what they were saying. The Holy Spirit was trying to get through to me, and He was using a source through which I would know He was speaking.

God does not always or even usually use the people with the most polish; as a matter of fact, it is often quite the opposite. First Corinthians 1:27-29 tells us that God purposefully chooses what the world would call weak and foolish, to put the so-called wise to shame. He uses what the world would discard, so no mortal man can have reason for glorying in His presence.

I am sure we often reject something God is trying to give us because we don't like the package in which it comes to us. As adults, it is hard on our pride to be taught by a child, or if we have been Christians for a long time, to be taught by a new believer. If we are teachers, it is hard for us to receive instruction from a student. But however God may choose to get through to us, it is His business, not ours.

The gifts function as the Spirit wills, not as man wills (see 1 Corinthians 12:11). We get into trouble when we try to operate the gifts instead of letting them operate through us. We also get into trouble when we try to choose the gift or gifts in which we would prefer to operate.

Many people want the "showy" gifts of healing or working of miracles. But the Bible tells us in 1 Corinthians 12:7 that each one of us is given the manifestation of the Holy Spirit for the good and profit of others. Each of us could have various gifts flowing through us to be used for the benefit of other people if we would just realize that we are vessels only. We should not desire a gift in order to appear important, but only for the good of others.

WORD OF KNOWLEDGE

And to another [the power to express] a word of knowledge and understanding according to the same [Holy] Spirit. (1 Corinthians 12:8)

The word of knowledge operates much the same way as the word of wisdom. There are a number of different interpretations of the word of knowledge, but one value is this: The gift of knowledge is in operation when God reveals something to an individual about what He is doing in a situation that he or she would have no natural way of knowing.[3]

Sometimes when God gives us a word of knowledge concerning other people, we know something is wrong with them, or we know that they need to do a certain thing in a specific situation. We should never try to force this kind of supernatural knowledge on anyone. Instead, we should present it humbly and let God do the convincing.

I remember a time when my husband received a word of knowledge concerning something in my life. When he shared it with me, it made me angry. He simply said, "You do what you want to with it; I am only telling you what I believe God showed me." He did not try to convince me; he just reported what God showed him.

Over the next three days God convinced me that the word He had given my husband was correct. I shed many tears because I really did not want Dave to be right about what he said.

Through the word of knowledge given to me by my husband I was able to know why I was having trouble in a certain area of my life. I had been seeking God about this situation and not getting any answers. Dave had given me my answer, but I did not like the answer he gave. That is probably why God gave it to Dave, because He knew I could not hear it from Him myself.

That word of knowledge convicted me of the sin of judgment and gossip, and I did not want that to be my

problem. I had been telling Dave that something wa
wrong, that I could not sense God's anointing when I wa
preaching, and that it was becoming quite frightening t
me. I wanted to know from God what was wrong, an
He told me through Dave. I had critically judged anothe
minister's preaching, and God was not pleased. I neede
to repent and not repeat the behavior.

I cannot tell you the impact this experience had on m
life. Had God dealt with me directly, I am sure I woul
have learned a lesson, but it would have been nothing lik
the lesson I learned when the word of knowledge came t
me through Dave. Not only was it embarrassing, but als
it was no longer hidden.

Sometimes we like to hide our sins. God knows wha
they are, but we certainly don't want anyone else to know
I remember throwing accusations at Dave, saying that h
had done the same thing I had done in being critical o
that minister's preaching. Dave's answer was, "You'r
right; I did. But I am not the one having problems, yo
are—you will have to work it out with God."

God led me to Scriptures in James chapter 3 abou
the words of our mouth and the fact that not many of u
should become teachers because we will be judged wit
a greater severity than other people (see v. 1). Here wa
my answer. God was dealing more harshly with me tha
He was with Dave. I am a Bible teacher and will not con
tinue to have a strong anointing upon my teaching if
am going to critically judge others who are functionin
under the same gift. All judgment—including criticism
negative opinions, and suspicion—is wrong, but it is espe
cially dangerous to judge another in the same professio
in which we wish to be or remain anointed.

I believe the word of knowledge has helped many people through me. I firmly believe that the word of knowledge operates through me quite frequently when I am teaching and preaching God's Word.

As I mentioned earlier, very often people to whom I have ministered a word of knowledge have said to me, "How did you know that about me, Joyce? It was as if you had been living in my house." Of course, what I told them I didn't know through natural means. God caused me to know what to say at just the right time. Although it seemed natural to me, it seemed supernatural to the listener.

While the word of knowledge is usually interpreted as a ministry tool to help someone else, I believe that this gift also helps us many times in our personal life. For example, I find this gift functioning in me frequently when I have lost or misplaced something. Suddenly the Holy Spirit gives me a mental image of where it is.

Once I could not find my glasses anywhere; I searched all over the house and was becoming frustrated, I stopped for a second and simply said, "Holy Spirit, please help me find my glasses." Instantly, in my spirit I saw my glasses between the couch cushions. I went to look and, sure enough, there they were. The Holy Spirit told me something in my spirit that I didn't know in the natural.

THE GIFT OF FAITH

To another [wonder-working] faith by the same [Holy] Spirit. (1 Corinthians 12:9)

I believe there are certain individuals to whom God gives the gift of faith for specific occasions such as a dangerous missionary trip or a challenging situation. When this gift is operating in people, they are able to comfortably believe God in or for something that other people would see as impossible.[4] They have total faith for something that others would be terrified of.

I believe my husband has the gift of faith in the area of finances. No matter what our situation has been in life concerning money, Dave has always been peaceful and sure that God will meet the need. Dave oversees all the finances at our ministry, Life In The Word, and is able to believe God for money to complete major projects that make the rest of us weak in the knees.

A person operating under a gift of faith must be careful not to think that others who do not have this gift are faithless or cowards, for when the gift is operating in a person, God is giving that individual an unusual portion of faith to ensure that His purpose in the earth is accomplished. As Romans 12:3 says, "For by the grace (unmerited favor of God) given to me I warn everyone among you not to estimate and think of himself more highly than he ought [not to have an exaggerated opinion of his own importance], but to rate his ability with sober judgment, each according to the degree of faith apportioned by God to him."

This Scripture lets us know that every person is given a certain measure of faith. We can all be assured that God will always give us enough faith to receive His grace for the fulfillment of every God-given task.[5] It is, however, unwise to compare ourselves with others or our faith with that of another person. We are responsible to use what God has given us and to strive to do the most we can with it.

I also believe there are people who have a gift of faith for certain things in life. Some may have a gift of faith to pray for the sick and believe they will be healed, or they may have a gift of faith for a specific area of healing such as cancer or some other disease. As I mentioned concerning my husband, there is a gift of faith that operates in the arena of finances. Some individuals are anointed and gifted to be givers in an extraordinary way. These people usually have a gift of faith that enables them to be entrepreneurs and make a lot of money. They can do things that others would be afraid to do.

The gift of faith makes a person unusually bold. Anyone operating in this gift must be sensitive to realize that their boldness is a gift of God and always give Him thanks for it.

THE GIFTS OF HEALING

To another the extraordinary powers of healing by the one Spirit. (1 Corinthians 12:9)

The gifts of healing work with the gift of faith. Although all believers are encouraged to pray for the sick and see them recover (see Mark 16:17-18), God may choose to use certain individuals in a special healing ministry.[6]

In our conferences we pray for people all the time and see many wonderful healings. I have stacks of testimonies that have come in over the years giving reports of confirmed physical healings. I pray the prayer of faith in our conferences and on television and often receive words of knowledge about certain healings that are taking place as I pray.

As believers, we can always pray for the sick, but the gifts of healing may not always be present, just as the gift of faith may not always be present. We can always pray in faith, using the measure of faith that God has given to every person, but the supernatural endowment of faith is given as the Spirit wills.

The late Kathryn Kuhlman was used by God in a healing ministry. When healings began to occur in her public meetings, she was as surprised as anyone. She came to be called a "daughter of destiny." A healing ministry was not something she sought out; it was her God-given destiny, and she simply walked in it with the guidance of the Holy Spirit. She always gave God all the glory and openly said that if it were up to her, she would heal everyone. She never understood why some people received healing while others did not. But she always knew for certain that she was functioning under a supernatural gift.

When someone is healed, their healing may not manifest immediately. Healing can be a process that works somewhat like medicine. It is necessary to take it by faith and believe it is working. Later, the results become visible.

When the gift of miracles is operating, we see more dramatic healings than usual, and they often appear instantaneously.

I have seen people try hard to make the gifts of healing work, but true gifts of the Spirit flow easily; they don't require a lot of struggle and human effort. For example, I have seen a minister pray for someone in a wheelchair, then try to force that person to get up out of the chair and stand. In Acts 3, we read about a man who was "crippled from his birth" and who lay begging at the temple gate "which was called Beautiful" (v. 2). As Peter and John were about to enter the temple to pray, the man asked them for alms (money). When he did so, Peter looked right at the man and told him that he didn't have money to give him, but that he would give him what he had. Peter then commanded the man to walk in Jesus' name:

> Then he [Peter] took hold of the man's right hand with a firm grip and raised him up. And at once his feet and ankle bones became strong and steady, and leaping forth he stood and began to walk, and he went into the temple with them, walking and leaping and praising God. (Acts 3:7-8)

Taking someone by the hand as Peter did in this passage is very different from trying to force people to do something themselves.

Once again, I want to make it clear: The gifts of the Holy Spirit cannot be forced. They can be coveted and developed through use, but they cannot be forced or falsified.

THE WORKING OF MIRACLES

> To another the working of miracles. (1 Corinthians 12:10)

Jesus worked many miracles. For example, He turned water into wine (see John 2:1-10) and fed a multitude with a little boy's lunch so that there were baskets full of fragments left over (see John 6:1-13). There are many kinds of miracles: miracles of provision and supply, miracles of deliverance, miracles of healing, etc.[7] We have already mentioned miracles in conjunction with healing, but now I would like to expound on that subject by telling you about a friend of ours.

We know a man who is a missionary, and God frequently uses him in miracles of healing. He held his first missionary crusade when he was just a young man. He had seen other men of God hold crusades and knew that the same call was on his life.

With no prior experience, no money, and no formal training, he set out on his first missionary journey. He went to a town in a foreign land and advertised that he was holding a crusade where miracles, signs, and wonders would take place. He shared with us that it never occurred to him how the crowd might react if no miracles happened.

He said that he was fine until he stepped out on the platform for the first time and saw all the crippled, blind, and deaf people in attendance. There were lepers and people with other terrible diseases, so as he looked around, fear struck his heart. He thought, *Oh, my God, what have I done? What if there are no miracles?* Then suddenly his heart filled with faith. He told God that he had come in the name of Jesus, not his own name. He further stated that it was God's reputation that was on the line, not his own.

With that declaration, he stepped out and began to preach. Then as he prayed for the sick, suddenly miracles began to happen—blind eyes were opening and cripples were walking. He said that he felt as if he were standing back as an onlooker. He saw what was happening, but he knew it had nothing to do with him. The gift of miracles started working then and has gone on working in his crusades ever since.

Like many other people, Dave and I have experienced miracles of supply over the years—times when God has provided so supernaturally that it is obvious that a miracle has occurred.

Miracles are things that cannot be explained, things that do not occur through ordinary means. We all can and should believe God for miracles in our lives, but some individuals are chosen by God to have the gift of the working of miracles flow through them. It may occur one or more times, or it may be a regular event; that is up to the wisdom of the Holy Spirit.

PROPHECY, TONGUES, AND INTERPRETATION

To another prophetic insight (the gift of interpreting the divine will and purpose)...to another various kinds of [unknown] tongues, to another the ability to interpret [such] tongues. (1 Corinthians 12:10)

Although much is said about speaking in tongues, as in this passage, and it is indeed a wonderful gift, in 1 Corinthians 14:1 Paul tells us that we should earnestly desire the gifts, especially the gift of prophecy. He felt that prophecy was more beneficial in a public meeting because all those present could understand it, whereas tongues could not be understood unless they were interpreted. However, in verse 5 he did go on to say that tongues with interpretation is equal to prophecy.

In verse 2 of that chapter Paul tells us that when we speak in tongues, we speak to God, not to men, and that we utter secret truths in the Holy Spirit. In verse 5 he says that he desired that all would speak in tongues, but "more especially" he wanted people to prophesy or "to be inspired to preach and interpret the divine will and purpose [of God]."

In these passages, Paul stresses the importance of all people being edified and built up. He emphasizes that all should benefit from what is being said. As he points out in verse 17, when someone speaks in tongues they may be giving thanks well, but the bystander is not edified; it does that person no good.

Then in verses 18 and 19, Paul says that he is thankful that he speaks in tongues more than all the others put together, but that in public worship he would rather say five words that can be understood by all present than ten thousand words in an unknown tongue.

Later in this same chapter, Paul goes on to give specific instructions about speaking in tongues in a public meeting:

> If some speak in a [strange] tongue, let the number be limited to two or at the most three, and each one [taking his] turn, and let one interpret and explain [what is said]. But if there is no one to do the interpreting, let each of them keep still in church and talk to himself and to God. (1 Corinthians 14:27-28)

I feel this letter written to the Corinthians was intended to instruct them in how to operate in the gifts of the Holy Spirit in public worship, not in their personal lives. There is a gift of tongues that operates in the church service and must be interpreted. I believe this gift of tongues is quite different from the private prayer language one receives upon being baptized in the Holy Spirit, as a sign or evidence of having received the fullness of the Holy Spirit. I don't mean the tongue is different, or sounds different, but the operation of it is different. Privately we may pray in tongues as much as we like, and as previously mentioned, when doing so, we edify ourselves and stir ourselves up in our faith.

With that understanding, let's look at the gifts of prophecy, tongues, and interpretation of tongues separately, as we have been doing with the other individual gifts of the Spirit.

PROPHECY

Eagerly pursue and seek to acquire [this] love [make it your aim, your great quest]; and earnestly desire and cultivate the spiritual endowments (gifts), especially that you may prophesy (interpret the divine will and purpose in inspired preaching and teaching). (1 Corinthians 14:1)

One may prophesy to another individual or to an entire congregation of people. Sometimes the prophecy is more general; at other times it is specific. It may come through a prepared message or sermon, or it may come by divine revelation. Prophecy concerns the will of God, is instructive or edifying, and may bring correction.[8]

Prophecy and the ministry of the prophet is definitely

important; however, I would be remiss if I did not issue a loving warning to be careful in this area.

This gift, in particular, has been abused and has caused a great deal of confusion in the church. There are false prophets as well as genuine ones. There are those who really mean no harm, who think they are prophets, but who are actually speaking out of their own mind, will, or emotions.

Probably the most harmful misuse of this gift occurs when one individual tells another that they have "a word" for that person. Often the one being prophesied to receives that word as being from God without trying the spirit or checking to see if their spirit bears witness with that "word" that it truly is from God (see 1 John 4:1 KJV; Romans 8:16 KJV).

Usually, true prophecy will confirm what has already been revealed to a person's heart, even if only vaguely. It witnesses to their spirit as being correct. Even if it is correction, it will be something God has already been dealing with them about. The prophecy just drives the point home or calls their attention to something they may have been ignoring.

A good example of the gift of prophecy being a benefit involves a time in 1985 when I was trying to decide whether I should leave my position as associate pastor of a certain church. I had worked there for five years and had enjoyed a successful ministry within the church. I loved the people and had great fellowship with the leadership, but I also had a strong desire to do other things that I could not do unless I stepped out into my own ministry. I did not want to make a mistake. I really felt that God was leading me to go, but I was afraid.

During this time of decision, many people prophesied to me, both people who knew me and people who did not know me. Basically, they all said the same thing: "God is calling you to go out. I see you going north, south, east, and west, and holding meetings. I see tremendous growth in your ministry. I see you reaching multitudes."

One woman I had never seen before came to the church to minister. She prophesied to me that someday I would be on television worldwide and that she saw me with a satellite. She prophesied to another woman that someday she would work for a large television ministry. Today the woman to whom this prophecy was given works for me, and I am on television with a potential audience of more than 2 billion people.

True prophecy comes true. One way to test prophecy is to see if it happens. The prophecies I received at that time all confirmed what I already knew in my heart. They increased my faith to step out and obey God.

I have also been given personal prophecies that were not a benefit. For example, some people I didn't even know have given me warnings of danger or "messages from God" that made it sound as if I was doing a lot of wrong things and making bad decisions. Such so-called words provoke fear and destroy boldness and confidence. It took me a long time to learn that the final decision lies in my own heart. If my spirit does not bear witness to a word I am given, I disregard it or place it on a shelf and leave it there for God to confirm it—if and when He is ready to do so.

I have received words of correction from people I did know. Even though I did not always like these messages emotionally, after a few days I would realize that God was indeed speaking to me. I hope I can always remain humble enough to receive correction if it is from God, but

I also desire to be wise enough not to believe every person who wants to tell me what to do.

I pray the same thing for you.

SPEAKING IN TONGUES

> I thank God that I speak in [strange] tongues (languages) more than any of you or all of you put together. (1 Corinthians 14:18)

Believers in some segments of the body of Christ are known for operating in the gifts of the Spirit perhaps more than those from other spiritual backgrounds. These church groups include teaching on the gifts of the Spirit as a regular part of their Bible instruction. Other groups of believers study the gifts, but are not as open about displaying those gifts, and some don't teach the subject at all.

I personally believe that many churches do not teach people to operate in the gifts of the Holy Spirit because either they don't understand them or they are afraid of them. They may have seen or heard of abuses and prefer to avoid the possibility of error or deception. I don't know what every church teaches. I only know what I was taught, and I do have the testimony of people from various backgrounds who tell me regularly that they have never heard of such things in their church.

Is it right for something to be in Scripture and yet people can go to church for years and never hear anything about it? Should we not all be taught everything the Bible discusses?

Ignoring the baptism in the Holy Spirit and the gifts of the Spirit may close the door to some problems such as excesses and abuses, but it also closes the door to countless blessings that people desperately need in their daily lives.

We need the gifts of the Holy Spirit. We are created by God with a desire for the supernatural, and if the church does not meet that yearning, sad to say, Satan is standing by ever ready to give us a counterfeit to meet our desire.

We have already discussed speaking in tongues in connection with the baptism in the Holy Spirit. The best and easiest way to describe this gift of the Spirit is to say it is a spiritual language, one the Holy Spirit knows and chooses to speak through you, but one you do not know.[9]

Like Paul, I have to say to my readers, "I am glad I speak in tongues." I speak in tongues a lot. It helps me stay in the Spirit, and it aids me in being sensitive to the leading of God. I am also edified and built up—made strong spiritually—as I pray in tongues.

Down through the ages, people who have spoken in tongues have been thought to be weird. Tongues have been given a "bad rap," so to speak. Those who personally know nothing about the gift of tongues have critically judged it.

Paul spoke in tongues. The 120 disciples who were filled with the Holy Spirit on the Day of Pentecost *all* spoke with other tongues. Other believers who received the baptism of the Holy Spirit as recorded in the book of Acts spoke in tongues. Why shouldn't you and I speak in tongues?

INTERPRETATION OF TONGUES

If some speak in a [strange] tongue…let one interpret and explain [what is said]. (1 Corinthians 14:27)

When a person speaks in tongues in public worship, the message must be interpreted, as Paul said in this passage. I often receive interpretations of messages given in tongues. They come to me as an impression or a knowing in my spirit of what God is trying to convey to the listeners.

The interpretation of tongues comes much the same way as tongues. A person may feel a stirring in their spirit, a knowing that they are to speak out in unknown tongues, yet they may have no idea what the message in tongues means. The one interpreting then gets an impression in their spirit of what God wants to say. Both parties must operate in faith, because their minds are not involved. What I mean is that the information being conveyed is not coming from their mind, but rather from God through their spirit.[10]

Paul encouraged believers to pray that they might interpret, and I believe we should do that. Doing so enables us to have better understanding of what we are praying about in private.

When I pray in tongues, I often have a sense of what general direction I am praying in without knowing precisely the details of how I am praying. I pray in tongues for a while, then in my native tongue (English) for a while. I pray back and forth in tongues and in English until I feel satisfied in my spirit that I have finished.

You may want to try that method of praying when you pray in your prayer language or you may be led to pray in an entirely different manner. The important thing is that you follow the leading of the Holy Spirit in this area.

DISCERNING OF SPIRITS

> To another the ability to discern and distinguish between [the utterances of true] spirits [and false ones]. (1 Corinthians 12:10)

I believe that the discerning of spirits is an extremely valuable gift, and I encourage you to desire and develop it.

Some people say that the discerning of spirits gives people supernatural insight into the spirit realm when God allows it. They believe that it is not exclusively the discerning of evil or demon spirits, as when Paul identified the spirit of divination in a girl who told fortunes at Philippi (see Acts 16:16-18); it is also the discerning of divine spirits, as when Moses looked into the spirit realm and saw the "back" of God (see Exodus 33:18-23), or when John was in exile on the isle of Patmos and had a vision of the resurrected Jesus (see Revelation 1:9).

Many believe that discerning of spirits also extends into helping us know the true nature of those we are dealing with, whether they are good or evil.[11] In other words, it can help us to know the motivation behind a person or the true nature of a situation.[12] For example, someone may appear to be doing a good thing, yet we may feel wrong about that person inside. That is often God's way of warning us that the person's intention is evil.

Many people today are not what they seem to be. The world is full of phony, deceptive people who are only out to get what they can—and they don't care how they do it.

In our ministry we have dealt with people who have all the answers, those who give the impression they would be a great addition to the workplace or church, group, or organization—the perfect person for the job, so to speak. They promise all kinds of things and then don't follow through with much of anything. They say whatever they think we want to hear to get our commitment; then they do what they feel like doing, making excuses each time for why they have not delivered what they promised.

There are people who are "wolves in sheep's clothing," and the Bible warns us about them (see Matthew 7:15). They act as if they want to help us, when in reality they hope to destroy us. Satan himself uses such people to deceive Christians and demolish their godly endeavors.

I have prayed a lot for discernment in my years in ministry. I never thought or knew to pray for such a thing prior to being baptized in the Holy Spirit, but since then I have learned about this wonderful gift—and I rely on the operation of it a great deal.

In our ministry, Dave and I have to make a lot of decisions, probably more than the average person does. Many of these decisions involve the destinies of other people, something we take as a great responsibility. We must make many decisions that concern those with whom we will or will not be involved on a ministry level. It is important whom we are involved with because spirits are transferable, so to speak. In other words, we can easily become like those we are around. For example, Elisha became like Elijah because he stayed in close contact with him (see 2 Kings 2:15).

The people with whom we are in fellowship affect us; and people also judge us by those with whom we keep company. If someone is known to be dishonest, and we are seen in the company of that person, people may easily think we are like that individual.

It is important for people to trust those who minister to them; otherwise, their hearts won't be open but closed by fear and suspicion. I want people to trust me; I want my ministry to be effective in their lives.

I used to quote frequently from a book written by someone I did not know. I received a letter asking me if I was aware that the person who wrote the book had divorced his wife and done a lot of dishonest things. Of course, I was not aware of those facts, and I stopped using the material for quotation because if other people knew this information, it could cause them to think less of me and have a closed heart toward me and my ministry. The information in the book was good, but the person behind it had backslidden. I needed to be careful about endorsing his materials to others.

We must make a lot of decisions out of love for others, caring about their spiritual well-being.

I remember a man who sat in my office applying for a job. Everyone thought he was the perfect person for the job, but something about him bothered me. There was no known reason for me to feel that way about him. His references and skills were good, and he attended my home church regularly. I tried to talk myself out of feeling the way I did, but I could not shake the feeling that something was just not right about the man. Despite my feelings, we hired him, and he turned out to be a big problem. I wished many times that I had followed discernment instead of reason.

Another time we hired a woman I felt the same way about, and she ended up starting a lot of strife in her department, even though on the surface she appeared extremely sweet and innocent.

On another occasion we hired a young woman who had recently graduated from college. She said she had gone to college with the desire to graduate and work for our ministry. She was very intelligent and capable, but something about her did not seem to be right. After we had hired her, people in her department began to quit, but no one ever complained about her. This went on for almost a year, and we ended up losing several good employees. Each resignation involved a unique situation. Even though I kept saying, "That many people can't be leaving from one department unless something is wrong," we still could not locate any natural reason for the problem.

Then through a series of other events that took place concerning this young woman, we discovered that she was purposely pitting employees against each other and enjoying watching them leave as a result of the lies she was telling about them.

I know it sounds bizarre that a Christian would do such a thing, but, believe me, there are all kinds and levels of so-called Christians. This young woman did believe in Jesus, but she was carnal and was having some emotional problems that only surfaced after a long time of dealing with her.

Some people are very expert at putting on a show. They can become whatever they think someone else wants them to be, but it is not the real them. The world is full of mixed-up people, and we need discernment to function among them and stay out of trouble.

In the case of that young woman who was causing all the problems for us, we could not find a reason for what was happening in her department. But down deep inside I knew that what was happening was more than mere chance.

Reasoning always robs us of discernment. We are
taught in God's Word not to lean on our own understanding, and not to be too wise in our own eyes (see Proverbs
3:5-7). In other words, we are to have a humble attitude.
We are not to trust our own thinking totally, but to trust
God to lead and guide us into all truth.

As I have said, discernment also helps us recognize
when something is of God. After seeing the damage that
one employee can cause in our ministry, it is tempting to
jump to wrong conclusions if someone starts aggravating
me in some way. If I get impatient with people, I might
entertain the thought to fire them, but God often inter-
venes and says, "No, I want you to work with them as I
worked with you." They may have an exterior that needs
change, but they have a heart for God and our ministry.
Then I realize that "there, but for the grace of God, go I."
I am sure other ministries I worked for at times wanted to
fire me due to some of my wrong behavior, but discernment from God told them to be patient and work with me.

This discernment is necessary to the body of Christ
today because the devil tries to separate people who are
called to work together toward a common goal. He creates some misunderstanding to offend them and destroy
the union between them in order to break up what they
might achieve if they remain in harmony with each other.

Satan knows full well the power of agreement, for in
Matthew 18:19 Jesus said, "Again I tell you, if two of you
on earth agree (harmonize together, make a symphony
together) about whatever [anything and everything] they
may ask, it will come to pass and be done for them by
My Father in heaven." Over the years I have learned the
hard way to follow my heart and not my head. I still make

mistakes at times, but I know firsthand the value of discernment in regard to both good and evil.

SEEK ALL THE GIFTS

> Now there are distinctive varieties and distributions of endowments (gifts, extraordinary powers distinguishing certain Christians, due to the power of divine grace operating in their souls by the Holy Spirit) and they vary, but the [Holy] Spirit remains the same. (1 Corinthians 12:4)

The gifts of the Spirit are difficult to explain because they operate in the realm of the Spirit. I hope and pray I have done an adequate job of describing them and their basic operation, I realize there is much more to be said about the subject, and as I have said, I encourage you to read other good books that are dedicated totally to teaching on the subject of the gifts of the Holy Spirit.

I also urge you to begin praying about the gifts of the Spirit. Ask God to use you in them and to allow them to flow through you as He sees fit. Don't seek just the "showy" gifts, but seek the gifts that are the most excellent.

Faith seems to be one of the greatest gifts. Wisdom is greater than knowledge or discernment, although they are all very important. Prophecy is greater than tongues or interpretation.

Some individuals make a big mistake in seeking the more flamboyant gifts and ignoring the gifts that will actually keep them out of trouble while using the others.

People can have knowledge, and yet not have wisdom

to know how to use it. They can have discernment, but no wisdom in how to handle the discernment they have been given. Others may speak in tongues all the time and edify themselves, but not be operating in love by not caring how it affects people around them. Some people may be used to work miracles, but not have enough faith to endure patiently if they have to go through something difficult.

Allowing the gifts of the Spirit to work through us helps us in our everyday life and demonstrates to unbelievers the power and the goodness of Christ who dwells within us. When the gifts of the Holy Spirit are operating in our lives, we reflect the glory of God's grace that is bestowed on us to others who desperately need to put their trust in Jesus. As Christ becomes visible in us, His body, we will illuminate the truth of His power as described in 1 Corinthians 1:4-10:

> I thank my God at all times for you because of the grace (the favor and spiritual blessing) of God which was bestowed on you in Christ Jesus, [so] that in Him in every respect you were enriched, in full power and readiness of speech [to speak of your faith] and complete knowledge and illumination [to give you full insight into its meaning]. In this way [our] witnessing concerning Christ (the Messiah) was so confirmed and established and made sure in you that you are not [consciously] falling behind or lacking in any special spiritual endowment or Christian grace [the reception of which is due to the power of divine grace operating in your souls by the Holy Spirit], while you wait and watch [constantly living in hope] for the coming of our

Lord Jesus Christ and [His] being made visible to all. And He will establish you to the end [keep you steadfast, give you strength, and guarantee your vindication; He will be your warrant against all accusation or indictment so that you will be] guiltless and irreproachable in the day of our Lord Jesus Christ (the Messiah). God is faithful (reliable, trustworthy, and therefore ever true to His promise, and He can be depended on); by Him you were called into companionship and participation with His Son, Jesus Christ our Lord. But I urge and entreat you, brethren, by the name of our Lord Jesus Christ, that all of you be in perfect harmony and full agreement in what you say, and that there be no dissensions or factions or divisions among you, but that you be perfectly united in your common understanding and in your opinions and judgments.

Yes, seek all the gifts, but be sure to earnestly seek the ones that are the greatest. Especially seek to walk in love, because love is above them all.

INTIMACY LEVEL
4

~⌒~

God's Everlasting Fruit

Dwell in Me, and I will dwell in you. [Live in Me, and
I will live in you.] Just as no branch can bear fruit of
itself without abiding in (being vitally united to) the
vine, neither can you bear fruit unless you abide in
Me. I am the vine; you are the branches. Whoever
lives in Me and I in him bears much (abundant) fruit.
However, apart from Me [cut off from vital union with
Me] you can do nothing. If a person does not dwell in
Me, he is thrown out like a [broken-off] branch, and
withers; such branches are gathered up and thrown
into the fire, and they are burned. If you live in Me
[abide vitally united to Me] and My words remain in
you and continue to live in your hearts, ask whatever
you will, and it shall be done for you. When you
bear (produce) much fruit, My Father is honored and
glorified, and you show and prove yourselves to be
true followers of Mine.

—JOHN 15:4-8

14

Gifts for Everyone

And His gifts were [varied; He Himself appointed and gave men to us] some to be apostles (special messengers), some prophets (inspired preachers and expounders), some evangelists (preachers of the gospel, traveling missionaries), some pastors (shepherds of His flock) and teachers. (Ephesians 4:11)

Having gifts (faculties, talents, qualities) that differ according to the grace given us, let us use them: [He whose gift is] prophecy, [let him prophesy] according to the proportion of his faith; [He whose gift is] practical service, let him give himself to serving; he who teaches, to his teaching; He who exhorts (encourages), to his exhortation; he who contributes, let him do it in simplicity and liberality; he who gives aid and superintends, with zeal and singleness of mind; he who does acts of mercy, with genuine cheerfulness and joyful eagerness. (Romans 12:6-8)

From these two passages we see that God's gifts are many and varied. Actually, each person receives some gift or gifts from God. People may have many qualities, but there is usually one primary gift that functions through them.

For example, I am a teacher and a preacher of the gospel. I go on missionary trips, but I am not a missionary in the true sense of the word. I help people, but I don't have a gift of helps (see 1 Corinthians 12:28 KJV) that lends itself more to the practical side of life. I know how to be merciful, but I don't function under a gift of mercy. I believe the same about the other gifts mentioned in these two passages as I do the nine gifts mentioned in 1 Corinthians 12: They may all function in us at various times as needed, but one may be a primary gift.

Administration and organization is also a gift. I am administrative, and I am not disorganized, but I don't love to organize things. One of my daughters has a strong gift in the area of helps; she simply cannot be happy for long unless she is helping someone. She loves to organize things. She once told me that one of her favorite things in the world is to make a list of things she needs to do and then cross them off her list as she accomplishes them. She particularly enjoys the "crossing them off her list" part. She said it gives her an amazing feeling of satisfaction.

As I thought about myself, I found that this would not thrill me. I rarely make lists, and when I do, I usually don't cross things off as I do them. I just look at the list to see what is left and then do it. When I am finished, I throw the list away.

The thing I enjoy much more than making lists and crossing off finished projects is giving other people jobs to put on their list. I am a boss; I was born to be a boss, and I will probably always be someone's boss—even if it is only the dog! I am a leader, and leaders want to tell other people what to do.

I am not lazy, and neither is any good leader, but I accomplish a lot by motivating other people to do things. A person like my daughter would rather do things herself because then she knows they will get done the exact way she wants them done.

It is truly amazing how different we all are, but based on the passages above, God creates and equips us that way.

THE FIVEFOLD MINISTRY

It was he who "gave gifts to mankind"; he appointed some to be apostles, others to be prophets, others to be evangelists, others to be pastors and teachers. He did this to prepare all God's people for the work of Christian service, in order to build up the body of Christ. (Ephesians 4:11-12 TEV)

The apostle, prophet, evangelist, pastor, and teacher gifts are often referred to as the fivefold ministry gifts. These are the five offices that should function in a church to bring a well-rounded ministry to the people.

The *pastor* should be resident within the local church most of the time to shepherd, train, admonish, edify, correct, and instruct the sheep (the congregation). The pastor is involved with their personal lives. This person knows them and their children and may perform weddings and funerals for the families, as well as aiding and counseling them in many other ways. The pastor loves the people and has a vision for the church he leads.

The other four offices may or may not function out of the local church. If they are not resident there, I believe that they should be brought in on some type of rotating basis so that the people are exposed to all the gifts. All of these offices are vocal offices, meaning that they speak into the lives of people. If the *missionary* (or the *evangelist*) never comes, people will lose sight of the importance of world missions. Their vision will become narrow and will not include others outside their own congregation, family, community, or nation.

The *apostle* is an establisher, one who may be used by God to start a new church or ministry. Apostles operate in a stronger gift of teaching than regular teachers and are frequently used to bring correction. Paul was an apostle. He established churches and believers, helping people get rooted and grounded in the Lord. He had a call to help the entire body of Christ, not just one local congregation.

The *prophet* sees and knows things. The message of the prophet can be but may not be as clear as that of the pastor or apostle, but it is often deeper. It may require discernment or an ability to read between the lines, so to speak, because prophets speak things they have seen in the spiritual realm. Prophets are usually not in-depth teachers. They can be good teachers, but usually they won't dig as deeply into a subject as apostles or teachers will.

I have a friend who is an exceptional preacher and teacher with a prophetic flair. In her teaching tapes she may share several powerful points, but not expound on any of them. I like to listen to her tapes because they give me new material. In them, she quickly presents several points for people to consider, while in my teaching I take the time to establish people in one thing. I could take each one of her tapes and make a four-part series of teachings out of it. She even tells me, "Joyce, you need to take this thought and do a series of teachings on it."

Prophets are often misunderstood because they see things that other people don't see. As visionaries, they may see what God wants to do, but not know how to get it done. Ephesians 2:20 says the church is built on the foundation of the apostles and prophets—the prophet sees what needs to be done, and the apostle knows how to do it.

In the Old Testament, prophets were frequently used to bring strong words of correction to kings, nations, and individuals. They were the mouthpieces of God. Nowadays, we can all hear from God for ourselves, so it is not as necessary to have a prophet telling us what to do all the time. But God still uses prophets to bring correction at times, as well as direction. They expound on the will of God through preaching and teaching.

The *teacher* may travel or be resident in the local congregation. For many years, I taught at one local church several times a week in its Bible college as well as in its regular weekly services. Then God called me to travel and teach in many places, establishing believers in the call of God on their lives and in the inheritance provided by the death and resurrection of Jesus Christ. It is one thing to have something, and quite another to know how to make proper use of it. I strive to teach people how to make use of what Jesus died to give them.

VARIED GIFTS OF THE HOLY SPIRIT

Now there are distinctive varieties and distributions of endowments (gifts, extraordinary powers distinguishing certain Christians, due to the power of divine grace operating in their souls by the Holy

Spirit) and they vary, but the [Holy] Spirit remains
the same. (1 Corinthians 12:4)

I have witnessed interesting and varied gifts of the Holy
Spirit working through people. The gift of exhortation always
interests me (see Romans 12:8). It is one of the gifts I don't
have, although I have developed an ability to be exhortative.

A true exhorter makes everyone feel like a million dollars, as if he or she is the most important, most wonderful
person in the whole world. And the exhorter does it naturally and continuously. I know several people with this
gift, and everyone likes to be around them. They are very
positive and usually in a great mood; they make everyone
happy. They are sometimes positive to a fault, in that they
actually don't see the problem, nor do they wish to deal
with it even if they do see it. Of course, not all exhorters
are alike. The degree of their exhortation depends on how
strong or how well advanced their gift is.

We actually grow in our gifts. We might say they are
"fine tuned" over the years. In time we learn our strengths
and weaknesses and how to avoid the pitfalls that go with
each of them.

A person with a gift of mercy, for example, feels sorry
for everyone, even those who don't need anyone to feel
sorry for them. A merciful person wants to help everyone.
I have learned it is not good to have a person with a gift
of mercy in charge of the benevolence ministry without
others involved because the merciful person may give the
entire ministry away.

Those with the gift of mercy don't use as much discernment
as they should sometimes. Their feelings of mercy toward
hurting people sometimes override even common sense.

Dave and I balance each other off in this area. We have found that when one of us is feeling rather strict and not inclined to be long-suffering with an employee any longer, the other will suddenly receive the gift of mercy. Sometimes it is Dave, and at other times I am the one. In this way God keeps us well balanced.

We need all the gifts working together. A person with a prophetic or apostolic bent may not be sensitive enough to the needy person and may need to be around or work with someone with the gift of mercy.

My husband is more patient than I am. He can wait forever for something and not even mind it. Sometimes he holds me back and keeps me from moving too fast, and at other times I light a fire under him and help him move a little faster. We need each other. The balance we provide each other helps keep us moving in God's timing, not ours.

It is easy to see the wisdom of God in distributing the gifts. He makes sure everything is balanced. Where would someone like me be without helpers, administrators, musicians, and so many others who support and encourage me in my life and ministry? We are not islands unto ourselves; we all need each other.

Dave and I frequently talk about the wonder of every job in the world being covered. There are people who like to sit on scaffolding all day and wash windows on tall buildings. I want my ministry windows washed, but I sure am glad someone else is doing it.

One of my sons has no fear of going anywhere in the world because he is missions-minded. The rougher the journey, the more excited he gets. I personally prefer hotels to huts. I don't like dirt. I want to know what I am eating. I don't like to sweat, and I am uncomfortable in places where I cannot understand the language. I do go on mission trips, because I want to do my part to help hurting people all over the world. I love people and enjoy seeing their lives changed through the power of God's Word, but I am not a true missionary.

I am glad I am comfortable knowing that I am not everything, that I don't have all the gifts. It is very liberating when we can know what our gifts are and what they are not. I have learned to staff my weaknesses. In other words, I surround myself with people who do well what I am not good at and don't enjoy. People who want to do everything themselves, and who don't know how to delegate or raise other people up and let them also be used by God, don't succeed at anything sizeable.

NO COMPARISON AND NO COMPETITION

However, when they measure themselves with themselves and compare themselves with one another, they are without understanding and behave unwisely. (2 Corinthians 10:12)

I believe one of the biggest mistakes we make is comparing ourselves with other people and our gifts with their gifts.

God is not going to help me be anyone but me and, likewise, He will not help you be anyone but you. He is not calling us to compete with others, but to love and help them. We should use our gifts to enhance other people's gifts, never allowing ourselves to fall prey to the spirit of jealousy that is so prevalent in our society.

It seems everyone is trying to outdo someone else. We think first is best, but really what is best is being wherever God wants us to be. Some people are intended to be number two, but they never become number one at being number two. They spend their whole life resenting the number-one person and being jealous.

There are some people who work for us who have been offered promotions to the number-one spot in their department and have turned them down because they have said they are better at working for the number-one person. They like to make the boss look good and assist that person in whatever he or she does. They are not comfortable with final responsibility.

I cannot tell you how much I respect people who are honest in their evaluation of their gifts and talents. It is painful to watch people try to be something they are not.

I did this for many years because of the mistaken idea that worth and value are tied to position. I am so glad that Jesus set me free to be me. I have learned that when we are jealous of someone else, that jealousy prevents us from fully enjoying the gift placed in him or her. Actually, God places gifts in others for our enjoyment, and He places gifts in us for the enjoyment of other people. If someone has a beautiful voice, for example, we appreciate his or her musical talent. When such individuals sing, they are working, but we are enjoying their God-given gift.

There was a time in my life when I was jealous of people who could sing well because I wanted to be able to sing as they did. Although I can make a joyful noise unto the Lord, I don't think anyone would want me to do a musical concert. In other words, I don't sing for the enjoyment of the public. I sound pretty good in the shower, but that is about as far as it goes. God showed me one day that as long as I was sitting and wishing I could sing like someone else, I was hindering myself from fully enjoying the gift He had placed in that person for my enjoyment. Since then, I have enjoyed the gifts in other people. John 3:27 says:

> A man can receive nothing [he can claim nothing, he can take unto himself nothing] except as it has been granted to him from heaven. [A man must be content to receive the gift which is given him from heaven; there is no other source.]

This tells us to be satisfied with the gift we have, because there is no source of gifts other than heaven. In other words, unless God sovereignly chooses to give us another gift or a different gift through the Holy Spirit, we may as well be satisfied with what we already have, because that is all we are going to get. We need to trust the Holy Spirit, believing that He truly does know the Father's plan and that He has been sent to earth to help make sure God's will comes to pass on the earth and in each of us.

Please meditate on the fact that God has sent the Holy Spirit to dwell in us. He actually lives inside every person who has truly accepted Jesus Christ as Savior and Lord. The Holy Spirit was sent to keep us until the final day of redemption when Jesus returns to claim His own. He is attempting to lead and guide each one of us into the fullness of what Jesus died for us to have. When we fight against our calling or are dissatisfied with what we are and what we have, we fight against the work of the Holy Spirit within us. Let us submit to Him, develop the gifts He has placed in us with His help, and live for the glory of God, not our own glory.

The only reason we are dissatisfied with the gifts we have is concern about what others will think. We compare and compete, and by so doing, lose the joy of being what God designed us to be.

Why should a secretary strive all her life to be an accountant if she is no good with numbers? Why should a chef struggle to be an athlete just because it is more glamorous or pays more money? If he loves to cook, then he should cook.

I once tried with all my might to learn to sew. A friend of mine made her family's clothes, and I wanted to be like her. I bought a sewing machine, took lessons, and undertook to make some clothes for Dave. I made a pair of shorts for him. When I had finished, the pockets hung below the hem in the leg. I hated sewing, but day after day I sat at the machine trying to be what I thought at that time was a "regular, normal woman." I had failed to realize I was normal to God. Although I had a different calling on my life than the other women I knew, that did not make me abnormal, except perhaps in the eyes of the world.

We are told in Romans 12:2 not to conform to the world, but to be renewed in our mind, so we can know what God wills for each of us personally: "Do not be conformed to this world (this age), [fashioned after and adapted to its external, superficial customs], but be transformed (changed) by the [entire] renewal of your mind [by its new ideals and its new attitude], so that you may prove [for yourselves] what is the good and acceptable and perfect will of God, even the thing which is good and acceptable and perfect [in His sight for you]." Unless we refuse to conform to worldly customs, we will never experience God's perfect will for us as individuals.

It is this same chapter in the book of Romans that speaks about the diversity of gifts given to individuals. We are all parts of one body in Christ, and He is the Head. In the physical realm, all body parts must respond to the head if everything is to be in good working order. The various parts of the physical body work together; they are not jealous or competitive. The hand helps the foot put its shoes on. The feet take the body wherever it needs to go. The mouth does the talking for the rest of the body. There are many parts to the body. They don't all have the same function, but they all work together for one combined purpose. The spiritual body of Christ should work the same way. That is why the Holy Spirit used the example of the physical body when He inspired Paul to write the book of Romans (see Romans 12: 4-7).

When we attempt to do things we are not gifted to do, it only creates pressure in our life. We should work with the Holy Spirit to discover what our unique, customized destiny is, and then do everything we can to fulfill it.

In addition to the gifts we have mentioned here, there are many, many others. There are those who are craftsmen, musicians, and singers. There are those with a keen mind for business. Many are gifted to entertain others, to make people laugh, to bring joy to people's lives. Still others are called and anointed to raise children.

There is no such thing as "just a housewife," or "just a mom or dad." I don't like to hear people say they are "just" anything. Each thing we are is important in God's eyes. We won't be judged for not fulfilling someone else's destiny, but we will have to give an account of our own gifts and talents and show what we have done with them.

Don't bury your talent because it is not the same as someone else's. Don't quench the Holy Spirit by quenching the gifts God has placed in you.

15

The Baptism of Fire

⁓

I indeed baptize you in (with) water because of repentance [that is, because of your changing your minds for the better, heartily amending your ways, with abhorrence of your past sins]. But He Who is coming after me is mightier than I, Whose sandals I am not worthy or fit to take off or carry; He will baptize you with the Holy Spirit and with fire. (Matthew 3:11)

As believers, we are called to do more than go to church on Sunday morning, do more than follow prescribed rituals, and certainly do more than have water sprinkled on our head or be immersed in a baptismal pool. All of the above are important and not to be ignored, but they must be followed up with a willingness to experience the "baptism of fire."

In Matthew 20:20-21 the mother of Zebedee's children came to Jesus and asked Him to order that her two sons be allowed to sit, one at His right hand and one at His left, when He came into His kingdom. Jesus replied that they did not know what they were asking. Then in verse 22 He asked, "Are you able to drink the cup that I am about to drink and to be baptized with the baptism with which I am baptized?"

What baptism was Jesus speaking of? He had already been baptized by John in the Jordan River and had received the Holy Spirit baptism at the same time (see Mark 1:9-12). What other baptism is available?

The baptism of fire is what Jesus was talking about. Fire is a purifying agent, something that causes discomfort while it does its work. Jesus was sinless and, therefore, did not need to be purified; but we do. John the Baptist said that Jesus would come to baptize with the Holy Spirit and with fire (see Mark 1:8; Matthew 3:11).

The fire of God burned in Jesus' life. He was on fire for the glory of God. He was required to go to the cross and pay a debt He did not owe. In His humanity He did not want to go, but He was willing to do the Father's will no matter how difficult it was (see Matthew 26:37-39). He experienced the pain of submission just as we do.

Jesus had feelings. We must remember that He came as the Son of God *and* the Son of man (see Matthew 12:8). And, yes, the fire of God burned in His life, just as it burned in the life of every other man or woman we see in the Bible who accomplished anything outstanding for God.

Jesus asked the Father to make us holy and unified as we reveal His glory in the earth, saying:

Sanctify them [purify, consecrate, separate them for Yourself, make them holy] by the Truth; Your Word is Truth. Just as You sent Me into the world, I also have sent them into the world. And so for their sake and on their behalf I sanctify (dedicate, consecrate) Myself, that they also may be sanctified (dedicated, consecrated, made holy) in the Truth. Neither for these alone do I pray [it is not for their sake only that I make this request], but also for all those who will ever come to believe in (trust in, cling to, rely on) Me through their word and teaching, that they all may be one [just] as You, Father, are in Me and I in You, that they also may be one in Us, so that the world may believe and be convinced that You have sent Me. I have given to them the glory and honor which You have given Me, that they may be one [even] as We are one: I in them and You in Me, in order that they may become one and perfectly united, that the world may know and [definitely] recognize that You sent Me and that You have loved them [even] as You have loved Me. (John 17:17-23)

Let me remind you that like Shadrach, Meshach, and Abednego in Daniel 3:20-27, we have to go through the fire. But also like those three Hebrew men, when we come out, we won't even smell like smoke.

God led the Israelites in the wilderness by a cloud of glory during the day and a pillar of fire at night. As I was meditating on this story in Exodus 13, God spoke to me and said, "Tell the people that they will never be led by the glory if they're not willing to be followed by the fire."

Everyone wants to enjoy God's glory, but few are eager to be pursued by His fire. But if you want to be led by the glory in the light of day where all can see you, then the fire of God is going to have to chase you in the dark places of your life. Learn to welcome both the glory and the fire of

God. This is vitally necessary to bring you into the highest level of intimacy with God.

The fire of God will burn the garbage out of your life. This purging is not a one-time experience. It is not like a wind that blows into your life to do a big work and fix you up so you never need anything else again. No, God's refining fire is more like a maintenance agreement on your car, which requires you to return to the dealer for regular adjustments and fine-tuning.

How many times a week, for example, do you need an attitude adjustment? If God's glory is shining through your life, Satan will set you up to upset you every chance he gets! Some week, keep a tally of every time something frustrates or irritates you, and you will see how many times in a month you need help concerning your mouth or your thoughts.

Sometimes God will use His Word to fall as refining fire on your situation. The more of His Word you learn, the easier it is for God to remind you of a Scripture that convicts your heart to repent of some reaction to life that is not Christlike.

Eventually, when you can see the fruit of His purging, you will actually welcome His conviction, saying, "Yes, Lord, You're right. I'm convicted, and I'm sorry. Thank You for showing me the way of escape from this bondage. I don't want to remain the way I have been."

I realize it isn't easy to change. I have been studying God's Word for twenty-six years, and I still have to work at many things. Change isn't easy, and I'm still not where I need to be, but I thank God that I'm not where I used to be.

If we get stubborn (unwilling to repent) when the Lord

reveals a behavior in us that needs to be modified—then love gets stubborn. As we have seen, God is love, and He is a jealous God. He doesn't want anything in us to occupy the place that belongs to Him. And love, God Himself, will be jealous enough and stubborn enough to stick with us until He gets His way. Love will show us things we don't want to see in order to help us be what we need to be.

God wants you! He wants full custody of your heart, not just visitation rights. People complain that they pray in Jesus' name and nothing happens—but considering the amount of time they spend with Him, it's obvious they're only dating Him. I didn't get my husband's name until I married him. Jesus wants a marriage relationship with His church so that we can use His name whenever we need to do so, and see His power working mightily.

Intimacy with God gives us everything we need, including power over evil that sets itself against us. Psalm 91:1-2, 9-11 says:

> He who dwells in the secret place of the Most High shall remain stable and fixed under the shadow of the Almighty [Whose power no foe can withstand]. I will say of the Lord, He is my Refuge and my Fortress, my God; on Him I lean and rely, and in Him I [confidently] trust!...Because you have made the Lord your refuge, and the Most High your dwelling place, there shall no evil befall you, nor any plague or calamity come near your tent. For He will give His angels [especial] charge over you to accompany and defend and preserve you in all your ways [of obedience and service].

Some people are like wild stallions unwilling to let a saddle be put upon them in order to carry a rider; they haven't learned that their own breakthrough to peace happens when they submit to God and obey Him promptly. They are like unbroken colts resistant to a bridle and bit in their mouths that could be used by God to guide them to a place of security and provision.

Some people are not willing to let God have the reins of their life because they want to control their own destiny. But they will never feel the security they long to have, or the peace that passes all understanding, until they give themselves over to the Holy Ghost. If you want that peace and security, pray like this:

God, I can't solve the crisis in my life; I can't change my circumstances. Do what You need to do in me and do what You need to do with my circumstances. I belong to You, and I submit myself into Your care. I want to be led by your glory, and followed by Your fire.

Fire devours all impurities and leaves all that remains on fire for God's glory. A lot of the old Joyce Meyer has been burned up in the baptism of fire over the years. It has definitely not been easy, but it has definitely been worth it.

THE REFINER'S FIRE

For our God [is indeed] a consuming fire. (Hebrews 12:29)

God desires to consume everything in our life that does not bring Him glory. He sends the Holy Spirit to live inside us believers, to be in close fellowship with us, and to bring conviction of our every wrong thought, word, or action. We must all go through the "refiner's fire" (Malachi 3:2).

What does that mean? It means God will deal with us. He will change our attitudes, desires, ways, thoughts, and conversations. Those of us who go through the fire instead of running from it are the ones who will bring great glory to God eventually.

Going through fire sounds frightening. It reminds us of pain and even death. In Romans 8:17, Paul said that if we want to share Christ's inheritance, we must also share His suffering. How did Jesus suffer? Are we expected to go to the cross also? The answer is yes and no. We don't have to physically go to a cross and be nailed to it for our sins, but in Mark 8:34 Jesus did say that we should take up our cross and follow Him. He went on to talk about laying aside a selfish, self-centered lifestyle. Believe me, getting rid of selfishness takes some fire—and usually a lot of it.

We are called to "walk in the Spirit," to "live according to God in the Spirit," and to "live the life of the Spirit" (see Galatians 5:25 KJV; 1 Peter 4:6 KJV; Romans 8:9). Making a decision to do this is the starting point, but I can tell you from the Word of God and experience that it takes more than a decision; it takes a deep work of the Holy Spirit in our life. He "operates" on us with God's Word, which divides soul and spirit (see Hebrews 4:12). He also uses circumstances to train us in stability and walking in love at all times.

These things we are called to do are not things that are

just given to us; they must be worked in us. Just as leaven or yeast must be worked into dough—it cannot be sprinkled on for results—so Christ must be worked in us.

In Philippians 2:12 KJV the apostle Paul teaches us to "work out" our own salvation with fear and trembling. That means that we are to cooperate with the Holy Spirit as He begins not only to live in our spirit, but in our soul as well. He begins in us a work of crucifixion or "dying to self." Paul said, "I die daily"(1 Corinthians 15:31 KJV). In other words, he was saying that he was constantly exposed to a "putting to death in the flesh." He was not speaking of physical death, but a death to his own will and ways.

SPIRIT, SOUL, AND BODY

And may the God of peace Himself sanctify you through and through [separate you from profane things, make you pure and wholly consecrated to God]; and may your spirit and soul and body be preserved sound and complete [and found] blameless at the coming of our Lord Jesus Christ (the Messiah) (1 Thessalonians 5:23)

We are spirit, soul, and body (1 Thessalonians 5:23 NIV). Our body is simply the vehicle for our soul and spirit—the parts of us that will live forever. When we die, our physical body returns to ashes and dust, but our soul and spirit live on.

Remember, when we invite Jesus to come into our heart, the Holy Spirit makes our spirit His home, His dwelling place. From that position in our heart, which is the very center of our being, the Holy Spirit begins a work, a purifying work, in our soul (and in our mind, will, and emotions). Our mind tells us what *we* think, not what God thinks. The Holy Spirit works with us to change that. According to 1 Corinthians 2:16, we have the mind of Christ. And Romans 8 teaches us that we have two minds—the mind of the flesh and the mind of the Spirit. We must be taught by the Holy Spirit how to think in agreement with God, how to be a vessel for God to think through. Old thoughts must be purified out of us.

Our emotions tell us how *we* feel, not how God feels about situations, people, and the decisions we make. According to Psalm 7:9, God tests and tries our emotions. He works with us through His Spirit until we are not moved by human emotion alone, but by His Spirit.

Living in the emotional realm is one of our biggest problems. Emotions have been nominated the believer's number one enemy.[1] More than anything they are used by Satan to keep us out of God's will. Feelings are strong and difficult to ignore or deny. They are fickle, ever changing, and therefore dangerous to follow. God has feelings about situations, but they are holy emotions, not carnal ones. We must learn to sense the heart of God and follow His leading in every situation.

Our will tells us what *we* want, not what God wants. We have a free will, and God will not force us to do anything. He leads us by His Spirit into what He knows will be good for us, but the final decision about what we do is up to us. God wants each of us to regularly make decisions that are in agreement with His will.

We are to use our free will to do the will of God. The will overrides emotions and even thoughts. It has the final vote in every decision that faces us. By an act of our will, you and I can choose to do the right thing even if we don't feel like it.

Once we allow these three areas—mind, will, and emotions—to come under the lordship of Jesus Christ, we are considered to be mature, or spiritual as Paul called it (see 1 Corinthians 2:15).

In 1 Corinthians 3:3 KJV, Paul wrote to the Corinthians, who had received the baptism of the Holy Spirit and in whom the gifts of the Spirit were in operation, telling them they were "carnal" because they were living out of the soul. As we read in *The Amplified Bible* version of this verse, they were following fleshly, "ordinary impulses": "For you are still [unspiritual, having the nature] of the flesh [under the control of ordinary impulses]. For as long as [there are] envying and jealousy and wrangling and factions among you, are you not unspiritual and of the flesh, behaving yourselves after a human standard and like mere (unchanged) men?"

The way we are to avoid being unspiritual is by allowing ourselves to be led by the Holy Spirit.

BE LED BY THE HOLY SPIRIT

But I say, walk and live [habitually] in the [Holy] Spirit [responsive to and controlled and guided by the Spirit]; then you will certainly not gratify the cravings and desires of the flesh (of human nature without God). (Galatians 5:16)

Paul did not say that the desires or lusts of the flesh would die and no longer exist for the children of God. He said that we should choose to walk in the Spirit, and that by making that choice, we would not fulfill the lusts of the flesh that continually tempt us.

There are many things available to lead us—people, the devil and his demons, the flesh (our own body, mind, will, or emotions), or the Holy Spirit. There are many voices in the world that speak to us, and often several at the same time. It is imperative that we learn how to be led by the Holy Spirit. Remember: He is the One who knows the will of God and who is sent to dwell in each of us to aid us in being all God has designed us to be and have all God wants us to have.

The Holy Spirit lives in each of us to help us!

His help may not always be welcome at first, but thank God, He is persistent and will not give up on us. We should lift up our entire life daily and say with all our might, "Holy Spirit, You are welcome in every area of my life!"

As I look back over the years, I can see that I have been on a fascinating journey with God. He has definitely changed me and is still changing me daily. I had many problems in my soul as well as in my circumstances at the time I received the baptism in the Holy Spirit. Little did I realize what was about to take place in my life. I was asking God for change, but I was totally unaware that what needed to be changed in my life was *me*.

God began a process in me—slowly, steadily, and always at a pace I could endure. As a Refiner, He sits over the fires that burn in our life to make sure that they never get too hot and that they never die out. Only when He can look at us and see His own reflection is it safe to turn the fire off, and even then we need a few alterations and adjustments from time to time.

When God was dealing with me about patience, I would have many circumstances in which I could either be patient or behave badly. Quite often I behaved badly, but the Holy Spirit kept convicting me, teaching me, and giving me a desire to live for God's glory. Gradually, little by little, I changed in one area and then another. I usually got to rest a little bit in between battles and often thought that perhaps I had finally graduated, only to discover there was something else I needed to learn.

Does that sound familiar to you? I am sure it does, because we all go through the same thing when we truly desire to come to the place of being led daily by the Holy Spirit rather than by the world, the flesh, or the devil.

Being led by the Holy Spirit means that He is involved in every decision we make, both major and minor. He leads us by peace and by wisdom, as well as by the Word of God. He speaks in a still, small voice in our heart, or what we often call "the inward witness." Those of us who desire to be led by the Holy Spirit must learn to follow the inward witness and to respond quickly.

For example, if we are engaged in a conversation, and we begin to feel uncomfortable inside, it may be the Holy Spirit signaling us that we need to turn the conversation in another direction or be quiet. If we are about to purchase something, and we feel uncomfortable inside, we should wait and discern why we are uncomfortable. Perhaps we don't need the item, or we may find it on sale somewhere else, or it may be the wrong time to buy it. Remember, we don't always have to know why; we just need to obey.

I remember being in a shoe store one time. I had chosen several pairs of shoes to try on when suddenly I started feeling very uncomfortable. This discomfort increased until finally I heard the Lord say, "Get out of this store." I told Dave we had to go, and out we went. I never knew why, nor do I need to know. Maybe God saved me from some harm that was coming my way, or perhaps the people in the store were involved in something perverse. Maybe it was just a test in obedience. As I have said, we don't always have to know why God leads us in certain ways. Our part is to obey, which honors Him. When we honor Him, He honors us (see 1 Samuel 2:30)!

Long after I had matured to a place where I no longer desired to push to get "things," God still used "things" to teach me valuable lessons. First of all, I learned that there is nothing wrong with wanting nice possessions as long as we aren't chasing after them.

In fact, if we chase after God, blessings and possessions will chase after us! Remember that Jesus said if we seek His kingdom, which is His righteousness, peace, and joy in the Holy Ghost, all the things we need (like food and clothes) will be added to us (see Matthew 6:32-33).

But I also learned we need to develop a mature sense of balance in all we do. Some people will go overboard to do for everybody else, but won't do anything for themselves. Excessive self-abasement is just as unbalanced as overindulgence. First Peter 5:8 says, "Be well balanced (temperate, sober of mind), be vigilant and cautious at all times; for that enemy of yours, the devil, roams around like a lion roaring [in fierce hunger], seeking someone to seize upon and devour."

To be in balance means that we don't dote on ourselves

and do everything for ourselves that we want to do, but it also means that we don't go to the other extreme and refuse to ever do anything good for ourselves. For example, I've learned to seek God's opinion when I shop.

I saw a ring that I really liked and could afford because I had saved some money. So I walked around the store for a while and prayed about it. It was a good price, and I knew it was something that I would continue to enjoy. I tested my own impulses by waiting at least half an hour; then I asked, "God, is it all right for me to get this ring? You know I'll do whatever You want me to do with the money, but I'd like to have it if it's okay."

I didn't have any conviction not to get it, so I bought it.

That would be a great ending to the story, but there was more—there was also a bracelet. The salesman prodded, "It's on sale just until tomorrow, and you ought to get it. It looks great on you."

When you *really* like something, it makes you forget everything about balance. I was hesitant, but I found Dave and asked, "C'mon, I want you to see this bracelet." I was thinking, *Maybe God will tell him to buy it for me.*

So he looked at it and said, "Well, yeah, you can get it if you want to. It's nice."

I knew in my heart that I should *not* buy that bracelet, but not because it would have been a sin to do so. There wouldn't have been anything wrong with buying it, but the greater benefit for me at that time was to develop the character I needed to be able to walk away from something that I really liked but didn't need.

I sensed that maybe at a later time God would release me to get it, if I still wanted it. But looking back, the self-control was more satisfying than the self-indulgence.

Dave took the salesman's card that day so we could call back to see if the bracelet would be on an upcoming sale at an even lower price, but I never had peace about it, and peace is more precious than any purchase. So I finally told Dave not to go back and get that bracelet.

Imagine his surprise! He said, "You don't want it?"

I said, "Yeah, I *want* it, but the greater thing for me this time is to resist it. That bracelet is not what I need right now."

The bottom line is, if we want to be truly happy, we need to listen to God. He will let us know whether something is right for us or not. God's Word gives valuable guidance in how to enjoy the abundant life: "Whereas she who lives in pleasure and self-gratification [giving herself up to luxury and self-indulgence] is dead even while she [still] lives" (1 Timothy 5:6). We can have all the world's goods hanging on our bodies, but be dead inside.

I had rather be full of life than adorned with fruitless baubles and bangles. I believe that if I had spent that money on the bracelet after losing my peace over it, I would never have been happy with it. I would have had an impressive bracelet to flash around, but its sparkle would have quickly dimmed my joy.

When we discipline ourselves not to purchase something we want but feel God is prompting us not to get, it is like sowing seed. When we sow, we always reap. I have probably received many bracelets since that time as gifts, not even realizing they were a harvest on the obedience I sowed long ago.

When we feel that God is not releasing us to spend money on ourselves, often it is because He wants us to sow it into someone else's life—and that is fine with me. I would rather have peace and joy than any material thing that money can buy. We can never give more to God than He gives to us anyway. He is never trying to take anything away from us. He is always trying to get us into a position where He can ultimately give us more. To those who are still carnal or unspiritual, this can seem like bondage. They may feel that they rarely get to do anything they want to do. However, for those of us who have chosen to follow the leading of the Holy Spirit, this crucified life is a joy. We can actually enjoy the suffering the flesh feels when denied its own way because we know a higher, even a holy, thing is taking place.

It is always better to please God than to please self; Romans 8:13 tells us why: "For if you live according to [the dictates of] the flesh, you will surely die. But if through the power of the [Holy] Spirit you are [habitually] putting to death (making extinct, deadening) the [evil] deeds prompted by the body, you shall [really and genuinely] live forever."

Those believers who remain carnal never really live, but those of us who work with the indwelling Holy Spirit and who form a habit of putting the flesh to death by saying yes to God and no to self, experience a quality of life that is wonderful. We have righteousness, peace, and joy in the Holy Spirit—and again I want to say, *it is wonderful* (see Romans 14:17)!

THE FRUIT OF THE SPIRIT

But the fruit of the [Holy] Spirit [the work which His presence within accomplishes] is love, joy (gladness), peace, patience (an even temper, forbearance), kind-

ness, goodness (benevolence), faithfulness, gentleness (meekness, humility), self-control (self-restraint,
continence). Against such things there is no law [that
can bring a charge]. (Galatians 5:22-23)

This passage describes the kinds of fruit we can bear
when we are filled with the Holy Spirit. In John 15:8 Jesus
told us that God is glorified when we bear fruit. He spoke
of fruit again in Matthew 12:33 when He said that trees
are known by the fruit they bear, and in Matthew 7:15-16
He applied this same principle to people. These verses
show us that as believers, we need to be concerned about
the kind of fruit we are bearing. How do we bear the good
fruit of the Holy Spirit?

We have seen that God is a consuming fire, and that
Jesus was sent to baptize us with the Holy Spirit and with
fire. Unless we allow the fire of God to burn in our life,
we will never exhibit the fruit of the Holy Spirit.

As we see by Jesus' words in John 15:2, fruit bearing
requires pruning: "Any branch in Me that does not bear
fruit [that stops bearing] He cuts away (trims off, takes
away); and He cleanses and repeatedly prunes every
branch that continues to bear fruit, to make it bear more
and richer and more excellent fruit." Just as fire is a way
of describing the work the Holy Spirit does in our life, so
is pruning. Fire is necessary for purification and death of
the flesh; pruning is necessary for growth. Dead things
and things that are going in the wrong direction must be
cut off so that as trees of righteousness we can bear rich
fruit for God (see Isaiah 61:3 KJV).

I will never forget when Dave decided that the old beautiful tree outside our home needed pruning. I didn't think

much about it when he said he was bringing professionals in to thin it out. But I was appalled when I came home and found that these saw-happy men had sabotaged my tree.

Dave said, "Just wait until next year, it will be beautiful again."

But I don't like waiting.

And I didn't like looking at those toothpick limbs that had once been lush and full. But now the tree is more beautiful than before and strong enough to withstand powerful winds for many more years. Galatians 5 gives us a list of sins of the flesh and a list of the fruit of the Spirit, or as *The Amplified Bible* puts it in verse 22, "the work which His presence within accomplishes." I really like that way of saying it. It is the fruit of *the [Holy] Spirit,* qualities we see in Jesus Himself: love, joy, peace, patience, kindness, goodness, faithfulness, gentleness (meekness or humility), and self-control. This is the goal of the Holy One living within us, to produce or accomplish this fruit in our life—big, luscious fruit for everyone to see and admire.

Love is the everlasting fruit that will not fade away. To bear fruit we must abide in God's love—to stay alert to His love for us, to dwell in His love by loving others, to endure testing by responding to trials with love. Jesus said that if we keep His commandments to love God and others, we are considered His friends.

I have told you these things that My joy and delight may be in you, and that your joy and gladness may be of full measure and complete and overflowing. This is My commandment: that you love one another [just] as I have loved you. No one has greater love [no one has shown stronger affection] than to lay down (give up) his own life for his friends. You are My friends if you keep on doing the things which I command you to do. (John 15:11-14)

How close to God do you want to be? Would you like to be His friend? Wouldn't you like to see Him and know Him as He really is? Loving people the way Jesus loved them makes us friends to God. So many people ask, "But who am I to be a friend of God?"

Jesus said, "You have not chosen Me, but I have chosen you and I have appointed you [I have planted you], that you might go and bear fruit and keep on bearing, and that your fruit may be lasting [that it may remain, abide], so that whatever you ask the Father in My Name [as presenting all that I AM], He may give it to you" (John 15:16).

These verses make it clear that if we love God and people, we will not ask for things outside of God's will. He will give us anything we ask for, if we put Him and people before all other desires. This loving attitude keeps us pure in heart. James made it clear that we fail to receive from God when we ask with wrong purpose and evil, selfish motives (see James 4:3); but love never fails (see 1 Corinthians 13:8).

When the Holy Spirit changes a proud, grouchy, stubborn, controlling, and manipulative individual into a humble, kind, submissive, and adaptable one, people take notice. The world today is looking for something real. It is tired of counterfeit spirituality, empty words, lifeless formulas that don't really work, and just going through

the motions. As believers in Christ, let's cooperate with
the Holy Spirit within us to give the world what it is really
searching for.

BE A FRUIT INSPECTOR

Therefore, you will fully know them by their fruits.
(Matthew 7:20)

Examine your own fruit and the fruit of others. Don't
examine others to judge and criticize them, but simply to
determine if they are what they claim to be. This is one
way we try or test the spirits and stay out of trouble.

For years I was like an apple tree that sat all day long
and yelled, "I am an apple tree," but I never produced any
apples.

One time my husband and I were in Florida, and I saw
a tree that I thought was very attractive. I asked, "What
kind of tree is that?" Before anyone could answer, I saw
oranges beginning to blossom on the branches, and I said,
"It's an orange tree." I knew it by its fruit.

Christians often carry outward signs attempting to tell
others they are believers. Bumper stickers on automobiles
are a good example. These signs say that the driver is a
Christian, but what kind of fruit do they bear in traffic?
Are they driving at or below the speed limit, or are they
speeding? How do they react to other drivers, especially
to those who cut them off in traffic? These are the true
signs of what they are.

You and I can carry a big Bible, wear Christian jewelry
such as a cross, have a bumper sticker on our car, own

a large library of Christian books and display them in a prominent place in our home. We can do all those things and still not be producing any good fruit. We must be concerned with the fruit of the Holy Spirit, because the Holy Spirit is concerned with it. One of His main purposes in making us His home is to continually work His fruit in us.

In John 15 Jesus compares us and our relationship with Him to that of a living plant. He is the Vine; we are the branches. Although it is not stated in John 15, we could also say the Holy Spirit is the Gardener who prunes us and keeps the weeds in us from choking the fruit.

God has planted a garden in each of us, and He has assigned the Holy Spirit the job of Gardener: *"For we are fellow workmen (joint promoters, laborers together) with and for God; you are God's garden and vineyard and field under cultivation"* (1 Corinthians 3:9).

A gardener aids in the production of fruit. That is what the Holy Spirit was sent to do in us—help us bear good fruit for God.

> He chose to give us birth through the word of truth, that we might be a kind of firstfruits of all he created. My dear brothers, take note of this: Everyone should be quick to listen, slow to speak and slow to become angry, for man's anger does not bring about the righteous life that God desires. Therefore, get rid of all moral filth and the evil that is so prevalent and humbly accept the word planted in you, which can save you. (James 1:18-21 NIV)

Examine your own fruit regularly. If any of it is diseased or rotten, ask the Gardener to help you get rid of it and produce a new crop. Perhaps you have some fruit that simply is not growing. It is on the branch, but it is very tiny, certainly not a size that would do anyone any good. Maybe you need a little more fertilizer. Jesus told a parable using this same kind of example.

BEAR GOOD FRUIT

> And He told them this parable: A certain man had a fig tree, planted in his vineyard, and he came looking for fruit on it, but did not find [any]. So he said to the vinedresser, See here! For these three years I have come looking for fruit on this fig tree and I find none. Cut it down! Why should it continue also to use up the ground [to deplete the soil, intercept the sun, and take up room]? But he replied to him, Leave it alone, sir, [just] this one more year, till I dig around it and put manure [on the soil]. Then perhaps it will bear fruit after this; but if not, you can cut it down and out. (Luke 13:6-9)

This is such a good example of what I am talking about. If we are not bearing good fruit, then we are just taking up room.

God has a plan for us after salvation; otherwise, He would probably take us out of the world. If we are not pursuing His plan, then we are simply taking up space and not doing any good for God, ourselves, or anyone else. If we strive against His blessings, it would be better for us if He took us on home to heaven! We certainly don't glorify Him, or show others His goodness, when we follow our own way instead of His.

I am so thankful that the Vinedresser (the Gardener) is always willing to work with us just a little bit longer. Even when we give up on ourselves, He refuses to give up on us.

Anyone who has the Holy Spirit living within can bear the kind of fruit I am speaking of: love, joy, peace, patience, kindness, goodness, faithfulness, gentleness (meekness, humility), and self-control. These things must be developed like any plant, but all of us believers have within us what we need to produce this kind of fruit.

As Jesus told us in John 15:4, no branch can bear fruit of itself; in order to bear fruit, it must abide in the Vine. For this reason, *fellowship and communion with the Father, Son, and Holy Spirit art of the greatest importance.*

We need to abide in the Lord's presence. It is the equivalent of a plant receiving sunshine, only we receive "Sonshine." Just as plants must be watered, so Jesus waters the church with the Word of God (see Ephesians 5:25-26).

If we follow the prescribed plan for fruit bearing—get planted, rooted, and grounded with plenty of "Sonshine," plenty of the water of the Word, and submit to the Gardener—*we will bear fruit!*

16

The Communion of the Spirit

~~~

> The grace (favor and spiritual blessing) of the Lord
> Jesus Christ and the love of God and the pres-
> ence and fellowship (the communion and sharing
> together and participation) in the Holy Spirit be
> with you all. (2 Corinthians 13:14)

The communion of the Holy Spirit refers to our fellowship with other believers and with the Spirit Himself.
Since the Holy Spirit lives inside us, we don't have to go
very far to have fellowship and communion with Him.

For years, in the church I used to attend, a benediction was spoken over the congregation at the closing of
the service. It always included these words: "May the
communion of the Holy Spirit be with you all." It sounded
spiritual, but I had no idea what it meant. I believe there
are many others who experience the same thing.

As I mentioned at the beginning of this book, I spent
years trying to "reach" God, without knowing that He
was in me all the time. I followed laws and rules, when I
could have been enjoying fellowship. I struggled and felt

like a failure, and all the time the Lord was in me to help me do what I was supposed to do.

The Holy Spirit comes to help us because He knows we constantly need it. There is no shame in needing help; it is part of our humanity.

First John 1:3 KJV says, "Truly our fellowship is with the Father, and with his Son Jesus Christ." This fellowship or communion is only made possible through the Holy Spirit living in us.

I live in a house with my husband, and we are very close. Dave and I work together and do most other things together. There are times when he goes to play golf, but we stay in close contact by phone. He may watch sports on television, and even though I am not particularly interested in them, I am still in the house. We eat meals together, sleep together, and share the bathroom in the mornings, as we get ready to go about our day. We spend a lot of time in each other's presence. We don't always talk, but we are always aware of one another. I talk to Dave about things that are important and things that are unimportant. I listen when he talks to me. Fellowship is not just talking; it is also listening.

Dave and I enjoy just being quiet together. We have often talked about how wonderful it is to be with someone with whom we can be comfortable in silence. We also consult each other before making any important decisions or major purchases, and we do it more out of respect than to get permission.

Proverbs 3:6 says if we will acknowledge God in all our ways, He will direct our steps. To me, acknowledging God means caring what He thinks about my actions and wanting His will more than my own.

In Jeremiah 2:13 the Lord said, "For My people have

committed two evils: they have forsaken Me, the Fountain of living waters, and they have hewn for themselves cisterns, broken cisterns which cannot hold water." The first and biggest mistake that anyone makes is to forsake God, to ignore Him and behave as if He does not exist. In Jeremiah 2:32 He says, "My people have forgotten Me, days without number." That is a tragedy; it sounds as if God is sad or perhaps lonely.

I sure wouldn't like it if my children forgot about me. I never go very many days without talking to each of them. I have two sons who travel extensively with the ministry. Even when they are out of the country, they call me every few days.

Recently, Dave and I had dinner with one of our sons two evenings in a row. Yet the next day he called just to see what we were doing and to ask if we wanted to do something together the next evening. One of the reasons he called was simply to say that he and his wife really appreciate all the things we do to help them.

These are the kinds of things that help build and maintain good relationships. Sometimes the little things mean the most. By my children's actions I feel loved by them. My logic may say I know they love me, but it sure is good to feel it also.

That is the way God is with us, His beloved children. He may know we love Him, but He also likes to experience our love for Him through our actions, especially through our fellowship with Him.

RENEWED BY FELLOWSHIP

Even when we were dead (slain) by [our own] shortcomings and trespasses, He made us alive

together in fellowship and in union with Christ.
(Ephesians 2:5)

Fellowship ministers life to us. We are renewed by it. It charges our batteries, so to speak. We are made strong through union and fellowship with God—strong enough to withstand the attacks of the enemy of our soul, who is Satan (see Ephesians 6:10-11).

When we are fellowshipping with God, we are in a secret place where we are protected from the enemy. In Psalm 91 we read of this secret place, and in verse 1 we are told that those who dwell there will defeat every foe: "He who dwells in the secret place of the Most High shall remain stable and fixed under the shadow of the Almighty [Whose power no foe can withstand]."

I believe the secret place is God's presence. When we are in His presence, we experience His peace. Satan just does not know what to do with a believer who remains peaceful no matter what the circumstances may be. This is hard to do at times, but we draw strength for stability as we have communion and fellowship with God through His Spirit.

Psalm 16:8 tells us that if the Lord is continually before us, we will not be moved. According to Psalm 31:20, when we are in the secret place of God's presence, we are hidden from the plots of men and from the strife of tongues. And Isaiah 54:17 tells us that tongues are weapons used against us. Satan tempts people to talk against those of us who are trying to go forward with God, hoping to discourage us and weaken us. But through fellowship with God, we are hidden from the negative effects of such attacks.

Satan despises our fellowship with God. He knows how

strong we are if we commune regularly with the Lord, and he fights against that fellowship with all his might.

Ask any believer if spending regular quality time with God is a challenge for them, and they will almost always say yes.

We find time for lots of other things on a regular basis (like watching television or engaging in some other form of entertainment), but we find it difficult to spend regular time with God praying, fellowshipping, and reading His Word. We need to take God out of our "emergency only" box and allow Him into our everyday life. How would we feel if our loved ones only talked to us when they had an emergency? Actually, it would ruin our relationship.

God taught me some valuable lessons about crisis management. Jesus said, "Come to Me," but He didn't say run to the phone and call up three of our friends. I am not against asking people to pray for us, but if we run to people, we won't find a cure, only a Band-Aid.

To avoid constant emergencies, the Lord impressed on me to seek Him continuously, or *diligently.* I used to seek time with God once in awhile or when my life was in big trouble. Eventually, I learned that if I ever wanted to get out of living in a state of emergency, I needed to seek God as if I were in desperate need of Him even during times of tremendous prosperity and blessings.

Just as the children of Israel forgot God in prosperous times, we too give God low priority in our schedule when things are good. Listen carefully to God's heart in the following principle: If the only time we seek Him is when we are desperate, then He will keep us in desperate circumstances because He is desperate for fellowship with us.

God will always rescue us and get us out of trouble

when we come to Him. But if we want to stay in a place of constant victory, we must diligently seek Him at all times. Solomon learned this vital truth, and expressed this wisdom saying, "I know that it will be well with those who [reverently] fear God, who revere and worship Him, realizing His continual presence" (Ecclesiastes 8:12).

We must never forget that *relationship is built on fellowship.*

GET PERSONAL

I do not call you servants (slaves) any longer, for the servant does not know what his master is doing (working out). But I have called you My friends, because I have made known to you everything that I have heard from My Father. [I have revealed to you everything that I have learned from Him.] (John 15:15)

God wants us to get personal with Him. He proves this by the fact that He lives in us. How much more personal can anyone get than to live inside another person?

If God had wanted some distant, businesslike, professional relationship with us, He would have lived far away. He might have visited occasionally, but He certainly would not have come to take up permanent residence in the same house with us.

When Jesus died on the cross, He opened up the way for us to get personal with Almighty God. What an awesome thought! Just think about it: *God is our personal Friend!*

If we know someone important, we love to have an

opportunity to say, "Oh, yes, he is a friend of mine. I go to his house all the time. We visit with one another often." We can say that of God if we follow through and do our part to fellowship and commune with Him regularly.

GOD IS JEALOUS OVER US

> Or do you suppose that the Scripture is speaking to no purpose that says, The Spirit Whom He has caused to dwell in us yearns over us and He yearns for the Spirit [to be welcome] with a jealous love? (James 4:5)

There we have it in one verse: The Holy Spirit wants to be made welcome; He yearns or longs for fellowship with us.

Open up your entire life and say with all your heart, "Welcome, Holy Spirit; I am glad You have made Your home in me!"

According to James 4:4, when we pay more attention to the things of the world than we do to God, He looks upon each of us as an unfaithful wife who is having an illicit love affair with the world and breaking our marriage vow to Him. To keep us faithful to Him, and in close fellowship and communion with Him, sometimes He must remove things from our life that are keeping us from Him.

If we allow a job to come between us and God, we may lose it. If money separates us from Him, then we may have to learn that we are better off poor than separated from God. If success comes between us and our heavenly Father, we may get demoted instead of promoted. If our friends take first place in our life, we may find ourselves lonely. Lonely people usually get very close to God. It is amazing how well we get to know someone when that person is all we have.

I went through a period of extreme loneliness in my life. I had my family, but I had lost all my friends. It seemed to me that God was purposely separating me from everyone I liked and enjoyed being with, and I did not understand it at all. Later, I realized that I depended too much on those friends. I was moved by what they thought and did. God wanted me to be led by His Spirit, not my friends. Had He not separated me from them and taken time to get me rooted and grounded in Him and His love, I probably would not have the ministry I have today.

Multitudes of people fail to realize that they never receive the things they want because they don't really put God first in their life, as we are told to do in Matthew 6:33 KJV: "But seek ye first the kingdom of God, and his righteousness; and all these things shall be added unto you."

In the gospel of Luke we find an example of someone who put the Lord first, and of someone else who allowed the cares of this world to interfere with close fellowship with Him.

MARY AND MARTHA

Now while they were on their way, it occurred that Jesus entered a certain village, and a woman named Martha received and welcomed Him into her house. And she had a sister named Mary, who seated herself at the Lord's feet and was listening to His teaching. But Martha [overly occupied and too busy] was distracted with much serving; and she came up to

> Him and said, Lord, is it nothing to You that my sis-
> ter has left me to serve alone? Tell her then to help
> me [to lend a hand and do her part along with me]!
> (Luke 10:38-40)

Jesus came to visit Martha and Mary. Martha was busy
getting everything ready for Him. She was cleaning
house, cooking, and trying to make an impression by having everything just right. Mary, on the other hand, took
the opportunity to fellowship with Jesus. Martha became
angry with her sister, wanting her to get up and help with
the work. She even complained to Jesus, requesting that
He instruct Mary to help her.

> But the Lord replied to her by saying, Martha,
> Martha, you are anxious and troubled about many
> things; there is need of only one or but a few things.
> Mary has chosen the good portion [that which is to
> her advantage], which shall not be taken away from
> her. (Luke 10:41-42)

When Jesus said, "Martha, Martha," there is more
implied in those two words than we realize. Martha was
too busy for relationships; she was choosing work over
intimacy. As such, she was misusing her time and missing
what was vital.

Mary was operating in wisdom; she was taking advantage of the moment. She could spend the rest of her life
cleaning, but Jesus had come to her house, and she wanted
Him to feel welcome. He had come to see her and Martha, not their clean house. This does not mean that a
clean house is not important, but there is a time for every-

thing—and this was not the time to be cleaning house. For much of my life I was like Martha. One regret I now have is that I did not take more time to play with my children when they were small. I was always busy when my son asked me to do something with him. Even five minutes would have made a difference in our relationship then, and would have produced a more fruitful relationship when he was older.

I am close to all of my children now, and 99 percent of the time I stop my work and take time for them, because I realize that relationships are important. In fact, one reason God gave us time is so we would use it to develop and enjoy close and abiding relationships. We are to love God and love others, but many, many Christians are overly busy, working instead of ministering to each other "as unto the Lord."

Let us use wisdom and not miss God's presence when it is available. There are times when we sense the Holy Spirit prompting us to pray, but we prefer to work or play. When He calls, we should respond immediately. How often do we tell the Lord we will spend time with Him in the morning or evening, and when the time comes, something gets in the way so that we fail to fellowship with Him as we promised?

The following blessing awaits those who diligently seek Wisdom (that is, God) at all times:

I love those who love me, and those who seek me early and diligently shall find me. Riches and honor are with me, enduring wealth and righteousness (uprightness in every area and relation, and right standing with God). My fruit is better than gold, yes, than refined gold, and my increase than choice silver. I [Wisdom] walk in the way of righteousness (moral and spiritual rectitude in every area and relation), in the midst of the paths of justice, that I may cause those who love me to inherit [true] riches and that I may fill their treasuries. (Proverbs 8:17-21)

Make regular time for God. Remember: you don't have to go far to find Him. Just close your eyes for a moment, and in the quietness of your own heart you will discover Him. His Holy Spirit is always there waiting for you. Don't leave Him alone without any attention from you. Make Him glad that He is living in you. Make Him feel welcome and at home. Make Him comfortable. Share everything with Him, because He has come to share everything with you.

17

The Wonder of It All!

~

That [Spirit] is the guarantee of our inheritance
[the firstfruits, the pledge and foretaste, the down
payment on our heritage], in anticipation of its
full redemption and our acquiring [complete] possession of it—to the praise of His glory. (Ephesians 1:14)

The Holy Spirit is our guarantee of the good things that
are to come. I often say, especially when I feel really filled
with the Holy Spirit, "This is so good, I cannot imagine
the glory of what the complete fullness will be like." If
we only experience 10 percent (a usual down payment)
of what is ours by inheritance, I am in awe when I think
of what it will be like to actually see God face to face, to
have no more tears, no more sorrow, no more dying—how
awesome!

In Ephesians 1:13-14 KJV, the Bible says that we are
sealed with the Holy Spirit, and He guarantees that we
will arrive safe, preserved from destruction on the final
day of deliverance from sin and all its effects. Think of
the wonder of it—the Holy Spirit is in us, preserving us

for our final resting place, which is not a grave but a mansion in heaven (see John 14:2 KJV).

As I approach the end of this book, I am in awe and wonder as I think of this great blessing of the indwelling Holy Spirit. He inspires us to do great things. He endues us with power for all of our tasks. He stays in close communion with us, never leaving us or forsaking us.

Just think about it—if you and I are believers in Jesus Christ, we are the home of the Holy Spirit of God! We should meditate on this truth over and over until it becomes a reality in our lives. If we do, we will never be helpless, hopeless, or powerless, for He promises to be with us to strengthen us and empower us. We will never be without a friend or without direction, for He promises to lead us and to go with us.

I am so excited about being able to share these things with you, and I sincerely pray that the things I am sharing are opening up your heart to the wonder of it all.

Paul wrote to his young disciple Timothy: "Guard and keep [with the greatest care] the precious and excellently adapted [Truth] which has been entrusted [to you], by the [help of the] Holy Spirit Who makes His home in us" (2 Timothy 1:14).

This truth I have been sharing is so precious I encourage you to guard it, to keep it in your heart. Don't allow it to slip away from you. Since you are a believer in Jesus Christ, the Holy Spirit is in you to help you not only to maintain this revelation, but to give you many others besides. Appreciate Him, honor Him, love and adore Him. He is so good, so kind, so awesome. He is wonderful!

THE TRINITY

So there are three witnesses in heaven: the Father, the Word and the Holy Spirit, and these three are One. (1 John 5:7)

Before I finish this book, I must mention again the Holy Trinity: Father, Son, and Holy Spirit. They are three, and yet They are one, as I have said. That does not compute for us mathematically, but nonetheless it is true according to Holy Scripture. By having the Holy Spirit living in us, we also have the Father and the Son living in us.

Oh, the wonder of it all. It is too awesome to explain. We must simply believe it with our hearts. Don't try to understand it. Be like a little child and just believe it because the Bible says it: The entire Godhead—Father, Son, and Holy Spirit—lives inside you and me and every born-again believer, all of us who have truly accepted Jesus Christ as Savior and Lord (see Colossians 2:9-10).

This truth should make us bold, fearless, and aggressive in a balanced way. We should believe we can do whatever we need to do that is part of God's plan for our life because the Holy Trinity equips us. He is our daily Manna,[1] our Portion in life (see Psalm 119:57). With Him, we have what we need and more besides.

Mark 10:27 says that with man many things are impossible, but with God all things are possible. Go forward in life, and go with a positive attitude, assured that God is with you and for you. He is on your side, and because that is so, it does not matter at all who or what may come against you (see Romans 8:31). You are more than a conqueror through Christ who loves you (see Romans 8:37). Greater is He who is in you than he (Satan) who is in the world (see 1 John 4:4 NASB). And the Greater One who lives inside of you wants you to get to know Him intimately through His indwelling Holy Spirit!

How totally awesome. As a believer in God through Christ, you are the home of God! This teaching should bring relief to your soul. I can almost hear you letting out a big sigh right now. I can see you lifting your hands and saying loudly, *"Thank you, Father, for your Holy Spirit! I am so grateful that you live in me!"*

CONCLUSION: REVELATION
ALLEVIATES AGONY

~

But when He, the Spirit of Truth (the Truth-giving
Spirit) comes, He will guide you into all the Truth
(the whole, full Truth). For He will not speak His
own message [on His own authority]; but He will
tell whatever He hears [from the Father; He will
give the message that has been given to Him], and
He will announce and declare to you the things that
are to come [that will happen in the future]. (John
16:13)

I cannot tell you how thrilled my heart was the first time I
read a book about the person and work of the Holy Spirit.
It seemed to me to be the most wonderful revelation I had
ever received—other than discovering that God was my
Father and Jesus was my Savior.

As we have seen, we Christians serve a triune God, and
the Godhead (Father, Son, and Holy Spirit) is referred to
as the Trinity. Usually when people are missing revelation
concerning one of the persons of the Godhead, it is revelation about the Holy Spirit of which they are deprived.
Why? Because Satan works very hard to make sure we

don't know all that is available to us today through the power of the Holy Spirit.

That is the whole purpose of this book—to let people know how to receive the power of the Holy Spirit that is available to us today.

I have endeavored to reveal the true nature and ministry of the wonderful Holy Spirit in people's lives. I encourage you to continue to learn everything you can about Him. Make Him feel at home in you and learn to live your life in such a way that He will always be comfortable in His home. Welcome Him into every facet of your life. Begin to daily draw upon His ministry that is readily available to you. Let Him be the Helper to you that He desires to be.

Don't struggle through things alone when you have a Divine Helper standing by just waiting for an invitation to get involved. Let revelation about the present-day ministry of the Holy Spirit alleviate the agony of going through life trying to do things on your own. When you give Him control of your life, He will lead you into the perfect will of God for you where you will experience exceeding, abundant blessings, peace and joy, and a greater closeness and intimacy with God.

NOTES

CHAPTER 1

1. James E. Strong, "Greek Dictionary of the New Testament," in *Strong's Exhaustive Concordance of the Bible* (Nashville: Abingdon, 1890), p. 77, entry #5479, s.v. "joy."

CHAPTER 2

1. Jesus substituted Himself for us. He took upon Himself our sins (which separate us from God) and died in order to restore our relationship with God. Jesus took our place by suffering on the cross, dying, shedding His blood for us, then rising from the dead. When we believe in Him and what He did for us, we receive eternal life.

2. James E. Strong, "Greek Dictionary of the New Testament," in *Biblesoft's New Exhaustive Strong's Numbers and Concordance with Expanded Greek–Hebrew Dictionary* (copyright © 1994, Biblesoft and International Bible Translators, Inc. All rights reserved). NT:907, s.v. "to baptize" John 1:33:...from a derivative of NT:911; to immerse, submerge; to make overwhelmed (i.e., fully wet); used only (in the N.T.) of ceremonial ablution, especially (technically) of the ordinance of Christian baptism.

CHAPTER 3

1. "The death, resurrection, and ascension of Christ were to inaugurate the new age of the Holy Spirit's ministry. Our Lord prophetically announced a drastic change in the Holy Spirit's operation in the age that was to begin. At Pentecost the Holy Spirit came...in a sense in which He was not here before and to perform all the ministries delegated to Him in this age; namely, regenerating, baptizing, sealing, and indwelling every believer with the added privilege of each believer's being filled with the Spirit...The experiences of OT [Old Testament] saints and all pre-Pentecost believers came short of these tremendous blessings that are the heritage of every genuine believer in this age." *New Unger's Bible Dictionary,* originally published by Moody Press of Chicago, Illinois. Copyright © 1988. Used by permission, s.v. "HOLY SPIRIT."

2. W. E. Vine, *Vine's Complete Expository Dictionary of Old and New Testament Words* (Nashville: Thomas Nelson Inc., 1984, 1996), "An Expository Dictionary of New Testament Words," p. 545, s.v. "SANCTIFICATION, SANCTIFY," A. Noun., *hagiasmos.*

CHAPTER 4

1. "In this quiet place of indescribable beauty, man was to enjoy fellowship and companionship with the Creator, and to work in accord with the divine blueprint to perfect His will." *The Wycliffe Bible Commentary,* edited by Charles E. Pfeiffer and Everett F. Harrison, Electronic Database. Copyright © 1962 by Moody Press. All rights reserved; "Genesis 2:8-17."

2. "Man's spirit was originally the highest part of his entire being to which soul and body were to be subject." Watch-

man Nee, *The Spiritual Man* (New York: Christian Fellowship Publishers, Inc., 1968), p. 43.

3. The immediate effect of sin on Adam and Eve was that they died spiritually and became subject to spiritual death." Lewis Sperry Chafer, revised by John F. Walvoord, *Major Bible Themes* (Grand Rapids, Michigan: Academie Books from Zondervan Publishing House, 1974), p. 174.

4. "This promise of eternal redemption is the essence of the promises to Abraham." *Biblesoft's Jamieson, Fausset and Brown Commentary,* Electronic Database. Copyright © 1997 by Biblesoft. All rights reserved; "Hebrews 11:13."

CHAPTER 5

1. "1. Behold, the veil of the temple was rent in twain…Just as our Lord Jesus expired, at the time of the offering of the evening-sacrifice, and upon a solemn day, when the priests were officiating in the temple, and might themselves be eyewitnesses of it, the veil of the temple was rent by an invisible power; that veil which parted between the holy place and the most holy. They had condemned him for saying, I will destroy this temple, understanding it literally; now by this specimen of his power he let them know that, if he had pleased, he could have made his words good. In this, as in others of Christ's miracles, there was a mystery." *Matthew Henry's Commentary on the Whole Bible: New Modern Edition,* Electronic Database. Copyright © 1991 by Hendrickson Publishers, Inc. Used by permission. All rights reserved; "Matthew 27:50-56."

CHAPTER 6

1. Strong, "Greek Dictionary of the New Testament," *Strong's Exhaustive Concordance of the Bible,* p. 9, entry #154, s.v. "ask."

2. Vine, p. 111, s.v. "COMFORT, COMFORTER, COM-FORTLESS," A. Nouns., *parakletos*.
3. Ibid.

CHAPTER 7

1. Vine, p. 267, s.v. "GLORIFY," *doxazo*.

CHAPTER 8

1. "[Praying in the Holy Spirit]...is the way to build them-selves up on their faith." *Robertson's Word Pictures in the New Testament* (Volumes 5 & 6). Copyright © 1985 by Broadman Press. Used by permission. All rights reserved; "Jude v.20."
2. Pat Boone, *A New Song* (Carol Stream, Illinois: Creation House, August, 1970), pp. 126-29.
3. See 1 Corinthians 14:14-15 MESSAGE; "In 1 Corinthians 14 Paul deals more specifically with the gift of tongues and its exercise in the church...Paul claims for himself the gift of tongues-speaking, but apparently he exercised this gift in private and not in public (14:18-19)...The person who speaks in an unknown tongue is to pray that he may interpret (1 Corinthians 14:13)." *Nelson's Illustrated Bible Dictionary,* Copyright © 1986 by Thomas Nelson Publishers. All rights reserved. Used by permission; s.v. "Tongues, Gift of."
4. "There will come a time when the gifts mentioned [in 1 Corinthians 12] will be done away with, or cease. (1 Corinthians 13 Verse 9-10). The [for] introduces the explana-tion of why the gifts will pass away. A time of perfected knowledge and prophecy is coming...The coming of that which is perfect can only be a reference to the Lord's sec-ond coming. That event will mark the end of the exercise

of prophecy, tongues, and knowledge." *The Wycliffe Bible Commentary,* "1 Corinthians 13:8-13."

CHAPTER 10

1. In view of the spirit that has been divinely given to Timothy (cf. v.7), he is urged not to be ashamed 'to testify about our Lord.'... Paul is not implying that Timothy was already guilty of doing this. But apparently he felt that his young colleague needed to have his courage strengthened... Paul... was now a prisoner of the emperor (probably Nero) and facing almost certain death. Timothy must not be so fearful as to be ashamed to visit Paul in prison. *The Expositor's Bible Commentary,* Volume 11 (Grand Rapids, Michigan: Zondervan Publishing House, 1978), "2 Timothy 1:8."

2. Webster's *II New College Dictionary* (Boston/New York: Houghton Mifflin Company, 1995), s.v. "stimulate."

CHAPTER 11

1. Vine, p. 558, s.v. "SEEK," *zeteo.*
2. Ibid.

CHAPTER 12

1. Webster's *New World College Dictionary,* 4th ed. (New York: MacMillan, 1999), s.v. "quench," "suppress," "subdue."
2. Vine, p. 492, s.v. "PROPHECY, PROPHESY, PROPHESYING," A. Noun., *propheteia.*
3. Ibid.
4. Ibid.
5. "This synagogue measured about seventy by fifty feet and had a balcony for women... The congregation sat in an appointed order, the most distinguished in the front seats,

the younger behind; men and women probably apart (see Matthew 23:6; Mark 12:39; Luke 11:43; 20:46)." *New Unger's Bible Dictionary,* s.v. "SYNAGOGUE."

6. "One must bear in mind here that during the era of time when Paul was writing, it was usually men who were the ones to receive an education." *The Complete Word Study Dictionary: New Testament,* p. 690.

7. See the discussion in *The Complete Word Study Dictionary: New Testament,* pp. 576-77.

8. Ibid., pp. 689-90.

CHAPTER 13

1. "Historians often trace the origins of Pentecostalism in the American context to a revival that began on January 1, 1901, at Charles F. Parham's Bethel Bible School in Topeka, Kansas. With the identification of speaking in tongues as the evidence of the baptism in the Holy Spirit, Parham...made a vital theological connection that has remained essential to much of classical Pentecostalism... The ensuing revival at the Azusa Street Mission (1906-09) represented an anomaly on the American religious scene... The gifts of the Holy Spirit (1 Corinthians 12), understood by most denominations as having ceased at the end of the first century, had been restored." *Dictionary of Pentecostal and Charismatic Movements,* eds. Stanley M. Burgess and Gary B. McGee (Grand Rapids, Michigan: Zondervan Publishing House, Copyright © 1988), pp. 2-3.

2. Ibid., pp. 890-92, "WISDOM, WORD OF."

3. Ibid., pp. 527-28, "KNOWLEDGE, WORD OF."

4. Arnold Bittlinger, *Gifts and Graces* (Grand Rapids, Michigan: William B. Eerdmans Publishing Company, Copyright © 1967), pp. 32-34, "(c) *The Gift of Faith.*"

5. "The measure of faith given corresponds to the task to be accomplished." *The Wycliffe Bible Commentary,* "Romans 12:3."

6. Gordon D. Fee, *God's Empowering Presence* (Peabody, Massachusetts: Hendrickson Publishers, Copyright © 1994), pp. 168-69. "(4) *Gifts of Healings.*"

7. Bittlinger, pp. 40-42, "(e) *The Working of Miracles.*"

8. Ibid., pp. 42-45, "(f) *The Gift of Prophecy.*"

9. *The Complete Word Study Dictionary: New Testament,* pp. 375-76, "1100 . . . Tongue."

10. Bittlinger, pp. 51-52, "(i) *The Gift of Interpretation.*"

11. "To another the discerning of Spirits, power to distinguish between true and false prophets, or to discern the real and internal qualifications of any person for an office, or to discover the inward workings of the mind by the Holy Ghost, as Peter did those of Ananias (Acts 5:3)." *Matthew Henry's Commentary on the Whole Bible: New Modern Edition,* "1 Corinthians 12:10."

12. Dennis and Rita Bennett, *The Holy Spirit and You* (South Plainfield, New Jersey: Bridge Publishing, Inc., 1971), p. 143.

CHAPTER 15

1. Nee, p. 191.

CHAPTER 17

1. *"Manna . . .* the supernaturally provided food for Israel during their wilderness journey (for details see Exodus 16 and Numbers 11) . . . The Lord speaks of it as being typical of Himself, the true Bread from Heaven, imparting eternal life and sustenance to those who by faith partake spiritually of Him (John 6:31-35)." Vine, pp. 390-91, s.v. "MANNA."

ABOUT THE AUTHOR

JOYCE MEYER is one of the world's leading practical Bible teachers. A #1 *New York Times* bestselling author, she has written nearly 100 inspirational books, including *Change Your Words, Change Your Life, Making Good Habits, Breaking Bad Habits*, the entire Battlefield of the Mind family of books, and two novels, *The Penny* and *Any Minute*, as well as many others. She has also released thousands of audio teachings, as well as a complete video library. Joyce's *Enjoying Everyday Life*® radio and television programs are broadcast around the world, and she travels extensively conducting conferences. Joyce and her husband, Dave, are the parents of four grown children and make their home in St. Louis, Missouri.

JOYCE MEYER MINISTRIES
U.S. & FOREIGN OFFICE ADDRESSES

Joyce Meyer Ministries
P.O. Box 655
Fenton, Missouri 63026
USA
(636) 349-0303
www.joycemeyer.org

Joyce Meyer Ministries—Canada
P.O. Box 7700
Vancouver, BC V6B 4E2
CANADA
(800) 868-1002

Joyce Meyer Ministries—Australia
Locked Bag 77
Mansfield Delivery Centre
Queensland 4122
Australia
(07) 3349 1200

Joyce Meyer Ministries—England
P.O. Box 1549
Windsor SL4 1GT
United Kingdom
01753 831102

Joyce Meyer Ministries—South Africa
P.O. Box 5
Cape Town 8000
South Africa
(27) 21-701-1056

OTHER BOOKS BY JOYCE MEYER

The Secret to True Happiness

The Secrets of Spiritual Power

Secrets to Exceptional Living

Seven Things That Steal Your Joy

Start Your New Life Today

Starting Your Day Right

Straight Talk Omnibus

Teenagers Are People Too!

Tell Them I Love Them

Weary Warriors, Fainting Saints

When, God, When?

Why, God, Why?

Woman to Woman

The Word, the Name, the Blood

JOYCE MEYER SPANISH TITLES

Come la Galleta... Compra los Zapatos (Eat the Cookie... Buy the Shoes)

El Campo de Batalla de la Mente (Battlefield of the Mind)

La Revolución de Amor (The Love Revolution)

Las Siete Cosas Que Te Roban el Gazo (Seven Things That Steal Your Joy)

Pensamientos de Poder (Power Thoughts)

BOOKS BY DAVE MEYER

Life Lines

* Study Guide available for this title